CONFLICT INTERVENTION IN SOCIAL AND DOMESTIC VIOLENCE

Executive Editor: Richard A. Weimer
Production Editor: Michael J. Rogers
Cover Design and Art Director: Don Sellers, AMI

Conflict Intervention in Social and Domestic Violence

CARMEN GERMAINE WARNER, RN, PHN

Conflict Intervention in Social and Domestic Violence

Library of Congress Cataloging in Publication Data

Conflict intervention in social and domestic violence.
    Bibliography: p.
    1. Victims of crimes—Counseling of—Addresses, essays, lectures.
2. Family violence—Addresses, essays, lectures.   3. Violence—Social aspects—Addresses, essays, lectures.   4. Crisis intervention (Psychiatry)—Addresses, essays, lectures.
I. Warner, Carmen Germaine, 1941-
HV6250.25.C66   362.8'8   80-29330
ISBN 0-87619-855-8 (casebound)
ISBN 0-87619-854-X (pbk.)

Prentice-Hall International, Inc., London
Prentice-Hall of Australia, Pty., Ltd., Sydney
Prentice-Hall of India Private Limited, New Delhi
Prentice-Hall of Japan, Inc., Tokyo
Prentice-Hall of Southeast Asia Pte. Ltd., Singapore
Whitehall Books, Limited, Petone, New Zealand

Printed in the United States of America

81 82 83 84 85 86 87 88 89 90 91   10 9 8 7 6 5 4 3 2 1

To Tracy Janee
and
Ryan Christopher

May they know a world
where love is lived
and not just spoken

CONTENTS

PREFACE

Violence and the impact on its victims is nothing new to the helping professional. Specific assessment and intervention has been addressed in Emergency Departments for years, but it has only been within the past decade that first responders have been challenged with the shared responsibility for the early stabilization and management of victims of violence. Accompanying this responsibility is the need for first responders to be prepared both educationally and emotionally to intervene in situations of violence. The first person who cares for victims of violence plays a critical role in not only establishing good lines of communication but possesses the potential for developing a trusting relationship. This element of trust helps the victim to remain open and creative throughout stages of short and long-term intervention. It is only with a comprehensive foundation of theory, specific causes, victim and family impact, along with conflict intervention that first responders will effectively be able to understand and properly manage victims of violence.

This text is designed to provide the reader with a firm knowledge base. The first section outlines some of the theories and philosophies concerning violence, why and how it occurs, specific learned behavior, and factors which influence evolvement, along with common threads in violent behavior.

The second section emphasizes definitions, general knowledge, statistical data, signs and symptoms, and the victim's specific transition sequences.

Section Three identifies specific intervention techniques which, based on the accumulated knowledge base gained in sections One and Two, will afford the reader a comprehensive, holistic approach to quality assessment and management.

Concomitant with detailed management is the importance of focusing on the commonalities rather than the differences. In an attempt to accomplish this goal, victims of social and domestic violence have been addressed collectively in a single text. The specific victims being considered include:

1) Victims of rape which include men and women of all ages.
2) Victims of molestation which consist of children 16 years of age and younger who are assaulted by someone outside their family unit.
3) Victims of sexual abuse focusing on the child who is sexu-

ally abused by someone within the nuclear or extended family.

4) Victims of child abuse which include physical and emotional abuse and neglect within the family structure.
5) Victims of domestic violence relating to all combinations of sibling, spousal, and elderly abuse.
6) Significant others who emphasize the indirect trauma felt by family, friends, and neighbors of the victim.

In essence, victimization extends far beyond the actual victim to include those who care for and about their loved ones.

First responders, for the purpose of this book include any helping professional who is the first individual to address the physical, emotional, or spiritual needs of a victim. Specifically, a first responder includes law enforcement personnel; fire fighters; on-the-scene medical personnel including Mobile Intensive Care Nurses (MICNs), paramedics and Emergency Medical Technicians (EMTs); Emergency Department clinicians, family practitioners; public health nurses and school nurses; nurse practitioners, social workers, crisis counselors, educators, and religious counselors.

Each of these helping professionals may provide valuable physical and emotional care for victims of violence. It is the hope of the author that through a thorough understanding and broader-based applied knowledge, first responders will be able to:

1) Identify a high level of comprehensive physical and emotional care to victims and significant others.
2) Introduce the concept of patient teaching regarding initial and follow-up intervention techniques.
3) Outline the necessary components of personal awareness and prevention techniques.

The ultimate state of recovery and eventual level of wellness will strongly reflect the degree of competence and empathy impacted by a knowledgeable, sensitive first responder.

CARMEN GERMAINE WARNER, RN, PHN

INTRODUCTION

The role of the first responder in emergency care has evolved from one of answering a plea for help and then calling the appropriate agency, to one of identifying the problem and stabilizing the victim until the appropriate care arrives. In many instances the first responder may be asked to manage the victim during transport. Police and fire personnel comprise the greatest number of first responders due to the population-based placement of their units. This placement pattern makes it easy for first responders to react quickly and efficiently. In large urban metropolitan areas Emergency Medical Technicians (EMTs) and paramedics may also be considered first responders. In less densely populated areas the role of first responders is filled by dedicated volunteers. As the need for immediate response increases, the lay public will become more involved in initial management. This will require the development and utilization of comprehensive, indepth educational materials.

A significant portion of the first responder's obligations is to interview and manage crisis situations. Police officers must deal with victims and perpetrators of violent crime on a daily basis. Domestic altercations are expected to be managed by the officers responding to the complaint. Increasingly, fire personnel are expected to initiate emergency care at the scene. This includes care of family members as well as the victim. Emergency Medical Technicians and paramedics are being asked to provide initial assessment and intervention for many psychiatric emergencies. Their hourly tasks include providing physical care and emotional support to all victims.

Every emergency encounter requires interaction with both the victim and the bystander. This interaction must be carefully handled to enable the collection of proper information needed to manage the situation. The victim and bystanders must be made to feel comfortable while providing this information. The first responder must feel as secure in the techniques of interviewing as he or she does in medical management. The first responder must also possess the ability to deal with his or her personal emotions while caring for victims of violence.

Unfortunately, the training received by police, fire fighters, EMTs, and paramedics places very little emphasis on crisis intervention and interpersonal relations. These individuals are expected, upon graduation, to be able to interact appropriately with all emergency situations. When a conflict arises at the scene it is frequently due to the inappropriate handling of people and not because of improper medical care.

This book addresses the psychology of violence and why it occurs. By assisting the first responder in understanding violent behavior, he or she will be holistically prepared to deal with the victim's personal emotions, physical trauma, as well as the needs of family and friends. Rape, child abuse, sexual abuse of children, and domestic violence, all highly charged emotional situations, are clearly identified. Victims are distraught and do not wish to be reminded of the incident through repeated questioning. Family members may be irate because the incident has occurred, hesitant to reveal correct information because of possible incrimination, or grieved because of the violence perpetrated against a loved one. The first responder must possess the necessary skills to control the scene in addition to specific care for the victim. At the same time, he or she must control personal feelings of anger toward the parents of an abused child, the sense of revulsion and helplessness at a suicide scene, or the futility of responding to a domestic altercation for the third time in a week.

As the demand for immediate medical care increases, the first responder will have to assume more of the initial management of emergency situations and scenes of social and domestic violence. The authors are to be congratulated for excellent contributions toward the advancement of quality care through an increased level of knowledge and understanding.

Mary Beth Skelton, RN
Director, Paramedic Training
Tulane University School of Medicine

Contributors

John (Jack) Michael Brazill
Health Care Consultant and Therapist
BA, MSW, and Ed.D.

M. Kathleen Collins
Registered Nurse
AA, BSN, MSN

Ronald James Cooper
Detective, Denver Police Department, Juvenile Division (Child Abuse Unit)

Drew E. Leavens
Mental Health Consultant II
Coordinator, DEFY Counseling Line
AA, BA, MA

Doris A. Spaulding
Director, Rape Emergency Assistance League
RN, BS

Linda J. Walker
Director, Family Stress Center
BA, MSW

Ashley Walker-Hooper, BA
Director, Battered Women's Services

I

ANATOMY OF VIOLENCE

1   THE NATURE OF VIOLENCE

by Carmen Germaine Warner, RN, PHN

"Human violence is that act which occurs when a blow is struck against life. Its roots lie not in man's aggressive behaviors, for these are normally applied toward constructive ends, but in the pain which affects men's hearts." David E. Sobel, MD, "Human Violence," *American Journal of Nursing* 76, No. 1 (January 1976): 69.

Acts of aggression and violence have always existed. Violence has been a means of communication, a mechanism of response; in essence, it is a way of life. Feelings of depression, frustration, anger, fear, stress, pressure, and jealousy can manifest certain behavioral characteristics shown through violent behavior. Violence is the language that speaks the loudest, carries the strongest message, and cries most desperately for help.

THE MEANING OF VIOLENCE

First responders answer a large number of calls each day. Calls relating to such emergencies as traffic accidents or heart attacks can be assessed quickly with minimal personal involvement; however, situations of social and domestic violence, along with unexpected causes are subject to personal feelings and interpretation. This may be based on a wide variety of factors ranging from an individual's past history and personal judgment, to religious beliefs and established social patterns.

To assist the reader in understanding not only the philosophy of this book but the author's basic premise, the following material is provided.

Commonalities of Social and Domestic Violence

Victims of violence constitute a wide range of individuals who may suffer from varying degrees of physical, mental, or social injury caused by a perpetrator or perpetrators. Recognizing this fact, the text is limited in its scope and only the victims of a common form of social and domestic violence will be discussed. These individuals include victims of rape (all ages and sex); child abuse (physical, sexual, and neglect); and domestic violence (spouse, grandparent, parent, and sibling).

There are several reasons why these victims show a common base for assessment and intervention. These similar features lie in their impact on other human beings and their later effect on how families function and communicate. Social and domestic violence, according to the author, is viewed as having eight common traits which weave a network of trauma and disruption (see Figure 1.1).

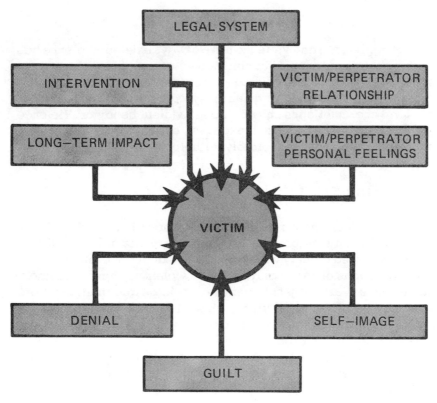

Figure 1.1.   Eight common traits of social/domestic violence.

These common traits include internal factors such as guilt, denial, and self-image in addition to external factors which include intervention and long term impact. Each of these traits play a role in the assessment and intervention process of victims of violence. Their signs and symptoms may vary but the important fact is that all victims experience or deal with each of the identified traits to some degree. This network of commonalities is designed to aid the professional in providing continuity of care, and developing an awareness of the similarities rather than the differences.

Victim/Perpetrator Relationship

In all cases of domestic violence, and in the majority of rape attacks (reported and unreported), the victim and perpetrator share a form of common awareness. As an example, these common awareness situations may involve a close relationship of cohabitation in cases of domestic violence and some cases of rape, or merely a friendship, social, or business association as noted in rapes involving co-workers, classmates, neighbors, dates, and others.

This means that the victims' areas of vulnerability, their concept and respect of self, and personal life patterns are well known. This also means in the case of the perpetrator that their individual mannerisms, weaknesses, and points of frustration are frequently known to the victim. Awareness of one's life patterns, habits, and feelings establish grounds for mutual trust. This factor of trust, along with a personal faith and belief in someone, is destroyed when an individual is victimized. In place of trust, feelings of doubt, fear, and anticipatory anxiety develop.

The song lyrics "You always hurt the one you love" are classic in many situations of violence. Perpetrators lash out at those closest to them, those who trust them, and those who believe in them. Afterwards, when they realize the pain and suffering felt by the victim, the perpetrator experiences feelings of remorse, embarrassment, and pain. Consequently, another person—the unsuspecting victim—has become the target for the perpetrator's personal feelings, needs, and inadequacies. The act of violence, as an attempt to gain power and self-worth, leaves the perpetrator with feelings of remorse not necessarily for the violent act, but for the resulting consequences afflicted on the victim.

Victim/Perpetrator Personal Feelings

The perpetrator's feelings before an act of violence are emotional and energy laden. Various stressors, anxieties, feelings of frustration, anger, or personal inadequacies accumulates, and their release results in injury to the victim. Perpetrators often feel the victim triggers the violence release mechanism through an action or comment or by nothing more than being present. This release mechanism is more sensitive to loved ones or close friends, which explains why most victims are known to the perpetrator.

The fact that the perpetrator has personal feelings for, or is aware of a victim's behavioral patterns, makes the victim an ideal target.

The perpetrator often unconsciously dismisses his or her lack of control and responsibility on the premise that the victim will understand and forgive them. This frequently provides the perpetrator with a crutch for justifying the actions.

Self-Image

Both the victim and the perpetrator are, in essence, victims. The nature of violence is a lose-lose situation where all parties are hurt—the victim for the obvious physical, emotional, and social reasons, and the perpetrator because the act of violence does not rectify or remove his or her original feelings or inadequacies. The episode only magnifies the issue.

A victim's self-image is injured because of the apparent vulnerability, the inability to abort the attack, and the resulting disgrace. The question of physical/emotional strength is frequently raised when the victim wonders how they could have prevented the attack. A perpetrator feels a low self-image because the real issue—the factor disturbing the person—was not addressed. If the perpetrator had a healthy self-image, they would confront their basic problems directly instead of victimizing another person and avoiding the issue completely.

Some factors which negatively influence the level of one's self-image include:

- Poor self-esteem.
- Desire for attention and recognition.
- Need for power and control.
- Feelings of frustration over employment, money, illness, and other factors.
- Poverty.
- Feelings of inadequacy.
- Accumulation of unattained goals.
- Perception of failure.
- Personal illness.
- Too many demands on ones self.

- Resentment and hostility toward an unrelated party.
- Lack of control over daily stressors.

Guilt

Feelings of guilt are evident in both the victim and the perpetrator in acts of violence. The victim tends to redirect feelings inward, which build into tremendous waves of guilt. They tend to accept the blame for the incident. Comments such as, "If only I had" or "If only I hadn't," are common examples in this "bearer of guilt" syndrome. This complicates the issue by relieving the perpetrator of all responsibility and accountability, condones the violent behavior, and provides a blanket of forgiveness.

. Feelings of guilt are evident in the perpetrator as well who, in an attempt to alleviate his or her personal feelings of inadequacy, reinforces the victim's guilt. They are unhappy with the hurt and pain they caused the victim, even though they may still harbor their original feelings of frustration and inadequacy.

Denial

Along with feelings of guilt there are feelings of denial. This tendency to hide from the fact that an act of violence has occurred becomes an automatic reflex. Embarrassment over the awareness that they had been victimized causes the individual to try to block the incident, to hide it from others, and to not report it.

Unfortunately, this burial process does not solve the problem. Denial only increases feelings of frustration and hurt which will eventually resurface.

The perpetrator manifests feelings of denial as well. The act itself, which did not resolve the initial feelings within the perpetrator, only compounds the problem, leaving the entire situation more complex and emotional with an additional unresolved issue.

Long-Term Impact

With the build-up of such feelings as guilt and denial comes a cancerous form of growth which eats away at, and eventually destroys, the family unit in general and the victim in particular.

By not addressing the issue and dealing with the necessary

recovery process, some of the following factors may evolve:
- Loss of self-worth.
- Dissolved life goals.
- Lack of motivation.
- Decreased level of physical wellness.
- Increased level of psychological problems.
- Tendencies toward retreat and isolation.
- Lack of trust.
- Tendency toward suicide.
- Reduction in responsibility for work, family, and self.
- Permanent disruptions in personal relationships.

As time progresses, without honestly addressing the real issue, symptoms of other problems begin to surface. The situation becomes more involved and intervention processes are more difficult.

The perpetrator discovers that not analyzing the main cause of the violent behavior only compounds feelings of poor self-image. With the passage of time, the original contributing factors become so ingrained in denial and isolation that they are very difficult to manage.

Despite the type of violence or the parties involved, intervention is difficult. When it is compounded by denial, the healing and recovery process is greatly extended.

Intervention

If the person is unwilling to share their feelings, discuss the situation with an uninvolved, helping person, and begin to develop a feeling of trust; recovery and regrowth will not occur. It is understandable that due to the nature of the violence and its accompanying feelings of embarrassment, guilt, pain, and isolation, it is extremely difficult to open up to an outsider. Disruption of the family unit is a frequently cited excuse for not seeking help, yet the mere fact that this isolation is allowed to continue insures ultimate family destruction.

Those closest to the involved persons become an integral part of the problem; thus, they are totally nonobjective to the causative factors. The first step toward victim intervention, that of open communication and honesty, is frequently overwhelming and very frightening, yet it is the only way the involved parties can honestly address all the issues and visualize the scope of the problem.

Legal System

The process of legal recourse and correction, by the mere fact of its complexities, poses tremendous barriers for many people. Recognizing that the perpetrator is often known to the victim, it becomes a stressful process to prosecute. The automatic tendency is to forget the entire issue, and not to face additional trauma. Yet making one accountable for his or her behavior is the only possible way to stop violent patterns of behavior.

Along with the overwhelming process itself is the tendency for the victim to be revictimized. The rehashing and reliving of a horrible experience is often as traumatic as the original incident. It is not uncommon for people to stop proceedings mid-way. Steps attempting to "prove" a certain behavior are a necessity which, by its nature, tends to destroy its effectiveness.

General Reactions of Victims

Despite the fact that each victim's experience is unique and individualized, there are several general reactions which maintain a common thread among victims of violence.

- The mind and body progress at separate distinctive rates. Mental thoughts develop much more rapidly than do bodily reactions.
- Physical actions follow a specific pattern.
  1. State of alarm—physical actions and reactions are nonoperative.
  2. State of resistance—strength is gained and a level of resistance emerges.
  3. State of exhaustion—physical exhaustion occurs with burn out resulting.
- Emotional reactions of victims fall into one of three categories.
  1. State of decompensation where one is totally nonfunctioning.
  2. State of physical nonaction, but the victim is mentally alert.
  3. State of physical and mental alertness.

Overview

Eight general commonalities of violence have been identified to increase the level of understanding concerning these victims and to emphasize that the origin, the intervention, and the outcome for victims are similar in many respects. Specific intervention techniques for each of the violent entities are identified in Section Three.

DISTINGUISHING CHARACTERISTICS OF VIOLENT BEHAVIOR

Developing a working definition of violence is deemed nearly impossible by all those attempting to write about it. Each author must determine what is the best working definition for their particular work, and relate this clearly to the reader. For the purpose of this text, violence is categorized in three areas: disciplinary violence, deliberate violence, and destructive violence.

Disciplinary Violence

Disciplinary violence is defined as "an act carried out for the purpose of instilling physical or emotional pain in an attempt to modify behavior or teach a lesson."

This is frequently the case when an individual chooses to stress a point or teach a lesson. As an example, a child's safety might be at risk when running toward the street. The child might be conditioned to pain in order to emphasize a point previously stressed. The argument of spanking and slapping as a form of violence is valid. The author, however, chooses to categorize this as a form of violence because, although frequently controlled, it may represent the first step toward an uncontrolled expression of physical force.

The dividing line between a slap and physical beatings is fine and undistinguishable. However, the progression rate is the critical factor. This is determined solely by the control and discipline of the initiator. It is also of value to raise the issue of slapping because it has been accepted as "natural behavior" and should possibly be reevaluated.

Physical punishment of children is used by 84 to 97 percent of all parents at some time during the child's life.[1] Even though these statistics do not provide specific ages of this behavior, they illustrate that those individuals most likely to be struck are usually the smallest and weakest members of a family.

Physical punishment or disciplinary violence may continue

well into the adolescent and early adulthood years. Mulligan reports that nearly 8 percent of high school seniors surveyed reported they had been physically injured by their parents during their last year at home prior to entering college.[2] In an attempt to create an understanding of violence, it is critical for the reader to seriously consider the correlation between physical punishment and its transition into ongoing physical abuse.

Deliberate Violence

Deliberate violence is defined as "an act initiated with the conscious, deliberate intent to cause physical or emotional pain and injury." Disciplinary acts are excluded, but acts which are premeditated and planned would fit this category. Examples of this include such actions as ongoing cases of child abuse and neglect, rape, and even murder.

Destructive Violence

Destructive violence is defined as "an act which does not manifest a conscious intent to cause pain or injury, yet a great possibility of injuring the person exists." Such acts as punching, hitting, biting, or even stabbing would be considered acts of destructive violence. In certain circumstances the individual might be severely injured, while in others the same act might produce only slight discomfort. Several factors influence this, such as the strength of the perpetrator, location of the perpetrator, tolerance of the victim, and the deliberate intent to hurt. The issue is not how severely the victim was injured, but that such an act should occur in the first place. The intent is the same whether the perpetrator makes contact or not.

VIOLENCE IS A REALITY

- 1979—more than one household in six witnessed a spouse striking his or her partner.[3]
- 1979—three households in five echoed the sounds of parents hitting children.[3]
- 1979—where there is more than one child in the home, three in five homes are the scene of violence between siblings.[3]
- 1979—overall, every other house in America is the scene of

family violence at least once a year.[3]
- 1979—child abuse is being reported over 300,000 times each year.[4]
- 1979—over one and a quarter million cases of child abuse and neglect are reported.[4]
- 1979—over 60,000 have significant injuries.[4]
- 1979—over 2,000 die and 6,000 have permanent brain damage.[4]
- 1978—one forcible rape occurs every eight minutes in the United States (this is reported cases).[5]
- 1978—an estimated 67,131 rapes occurred in the United States (reported cases).[5]

Statistics show that violence is a way of life. This is true today as in the past—the only difference being the increased awareness and openness of its existence. As the news media continues to reverberate the shocking results of current research, the public is just beginning to comprehend its scope and intensity.

Accounts of brutal rapes on men and women are an everyday occurrence which, due to their frequency, do not make the bold headlines any more. Cases of family violence, which inundate community shelters and counseling services, reiterate the fact that family violence is *not* the exception.

Stereotypic beliefs of the "types of people who are raped" or those "particular social class families who hit each other" have been blown apart by this shocking reality. To confirm this, intensive research by Straus, Gelles, and Steinmetz has just been completed which clarifies some of the following points.[6*]

Region

- Southerners are *not* more prone to engage in abuse or domestic violence.
- Rates of violence are very evenly distributed throughout the United States.

---

* This study involved 2,143 completed interviews conducted with 960 men and 1,183 women. Each interview signified a couple who identified themselves as married or being a couple. There were 103 primary areas chosen as a national sample, stratified by geographic region, type of community, and other population characteristics. Three hundred interviewing locations were chosen for the study.

City and Country

- Families in large cities (one million population or more) have higher rates of abusive violence toward children and between husbands and wives.
- Wife abuse is one-half the rate in the suburbs, compared to large cities.
- Sibling and wife abuse are as common in rural areas as in large cities.

Race†

Child abuse. Blacks and other racial minorities are inaccurately presented as child abusers.

Parental abuse. Highest among American Indians, Orientals, and other racial minorities; there is no difference between blacks and whites.

Wife abuse. Highest among blacks (400 percent higher than in white families).

Husband abuse. Highest among racial minorities; twice as common in black families as in white families.

Sibling abuse. Highest in families of racial minorities; lowest in black families.

Religion

Sibling abuse. The rate is lowest among families where the mother is Jewish. The rate is highest among minority religions (other than Catholic, Protestant, or Jewish).

Child abuse. The rate is lowest among Jews. The rate is highest for those families where one or both parents have minority religious affiliations.

Wife abuse. Jewish husbands have the lowest rates; minority religious husbands are the highest.

Husband abuse. The rate is lowest among Protestants and highest among minority religious groups. Jewish women abuse their husbands more than twice the rate of Protestant women.

---

† Categorized in three racial groups: black, white, and others—Indian and Oriental.

In families where both husband and wife were of the same religion, the rates of violence were less than those families with mixed religious marriages.

Age

Couples under 30 years of age are more violent than older couples.

Education

- The most violent fathers and husbands were those who graduated from high school. The least violent were grammar school dropouts and men with some college education.
- Men who did not complete high school are most likely to be victims of wives' violence.
- Men with the most education have children most likely to use violence on siblings.
- The most violent mothers are those who graduated from high school. The least violent are those who did not complete grammar school or those who secured some college education.
- College educated women are least likely to be abused by their husbands. Women not possessing a high school diploma are most likely to be physically abused. The most violent wives are those who did not complete high school.
- Women without a high school diploma and women who had some college education have the most violent children.

Income

- Families living at or below the poverty line (under 5,999 dollars) had a rate of violence between husband and wives of 500 percent greater than spousal violence in families of 20,000 dollars and over.
- Families earning under 5,999 dollars had a rate of child abuse twice that of families earning 20,000 dollars or more.

Occupation

- Except for violence among siblings, men and women who held blue collar jobs had a higher rate of violence than white collar occupations.

- Violence between spouses was twice as high in blue collar families, compared to white collar workers.
- Severe child abuse was twice as high in blue collar homes than in homes of white collar workers.

Unemployment

- If a man is employed part-time or unemployed, there is more severe violence in the home.
- Unemployed men are violent toward their wives twice as often as employed men.
- Men employed part-time beat their wives at three times the rate of fully employed men.
- Unemployed or partially employed men are three times more likely to be beaten by their wives.
- Severe child abuse occurs twice as often in homes where the father is partially employed, compared to full-time employed men.
- The least amount of violence occurs in homes of retired men.

THE CONCEPT OF FORCE IN VIOLENCE

Society, its inner actions and communications, together with family systems, rests primarily on customs, tradition, personal beliefs, and values, not calculated obedience or compliance. Thus, in acts of rape, child sexual abuse, child abuse, spouse, parent, and sibling abuse, individuals become both hurt and angry concerning the force to which they are subjected. This force, according to Goode, constitutes three main faces of power: " . . . structure, socialization, and violence."[7]

Family and societal structures are ultimately backed by force. This force is invisible, but should the written or unwritten lines of agreement be crossed or violated, force in the form of court, police, and institution correction is put into action. Despite the personal feelings one might have regarding these facets of force, when the need arises they are frequently considered as a means of support and security.

Socialization is based on overt physical force or threat. One originates from the point of zero commitment or value structure. The learning process begins with the withdrawal of items of pleasure and develops into the use of physical punishment and threat.

The learning process demonstrates that violation of rules will be met with force.

Violence, as the third aspect of power constituting force, stems from the development of imbalance. This imbalance results from an unequal exchange of such things as income, household tasks, affection, loyalty, obedience, and respect. What one gives may not be equal to what one gets and vice versa. As this imbalance increases and intensifies, violence is used as a means of resolution. Even though society balks at the degree of force prevalent in families and society, it appears to be the tool sought after immediately to afford needed control and restraint.

VIOLENCE TODAY

In earlier times, violence was a common means of control. Corporal and physical punishment, together with brutal forms of death, were used by the courts, prisons, slave owners, and churches as a means of social control. Today, only law enforcement officials and parents possess a legal mandate for the use of violence in obtaining social control.

Despite the disagreement regarding physical punishment as a form of violence, parents who use physical punishment to control aggressiveness in their children are probably increasing rather than decreasing the aggressive tendencies for their children." Violence begets violence, however peaceful and altruistic the motivation."[8]

Violence can be viewed as an interlacing mechanism of mutually influencing and interacting actions. Each action or direction affords a mechanism for feedback and reinforcement to others.[9]

Social and domestic violence is a two-way interaction. Societal violence influences the type of violence in families, and domestic violence affects the pattern of violence in society as a whole.

SUMMARY

In order for first responders to effectively relate and respond to the needs of victims of violence, a comfortable working knowledge of violence, its manifesting characteristics, its developmental patterns, and resulting consequences must be understood and respected. Change in attitude and behavior is a slow, deliberate process which requires the combined efforts of both the victim and responder. Only when this process has occurred can intervention be appropriate, effective, and on a cooperative basis.

REFERENCES

1. Stark R, McEvoy, III J: Middle-class violence. Psychology Today, Vol. 4, November 1970, pp. 52-65
2. Mulligan MA: An investigation of factors associated with violent modes of conflict resolution in the family. University of Rhode Island, master's thesis, 1977
3. Straus MA, Gelles RJ, Steinmetz SK: Behind Closed Doors: Violence in the American Family. New York, Anchor Books, 1980, p. 3
4. Gray JD, Cutler CA, Dean JG, Kemp CH: Prediction and prevention of child abuse and neglect. Journal of Social Issues, Vol. 35, No. 1, 1979, pp. 135-136
5. Cryer L, McDowell JH: Rape prevention. Your Health, Vol. 2 No. 1, February 1980, p. 6
6. Straus MA, Gelles RJ, Steinmetz SK: Behind Closed Doors: Violence in the American Family. New York, Anchor Books, 1980, pp. 126-152
7. Goode WJ: Force and violence in the American family. *In* Steinmetz SK, Straus MA (eds): Violence in the Family. New York; Dodd, Mead and Company, 1974, pp. 41-42
8. Steinmetz SK, Straus MA: Intra-family violence. *In* Steinmetz SK, Straus MA (eds): Violence in the Family. New York; Dodd, Mead and Company, 1974, p. 3
9. Heil R: Modern systems' theory and the family: A confrontation. Social Science, 10, October 1970, pp. 97-110

2 LEARNED BEHAVIOR: ITS IMPACT ON VIOLENCE

Jack Brazill, Ed.D.

There are numerous theories regarding violence, a subject which society is only beginning to acknowledge. Violence, on a broad level, has become widespread and can be seen in the form of wars, riots, murders, and gang fights. These examples have appeared on television and in newspapers. Violence in one area has also been one of society's best kept secrets. This violence—which originates in the home—is seen in wife and husband beatings, child abuse, sibling abuse, and abuse of the elderly.

In a study conducted by Richard J. Gelles in Michigan, it was determined that half of the families suspected of violence did indeed participate, and over one-third of the 40 neighbors in the control group had experienced spouse assault.[1] Flynn noted that 10 percent of the families experienced some form of domestic violence within this specific geographic area in Michigan.[2]

The problem of violence appears to cut across all socio-economic lines. However, lower socio-economic groups seem to show a higher percentage of problems. This could be due to greater stress factors and more involvement with social agencies and/or police.

The range of theories regarding violence run from community attitudes supporting and approving the practice of wife beating, male domination, and sexist attitudes fostering and condoning domestic violence, to social learning theory of aggression, social structural theory of intrafamily violence, and psychological theory of violence.

Community attitudes supporting certain role identification can spring from such things as "a man's home is his castle" and "he can do what he wants within," to the violence one views on television. The male sexist theory is represented in the idea that men are superior, that they do and should dominate the world and women, and that women are property to do with what men choose. Social learning comes from what one sees and hears commencing with birth, such as violence from television, parents physically abusing each other, and parents abusing children. The social structural theory of violence springs from the position that the sources of family violence are not a psychological phenomenon of each individual, but rather ". . . complex structural circumstances creating environmental stresses that are distributed unevenly across the social structure. Poverty is one such environmental stress."[3] The psychological position would be an individual problem starting with a poor self-concept, lack of impulse control, and moving to aggression, destructive rages, intrapsychic conflicts, and other factors. One other prospective similar to the social structure theory is that with the exception of food, shelter, and clothing, it is not the absence of resources alone that brings on violence, but coupled with the knowledge that somebody else has these resources and you do not; activates the violent behavior.

One's perspective regarding which theory is correct will probably depend on individual education, its level, and the discipline pursued. The author will intermingle concepts throughout this chapter, believing violence flows from a variety or combination of factors and forces which come into play and, at a given time, will trigger violence. Violence does not seem to come from one factor. It is encompassed within psychological, environmental, modeling and other forms of learning, and biological and social factors which, when combined, will explode into **violent** behavior.

SOCIAL FACTORS INVOLVED IN LEARNING VIOLENCE

Tord Høivik, who wrote on "The Demography of Structural Violence," was summarized as saying:

> The distribution of society's resources affects not only the standard of living, but the chances of survival itself. A more equal distribution will normally increase the average length of life in society as a whole. The loss of life from an unequal distribution is an aspect of structural violence, i.e., violence inherent in the social order.[4]

Several points are identified by Høivik, but an example of the idea is that if a society is starving, that is violence in itself.

Two other perspectives or theories are as follows: violence is an expression of the antagonism between the will (social and individual) to live and the necessity of a real concern about society. This represents the eternal confrontation of values. Violence can be creative in that it can be a stimulus needed for revitalization of a moribund social structure. This obviously is learned, but usually not on a conscious and direct level. It also indicates that some violence in a society may be its salvation.

Another theoretical position by Schaffer is that:

> . . . the imposition of structured forms of order by a political-legal
> system (the 'structuring' function) in conflict with the system's role of
> preventing acts of victimization (the 'hygienic' function) produces a
> frustration of citizens' personal, economical and social expectations.
> This frustration, as a result, may lead to aggression and violence. [5]

This reemphasizes a point made in the previous theory that distribution of society's resources affects not only the standard of living, but the chances of survival itself. It also indicates that one needs to have an order in society, but at the same time this order can create victims, who, when frustrated, can create violence. This points out two things: many forces are in operation when violence erupts, and if one reviews these theories from a systems point of view, one can see that when the system is reduced to a lesser level, it can be applied to the family system. This system, while socializing children, can create conflict situations, many with the potential for violence.

Socialization of Violence in Children

A prime influence in the socialization of violence to children is the media. Children frequently control the quality and quantity of television watched. Children watch television many hours a day and are exposed to a great deal of violence. They also learn violent behavior through other forms of media, but television is the primary source.

Children, as well as adults, become desensitized to violence. In research conducted by Berges (1962), Lazarus (1962), Lazarus and Alfert (1964), Speisman (1964), Goranson (1970), Bandura, Blanchard, and Ritter (1969), Bandura and Menlove (1968), Brabamn and Thomas (1974 and 1975), and Cline, Craft, and Courrier (1973), it has been shown that after watching violence on television, children are more likely to participate in violent behavior and less likely to prevent it in others. Further, the approval or disapproval they rece from adults regarding participation in, or observation of violence, contributes to developing children's attitudes toward violence. Most television viewing by children occurs in the absence of an adult. In addition, adults observing violence in the presence of children, without signs of disapproval, automatically condones violence to a child. Violence certainly can look exciting and, at times, even romantic in the eyes of a child.

Other factors in a child's disposition can lead to violence. However, when experienced separately they usually do not trigger violent behavior: (1) unable to cope with stress, (2) poor self-concept, (3) deprivation, (4) poverty, (5) lack of constructive attention, (6) unstable parents, and (7) broken homes. It is usually a combination of these factors and not any single one which precipitates violent behavior.

Timing and Situation

Timing seems to be an important factor in violence. For example, most conjugal violence usually takes place in the evenings, in the home, or on a weekend with only family members present. Christmas and New Years seem to be particularly stressful times of a year and produce more family violence. Further, violence appears to be more common in families where members have less education, low income, and low occupational status.[6] However, it should be noted that conjugal violence is not confined to this group; it spans all socio-economic lines. It may be more prevalent in the above-mentioned categories, but lower socio-economic groups establish linkages with the reporting mechanisms more frequently.

The inability of people to handle stress may result in violence. A violent family is frequently characterized by the husband often having less education and occupational prestige than his wife. These families are usually isolated from their neighbors. The partners are of differing religious backgrounds, and partake in frequent disputes over sex. Another significant phenomenon is that numerous wives are beaten while pregnant. In a situation where a child is not wanted, pregnancy can cause a major crisis.[7]

There is a disagreement among experts regarding a woman's role in family abuse. Some groups say a woman plays no role in spouse abuse, while others say it is partly or all her fault. This author feels abuse is the responsibility of both partners. The woman has responsibility for her actions, and her partner has responsibility for his. Most physical assaults start with verbal arguing. If the wife is nagging or "putting down" her mate, she has set up the possibility for violence. Again, it seems to be only a part, not to be ignored nor seen as the major reason for violence. Females tend to develop earlier and possess better verbal skills than males. This is more noticeable in situations where the female has a better education. A male who has a weak ego is unable to compete verbally and becomes threatened by a woman, thus frequently reacting violently.

The threat or actual loss of power, status, or even one's partner may trigger violence in an inadequate male. This can be true for females, but is not as likely.[8] Elaborating on an earlier statement:

> Gelles reported an inverse relationship between a high incidence of spouse assault and a husband's educational and income levels. On the other hand, he found a higher level of violence among couples in which the wife had at least some high school education or was a college graduate. Intrafamilial violence was said to more likely occur when the level of education and occupational status of the husband was lower than that of the wife.[9]

More and more, society is coming to understand that family violence is passed on from generation to generation. The rationale behind this is that people exposed to a high degree of physical punishment as children are more likely to resort to family violence as adults. Further, people who were brought up in an environment characterized by either low family warmth or high stress, in combination with exposure to a high degree of parental punishment, were considerably more likely to partake in physical punishment in their own families. In addition, family violence was more likely to be transmitted in same-sex rather than cross-sex linkages.[10]

BIOLOGICAL AND ORGANIC FACTORS IN VIOLENCE

There seems to be some conflicting information about our biology and the effect it has on propensity for violence and its opposite altruistic behavior. Most research has consistently indicated that the male sex is more assertive, aggressive by nature, and partakes in more violence than females. This is noted from the time of birth until the time they die. Even in studies with infants, males will try to push their way through physical obstacles more frequently and persistently than females. These studies, documented on film and shown in college psychology classes, might imply that males are born more aggressive than females and it is also thought that males may not have the capacity for the counterpart of violence which would be altruistic behavior.

Altruistic studies may be providing a new perspective regarding a source for our behavior other than learned behavior. At the same time, the studies may be showing the role of learned behavior in altruistic behavior in very young children. However, caution should be noted. Altruistic behavior may not eradicate violence, but may coexist with it. Two researchers—Marian Yarrow and Carolyn Zahn-Waxler—found in their study of infants performing altruistic behavior that:

> . . . neither the children's sex nor the size of their families made any difference in the amount of sympathy or help they offered to people in distress. [11]

Even if there is something biological in males making them more prone to violence, they seem to carry the same capacity for altruistic behavior as females from ten months of age when it first may be exhibited. It would appear that if male infants by nature are more aggressive than females but carry the same capacity for altruistic behavior and at the same time act out more violence than females, that learned violence and sex-role definition may play a larger role in becoming violent than males "nature" or biological make-up.

One study conducted in England and Wales in 1957 through 1972, using teenagers 14 and 17 years of age, indicated each year that at all ages males committed more murders than females. In fact, only one female, 17 years of age, committed murder.[12] Due to consistent differences in males and females, such as noted above, it has been hypothesized, based on outcome, that biological differences have to be part of the reason. The aggressive tendencies may be more pronounced in males. This, along with differences in sex role learning and learned violence, has to be considered among the contributing factors to a greater incidence of violence in males.

Another factor affecting violence concerns disease entities, specifically a neurologically based disease. This is called Organic Dysfunction Syndrome (ODS). One symptom is the attack of unwarranted, explosive anger directed at others. Most of the time it is the product of a damaged limbic system. Some people manifest temper tantrums beginning with infancy; in other cases, it appears following some injury or illness. Etiology will include such things as epilepsy, minimal brain dysfunction, head trauma, infection, brain tumor, cerebral vascular disease, other neurological diseases, and endocrine and metabolic disorders.[13]

PSYCHOLOGICAL ASPECTS OF VIOLENCE

In Children

In a 1977 article, L. S. Walske-Brennan cited a ten-year study conducted by Johnston (1955) in which psychopathy was related to home background and concluded that children who are aggressive, homicidal, arsonists, or exhibitionists " . . . are usually doing what their parents subconsciously wish."[14] Johnston believed that:

> . . . the child's defective conscious is traceable and is a like defect in the parents' own poor resolution of unconscious impulses to similar antisocial behavior.[15]

Children cited in this article were not overt attention seekers, were more cooperative than noncapital offending children, and were polite and cooperative to work with. It would appear that these children were people who generally used avoidance as a coping mechanism. They avoided and were out of touch with their feelings, "stuffed" them and did not communicate their feelings, and felt alone and isolated. Instead of verbally relieving their frustration, anger, and rage, they would "stuff it," collect it, and when their feelings did explode, they were usually out of proportion to the triggering incident. Basically, communication skills, coping skills, and constructively dealing with feelings are learned. They are learned early in life and many times are modeled by one or both parents. The psychological make-up of a person affects learning patterns which in turn affect the psychological aspects of a person. Repetition of this pattern starts very early in life.

All but two of the boys in this study were shown to have mothers who were overdominant. Children who had killed showed other psychological factors such as being nervous, fast to cry, anxious, fearful, depressed, isolated, overcontrolled, covertly hostile, and having poor stress-related coping skills, manifesting a poor self-concept, and poor self-esteem.[16]

Children's psychological make-up will greatly reflect the emotional composition and degree of stability of their parents. When one or both parents are unstable, emotionally erratic, unpredictable, disturbed, and violent, the psychological development of a child is influenced. Concomitant with this is the role modeling of the parents' behavior resulting in a very poor potential for developing stable, nonviolent children/adults.

In Adulthood

By the time a person reaches adulthood, they are capable of carrying a lot of psychological scars from childhood. Their personality has been formed for years. A common ingredient for the adult who was abused as a child, and who may now be the abuser, is a poor self-concept with low self-esteem. An obvious clue that one does not like oneself is noted by their actions toward themselves and others. An adult who possesses a good self-respect will not emotionally or physically abuse themself or other people.

Common ingredients in the psychological make-up of these adults are insecurity, fear, easily threatened, paranoia, domineering, weak, powerless, helpless, inability to communicate, out-of-touch with feelings, and/or fearful of expressing themselves, hostile, poor ego control, and being quick to anger. In males their sense of masculinity is also questioned.

There are a lot of psychological similarities between the abuser and the person they are abusing. The person being abused (usually an adult female) will generally have a poor self-concept. No person with a positive self-concept will allow an abusive situation to continue. Victims of abuse manifest a common psychological make-up which includes insecurity, fearfulness, intimidation, weakness, powerlessness, helplessness, hostility, and anger. Some differences which distinguish them from the abuser are their passive or passive/aggressive behavior, a strong sense of shame and self-blaming, dependence, and certain masochistic tendencies, most of which can be traced to childhood experiences, particularly neglect or abuse. Generally, the abused is better able to communicate than the abuser, is more in touch with their feelings, and better able to express themselves. Consequently, they function better in verbal fights, and their partners choose to become physical in order to maintain their (usually his) "dominant" position. Another ingredient for triggering violence is the use of chemicals. Alcohol, which is the most commonly abused drug in our society, is a prime example.

CHEMICAL ABUSE (ALCOHOL) AND ITS RELEVANCE TO VIOLENCE

Usually the person being abused has been found to possess a low abuse of alcohol and other drugs. However, the abusers are found to have a much higher incidence of alcohol and drug abuse. One study indicated that the victim's assailants were alcohol abusers in 60 percent of the cases and 21 percent were drug abusers.[17]

In many situations one partner will initiate a verbal argument over the other partner's drinking—the male usually being the abuser. These arguments frequently take place when the partner has been drinking. The " . . . alcohol-related violence allows family members to 'disavow' the deviance of violence. Furthermore, offenders may drink and hit because they know that they will not be held responsible for their actions."[18]

Many "experts" view alcoholism as just a symptom of other psychological and/or social structural stress problems. What is overlooked by many "experts" is that by the time drinking has reached the alcoholism stage, it is a problem in and of itself. However, it does not mean that there are not other problems to be dealt with.

John P. Flynn stated that:

> . . . of all the precipitating factors mentioned in other studies, the escalation of argument seems to be frequently associated with excessive use of alcohol which, in turn, increases the probability of violence.[19]

He added that the same association is often found in child abuse literature. Based on this and other data, the author would say that men in particular who are alcohol abusers are a high-risk group for domestic violence.

Of the individuals in the juvenile population who had committed crimes of violence, the use of drugs—especially alcohol—was found to be used prior to the violent act in approximately one-third of the cases. Juveniles and adults will experience the same thing when they drink. The alcohol will block the inhibitions people normally have. This results in certain acts which normally would not occur; one of those acts is the use of violence.

EARLY PATTERNS OF INFLUENCE: ITS RELATIONSHIP AND EFFECT

As was indicated previously, the abused and abuser often have experienced violence in their own childhoods. They experienced learning patterns from authoritarian and punitive parents, and felt the loss of one or both parents.

An example of the effect of early learned patterns on life is women who lived with alcoholic, abusing men. The women were found to come from three different:

> . . . family background types characterized by a subtly controlling mother/dictatorial father; submissive mother/dictatorial father; or disturbed mother/multiple fathers. It is suggested that the women carry the conditions of their early family situation into the marriage.[20]

Early childhood and what one is exposed to during the formative years seems to dictate future patterns. If a child is exposed to abuse from a parent or parents and/or is a witness to spouse abuse, he or she is likely to play out that same action in their sex role. A female, as a mother, may abuse her own children and/or be abused by her husband because she was either abused as a child and/or had a father who abused her mother. If her mother did not abuse her but her father did, she is less likely to abuse her own children. However, she is more likely to marry a man who will abuse her. That is what she has come to expect from males and thinks that is what she deserves.

If a boy is abused by either sex, he is likely to abuse his children. If he sees his father abuse his mother, he is very likely to abuse his wife or mate. This is documented in numerous studies. One additional recurring theme is where:

> . . . . child abuse in the family is associated with wife beating when the wife is the more passive parent. Another theme is that of displacement of hostile feelings in which the assaulted parent is observed to displace those feelings upon the child who is consequently and subsequently abused in turn.[21]

This is a generation-to-generation sickness. In this pattern, everyone is a victim; the abused and the abuser both are victims of his or her socialization; however, this does not negate their responsibility for taking corrective action.

Another and more subtle, less direct way in which children will learn patterns of violence is to observe and/or partake in violence as a child and not pay the consequences for that act. Seeing somebody else nonaccountable for their violent act has a direct affect on what the child builds for a belief system concerning violence. The belief system will directly affect a person's value system. Children learn to believe and value violence as an acceptable solution to childhood or adult problems. Conversely, if a male child is abused or witnesses his mother being abused, he believes he too can perform this act. He can do it as a child and he can do this to women and children when he is an adult. This attitude has become part of his belief system. If the person is female and she was abused as a child, particularly by her father, she will likely tell herself that being abused is what to expect, accept, and deserved from her father and later from a mate. Based on such a belief system, one is more likely to become involved and remain in an abusive situation.

In an article by James M. Sorrells entitled "Kids Who Kill," it was noted that the families of these kids were typified as chaotic and violent, with parent(s) possessing a history of crime, alcohol abuse, and violence. Youngsters in the study:

> . . . . *seemed to have been deprived of models for controlling impulses, and their family experience had not generated compelling hopes and goals. In the absence of internal restraints and goals, juveniles can be profoundly influenced by popular media which teach that life must be exciting to be worthwhile. Violence is a cheap form of excitement, and excitement is a cheap form of gratification. For these youngsters, the adults in their families and the adults in popular entertainment usually choose violence over long-term gratification. So did the youngsters.*[22]

Lack of impulse control, the ability to assess a situation and to reach a constructive conclusion, resulting consequences, and loss or gain resulting from the behavior are all learned behaviors. Even a lack of learning is learned; it forms early and late life patterns. A child's family, his or her peers, and the media are the biggest influences on these patterns. In turn, they may or may not impact violence. A child will always learn more from personal observations and exposure than from what they are told. This is called modeling. Dr. Sorrells added that children ". . . . learned from their parents that to feel is to act and that being out of control is the expected state of affairs."[23] In essence, the family affords the basic training model for learned violence.

There seems to be no question that children influence their peers. However, in the literature and based on the author's clinical experience, this actually plays a lesser part in learning patterns of violence. If the family is really stable, solid, caring, loving, nurturing, and nonviolent, this will be reflected in most children. This does influence the child when choosing peers as associates. Children, as adults, act as a mirror for each other. Many times they will seek out another person who acts as they do and feels about themselves as they do. This can be positive or negative, depending on the way one feels about themself. When parents exercise minimal control over the child and model destructive and violent behavior, the child will likely dislike themself and will act out negative behavior which mirrors the parent(s). In addition, they will seek out peers who act and feel much about themselves as they do; this is another mirror.

Television is another influencing factor on a child's learning, behavior, and patterns relative to violence. Television depicts great violence and many unrealistic expectations regarding violence and life. This violence is portrayed as romantic and exciting. Violence is not as "neat and clean" in real life as portrayed on television. "In peddling 'excitement' as a desired end, television is also teaching the young viewer implicitly that his/her life must be exciting in order to be worthwhile. Nonviolence is equated with boredom, and boredom is deemed intolerable."[24]

Observing violence on television appears to decrease the viewer's anxiety regarding aggressive behavior. Also, television violence, ". . . decreases the speed and willingness of children to intervene in other children's altercations."[28] This author believes that this strongly points out how one learns violent behavior and reacts accordingly. The reader can observe how this will influence patterns throughout one's life. With the desensitization to violence people have gone through by the time they reach adulthood, it is not difficult to understand why groups of adults have stood witness to violent acts in progress and have done absolutely nothing to aid the victim.

The above ideas provide a glimpse into the effect television has on violence. The more exposure a child has to violence, the more desensitized he or she becomes. Literature on systematic desensitization therapy points out that after a person emotionally reacts to a particular behavior, the behavior is reduced or eliminated. This leaves the person free to partake in the previously anxiety-provoking activity. This was shown in studies using television and television's relationship to learned violence.

> *The more violence the child watched, the less responsive he/she was to either violent television drama or 'real life' aggression. When total viewing time was statistically controlled, their relationships were even more pronounced.*[25]

Studies conducted by these researchers using galvanic skin responses (GSR) to measure responses to violence indicated that both men and women responded to violence. They became more excited and, at the same time, the respondents showed that exposure to aggressive drama blunted the feelings and emotional sensitivity to aggressive actions.[26] Further, while watching films, ". . . . children and adults were found to be less emotionally responsive to films depicting real-life aggression after watching a violent crime drama than were subjects who had seen a neutral film."[27]

Societal institutions such as families, schools, sports, the military, and others teach values which support violence. For example, boys-men are supposed to be better achievers, to be dominant, and to take care of women, especially after marriage. These are sexist values which set up the potential for violence. When one adds another ingredient—such as an adult male who is not living up to these values, who feels inadequate, is insecure, and easily threatened—he is more likely to physically abuse a woman in order to keep this mythical position. This is especially true when a man is threatened by a woman. If a man has been a victim of child abuse or witnessed spouse abuse, he is even more likely to manifest this behavior toward his mate. This is especially true if he believes in the values just outlined. These values are taught.

As long as one continues to learn the value of violence and believes that when frustrated or under stress it is all right to perpetuate aggression and violence, the problem of abuse and battery will continue.

How Can the Pattern Be Corrected?

Because considerable violence is passed from one generation to another, intervening at either level (child or adult) will affect the other level. Working with adults will affect the present generation of children; dealing with children will affect future adults and the next generation of children. In either case, intervening effectively will help break up the continuous cycle of violence our society is going through.

We need to replace some of the values and beliefs our society persists in retaining. These include: (1) teaching that men have to be dominant, (2) violence is romantic, and all right to partake in, and (3) a lot of negative reinforcement and feedback to children will build character and good self-concepts. We need to replace the role modeling of violence.

Bonnie E. Carlson noted that:

> . . . . efforts should be made to eradicate the beliefs that (1) men's status must and should be higher than women's, (2) men who are not dominant are in some way not masculine and not adequate, and (3) physical power and coercion are valid means of solving disputes in the family or in any other interpersonal relationships.[29]

Her statements focus on values and beliefs which are openly taught, modeled in the home, at school, and on television. However, the vast majority of society appears to operate with very little awareness of the values and beliefs which they allow to run their lives or which are passed on to their children.

The author is convinced that change is only affected on a personal level, not on a large social scale. If that is the case, then each person examining his or her own value and belief system regarding violence, sex role, and self-concept will be needed. Out of this will have to come a decision to change. To aid in the change, one will have to discuss themself openly, practice the change, take risks, be honest with and about self, take classes, participate in workshops, self-help groups, or in therapy. Discussing personal behavior, feelings, beliefs, and values raises one's awareness and, at times, the awareness of others. It opens the opportunity for each individual to make a decision about change and its implementation, and if necessary to seek professional assistance.

Society must discontinue rewarding uncontrolled violence, whether it is a child acting out or a violent television program.

Another value that must be stressed as positive is that it is ,re exciting to learn about oneself, develop oneself, experience personal growth, build relationships with other people, and learn how to love oneself and others. It will have to replace acts such as constant viewing of violence on television or precipitating violence in order to gain excitement.

Another option is for certain people to remain childless. In numerous cases this would be the best way to disrupt the violence cycle. Some people may not be able to stop the cycle any other way. Reducing the pressure for everyone to have children would help this situation. In more recent years it has been reduced, but there is a need for reduction on a more selective basis.

Another idea is for people to become more selective when choosing partners. Selecting partners out of a desperate need to be loved, married, taken care of, or removed from something is dangerous. Certain people are higher risks. Examples include people who use a lot of sarcasm in their communication, and men and women who were beaten as children (men in particular). Other high-risk groups include people who as children watched their parents abuse each other and chemical abusers, particularly alcohol abusers. People who fall into these categories should be considered carefully and avoided, or at least have some counseling together and individually prior to coupling up.

As women become more self-reliant and stop playing the "take care of me game," they are less likely to become involved in situations of abuse. When women learn to stand on their own, they will be far less likely to become involved with and remain in abusive situations. Society needs to reward women for developing self-respect and financial independence. Strong encouragement should be given to victims (abused and abuser) to go into therapy. Human potential and development groups can also be of value.

Openly discussing domestic violence, dealing with it in the class room, and presenting it in the news and documentaries are ways of raising the consciousness level of the public to the magnitude of the problem. If people recognize they are not alone with this problem, they are more likely to come forward and seek assistance. Adults can receive help from counselors, social workers, psychiatrists, psychologists, and organizations like Parents Anonymous. These can be valuable on a long-term basis.

What First Responders Can Do

The ideas presented in this chapter can be of assistance as a knowledge base for a person(s) responding to a violence crisis. The primary consideration is the physical safety and well-being of the abused person(s) and of the responders. Police, sheriffs, and paramedics dislike and fear the call to a domestic quarrel or violence situation. It has a high degree of danger, and law enforcement officers have a high number of injuries to themselves in these situations.

If the combatants are still together, whether it is in their home, a clinic, or Emergency Department, it is best to separate them. The first thing to do after carefully separating them is to take care of the physical problem(s).

In dealing with the abused person, one thing to keep in mind is that if this is the first time this secret has come into public view, the victim will feel upset about its discovery. They need to be reassured that it is best to have this out in the open, that they are not alone in the beating, and are in safe hands. The abused person will likely feel ashamed. Again, they will need assurance and emotional support in dealing with this feeling of shame. Whatever feelings the abused person has, they need to be allowed to ventilate them. If the abuser has threatened to kill the abused, believe the threat and, if at all possible, remove the abused from the scene. Also, while the crisis is still in process, people are most responsive to help. Use this knowledge to get the victims linked to support systems, whatever is appropriate to their situations, such as a shelter for women and/or children, Parents Anonymous, psychotherapy, and other measures.

If the respondent has the opportunity to deal with the abuser, again, be aware of one's own safety, especially if the person is on drugs or has been drinking. If the abuser is coherent and can communicate, try and get them to talk about their feelings and what they are experiencing. *Do not judge them*. If the abuser is aware of what is going on, they will feel guilty but may not express this or any feelings of hurt, anger, or other emotions. Remember, if these people had good verbal communication skills and were in touch with themselves, the situation would not have occurred. If the abuser is drunk, the best time to approach them about getting help is when they are coming out of the drunk and have a severe hangover. It is a time they feel their worst and can be strongly encouraged to make a choice to secure professional help, get involved in AA, Narcotics Anonymous and soon, when the abuser makes the choice to obtain help, make sure someone assists with making appropriate referrals. Finally, remember that the abuser is going to feel very inadequate and not like themselves. They need to be supported, understood, and shown they can be cared about. They need to know they can be helped.

Responders in the Role as Educators

Responders to domestic violence can play a primary role in educating the victims (abused and abuser) and the general public. In the selection on "What First Responders Can Do," the author believes the reader can view his or her role of responder as one of an educator. Good treatment always has an educational foundation. Helping victims understand that they are not alone in their experience can be enough to motivate the victim(s) to seek further help.

Responders are in a unique position to educate the public. They need to conduct seminars, forums, and workshops whenever possible. Further, they need to use the media to disseminate the message. If respondents seek out the media, they may be surprised at how easy it is to get a human interest story in the newspaper or on television. The electronic media (radio and television) is required to give a certain percentage of their air time to public service announcements. It can be used for this subject. Further, responders will find they can participate in radio shows, on television specials, or on live talk shows. In addition, television stations have a certain amount of programming devoted to local news and events. Finally, if one believes strongly about some subject, write about it.

SUMMARY

For the vast majority of people, the most influential factor in domestic violence is learning. It develops in the form of values and beliefs which are manifested in attitudes and behaviors. It is carried to people through several sources, with the six primary means being religion, schools, television, parents, verbal communication, and role modeling by all adults.

Domestic violence is passed on as a generation-to-generation sickness. If one witnessed violence while growing up or was a victim, he or she is a prime candidate to be involved in violent behavior as an adult.

Sarcasm, arguing, being pregnant, alcohol abuse, stress laden, feeling inadequate, disliking oneself, poverty, and/or being a poor verbal communicator are but a few of the variables involved in the outbreak of domestic violence.

If we believe that most domestic violence is learned, then we must believe it can be unlearned. Violence must stop being made an acceptable method for the settlement of disagreements. Further, a basic change in the values and beliefs about male dominance and female helplessness and dependency must occur. Finally, as a respondent, one can aid in the prevention and education of violent behavior.

REFERENCES

1. Gelles RJ: The other side of the family: Conjugal violence. Dissertation Abstracts International, 34, 9-A, P+2, March 1974, pp. 6141-6142
2. Flynn JP: Recent findings related to wife abuse. Social Casework, Vol. 58 No. 1, January 1977, p. 16
3. Carlson BE: Battered women and their assailants. Social Work, Vol. 22 No. 6, November 1977, p. 458
4. Høivik T: The demography of structural violence. Journal of Peace Research, Vol. XIV No. 1, 1977, p. 1467
5. Shaffer BD: Violence as a product of imposed order. University of Miami Law Review, Vol. 29 No. 4, Summer 1975, pp. 732-763
6. Gelles RJ: The other side of the family: Conjugal violence. Dissertation Abstracts International, 34, 9-A, P+2, March 1974, p. 6141
7. Gelles RJ: The other side of the family: Conjugal violence. Dissertation Abstracts International, 34, 9-A, P+2, March 1974, p. 6141
8. Ball M: Issues of violence in family casework. Social Casework, Vol. 58 No. 1, January 1977, p. 10
9. Flynn JP: Recent findings related to wife abuse. Social Casework, Vol. 58 No. 1, January 1977, p. 17
10. Carroll JC: The intergenerational transmission of family violence: The long-term effects of aggressive behavior. Aggressive Behavior, Vol. 3 No. 3, 1977, pp. 289-299

11. Pines M: Good samaritans at age two. Psychology Today, Vol. 3 No. 1, June 1979, p. 70
12. Brennan KS: A socio-psychological investigation of young murderers. British Journal Criminol, Vol. 17 No. 1, 1977, p. 59
13. Elliot FA: Neurological factors in violent behavior (the dyscontrol syndrome). Bulletin of the American Academy of Psychiatry and the Law, Vol. 4 No. 4, 1976, pp. 297-315
14. Brennan KS: A socio-psychological investigation of young murderers. British Journal of Criminol, Vol. 17 No. 1, 1977, p. 59
15. Brennan KS: A socio-psychological investigation of young murderers. British Journal of Criminol, Vol. 17 No. 1, 1977, p. 59
16. Sorrells JM: Kids who kill. Crime and Delinquency, 23, July 1977, pp. 312-320
17. Carlson BE: Battered women and their assailants. Social Work, Vol. 22 No. 6, November 1977, p. 457
18. Gelles RJ: The other side of the family: Conjugal violence. Dissertation Abstracts International, 34, 9-A, P+2, March 1974, p. 6141
19. Flynn JP: Recent findings related to wife abuse. Social Casework, Vol. 58 No. 1, January 1977, p. 18
20. Hanks SE, Rosenbaum CP: Battered women: A study of women who live with violent alcohol-abusing men. American Journal of Orthopsychiatry, Vol. 47 No. 2, April 1977, pp. 291-306
21. Flynn JP: Recent findings related to wife abuse. Social Casework, Vol. 58 No. 1, January 1977, p. 17
22. Sorrells JM: Kids who kill. Crime and Delinquency, 23, July 1977, pp. 312-320
23. Sorrells JM: Kids who kill. Crime and Delinquency, 23, July 1977, pp. 312-320
24. Sorrells JM: Kids who kill. Crime and Delinquency, 23, July 1977, pp. 312-320
25. Thomas MH et al: Desensitization to portrayals of real life aggression as a function of exposure to television violence. Journal of Personality and Social Psychology, Vol. 35, No. 6, 1977, p. 454
26. Thomas MH et al: Desensitization to portrayals of real life aggression as a function of exposure to television violence. Journal of Personality and Social Psychology, Vol. 35, No. 6, 1977, p. 456
27. Thomas MH et al: Densensitization to portrayals of real life aggression as a function of exposure to television violence. Journal of Personality and Social Psychology, Vol. 35, No. 6, 1977, p. 457
28. Thomas MH et al: Desensitization to portrayals of real life aggression as a function of exposure to television violence. Journal of Personality and Social Psychology, Vol. 35, No. 6, 1977, p. 457
29. Carlson BE: Battered women and their assailants. Social Work, Vol. 22 No. 6, November 1977, p. 466

3 INFLUENCING FACTORS OF VIOLENT BEHAVIOR

Carmen Germaine Warner, RN, PHN

Lizzie Borden . . . took an ax
And gave her father 40 whacks.
When the job was neatly done,
She gave her mother 41. 1892—famous rhyme

Violence and aggression are not hereditary. No one is born violent. Yet, over the course of years, with direct and indirect forms of influence, one may become conditioned and accept violence as a way of life. With the daily occurrence of political assassinations, urban riots, prisoners held hostage, military invasions, escalation of crimes involving personal injuries, physical rape and assault, mass murders, domestic beatings, and killings it is no wonder violence is a part of one's everyday life. In addition to this public exposure, there are a number of influencing and contributing factors which help pattern an individual's way of living and acceptance of personalized behavior.

INFLUENCE OF THE SUPER EGO ON BEHAVIOR AND VIOLENCE

One's super ego is the structure responsible for the good and bad, right and wrong, and the should and should nots. It is a blending of one's ideals and conscience, basic drives, and personal desires which ultimately determine what channels of aggression are chosen as acceptable for life.

The super ego begins to develop early in life and is strongly influenced by parental guidance. Throughout one's development, an individual learns the things to say and do which, according to Steele, is accomplished largely through two means of indoctrination.[1] One is the promise of love and approval upon acceptance of certain standards, and the other is the threat of punishment if one does not behave properly. These methods are quite effective, especially during childhood, and adult reorientation is not uncommon. The role of the first responder can openly extend to intervention with the perpetrator as well.

In addition to the instillation of violence in the growing child through cultural and familial standards, it also can develop in the child's own psyche. When a youngster is attacked, feelings of helplessness and weakness develop. In an attempt to avoid a hopeless, passive, helpless feeling, the child may decide to become strong like the attacker. Thus, the person who experiences violence in his or her own family will inevitably follow this same example as a manner of problem solving and dealing with personal feelings. Unfortunately, the adult who is the aggressor is frequently the model for the final developmental stages of the super ego's formation. Consequently, the ideals and categorical imperatives taught to children and infants are crucial.

DIRECT INFLUENCE ON VIOLENCE

Acceptance and approval by other human beings is based on such factors as power, wealth, prestige, influence, and notoriety. The greater accumulation one has of these characteristics, the more one presumes they will be liked, respected, and admired. Unfortunately, the manner in which an individual attempts to gain these characteristics may sometimes be destructive and at the expense of others.

Rape and sexual assault are blatant examples of the perpetrator's desire and need for power. The rapist interprets his ability to intimidate, induce an element of fear and guilt, physically and emotionally overpower, and project feelings of hostility over his victim as a means of gaining and expressing power.

With few exceptions, the acquisition of great wealth, prominence, and influence is not without the effect of aggression and violence. Organized crime and gang struggles for position are indicative of the "accepted manner" of attaining personal goals. Awareness of such factors is important in acquiring a general understanding of violence.

The family unit itself serves as a training ground for toughness and violence. Common acceptance that boys should have a few fist fights while growing up; the encouragement of children to become tough, athletic and aggressive; the approval of violence as an instrument of public policy; international relations; punishment of criminals; and control of social deviants are all examples of direct influences on violence.

INDIRECT INFLUENCE ON VIOLENCE

Even though a family might be outwardly opposed to violence as a matter of principle, a violence-prone child may develop due to the structure of relationships within the family unit.

One of the efficient methods of indirect violent training, such as spanking and slapping a child, is a common means of controlling a child's behavior.[2] As a result of this behavior, the child learns that violence can be an effective manner of dealing with others.

Other contributing factors could be the parents' moral outrage over social and economic injustices, the resulting feelings of helplessness regarding these issues, and one's inability to engage in socially constructive activities. Problem solving on a family or social level may utilize violence as the only known alternative to resolution.

Early family pressures such as being an active, creative, or positive force in society, according to Steinmetz and Straus, represent a combination of family experience and social position which influence violence.[3] Lack of self-worth among adolescents is a source of frustration for many youth. Violent reactions are not uncommon when dealing with certain pressures, and these reactions have caused society to recognize the intense needs of today's youth.

THE NATURE OF CONFLICTING ISSUES

Any topic of discussion could be a potential issue for conflict. Money, employment, education, vacations, recreation, entertainment, social activities, cooking, housework, house repairs, sex, discipline, and affection are some common issues.

In a recent study by Straus, Gelles, and Steinmetz, a total of 2,143 couples were questioned on issues over which they *always* disagreed. Thirty-four percent disagreed over housekeeping issues; 29 percent disagreed about sex; 27 percent disagreed on social matters; 26 percent disagreed over money; and 20 percent disagreed concerning the children.[4]

These data measurably contribute to the conflict-violence relationship. It has been a general assumption that the greater the conflict, the greater the incidence of violence. Further research conducted by Straus, Gelles, and Steinmetz identified results which clarified that assumption.

- Couples with the most conflicts had a violence rate of 43.9 percent.
- Nonconflict couples had a violence rate of 2.3 percent.
- Thirty-nine percent of the husbands in conflict marriages were violent.
- Thirty-three percent of the wives in conflict marriages were violent.[5]

Conflict can also be a signaling device, alerting individuals to the existence of certain issues which need attention. Instead of dealing with them in a physical, violent manner, individuals can use more constructive tactics such as negotiation or reasoning. Thus, conflict dealt with in a constructive manner can be viewed as a signal for needed communication.

The concept of catharsis as a method of working with conflict affords an additional approach for consideration. In some individuals, their inherent aggressive drive is suppressed or withheld. Natural aggression is manifested in nonviolent ways until an overload is reached and a bursting, explosive, severely destructive action results. The catharsis theory recommends avoiding violence by verbally expressing aggression or by attacking inanimate objects. This method will serve as a means of ventilating feelings short of physical attack.

According to the Straus research, the concept of catharsis does not work. In fact, they discovered the more verbal aggression couples expressed, the more physically violent they became. To clarify this, the study found that in the top 5 percent of couples who expressed verbal aggression, 83.3 percent engaged in one or more physical fights during the study period.[6]

SOME CAUSES OF DOMESTIC VIOLENCE

Children demand a great deal of attention. Caring for a child is a full-time job, and when there are two, three, or more children in the home, the demands, frustrations, and pressures increase markedly.

According to Straus,[7] the highest incidence of child abuse occurred in families with five children. In families with more than five children, there appeared to be a concept of child sharing and child caring which tended to minimize the responsibility and frustration for the parents.

Financial responsibilities, living accommodations with available privacy, and outside commitments with needed transportation are, according to this author, other factors to be considered in the assessment of potentially abusive homes. There appears to be a similar thread of violent behavior between child abuse and spouse abuse with respect to the number of children in the home.

As previously noted, child abuse occurred most frequently in homes with five children. The greatest incidence of spouse abuse also occurred in homes with five children.[8] If the family had six or more children, there appeared to be a leveling off syndrome utilizing more family sharing and helping skills on a daily basis.

Life Stressors

The impact of stress on one's life is a common topic of discussion. Considerable literature has come forth identifying common stressors, their causes, and possible solutions. It is not surprising that these same stressors also influence the rate of violence in our society.

Inner stress and strivings for power and control lead to the high incidence of rape and sexual assault. The need for self-identity, recognition, and the acquisition of status culminate in aggressive behavior directed at the individual deemed vulnerable and easy to conquer.

In situations of family violence, an excess of stress-producing factors accumulate and multiply producing a media for violence. Some of the contributing factors include:

- Escalating inflation rates
- Inability to increase family income
- Work related problems
- Unemployment
- Medical expenses
- Serious illness or accident
- Death in the family
- Pregnancy
- Foreclosure of loan on home
- Problems with relatives
- Sexual problems
- Separation or divorce
- Relocation of home
- Relocation of school
- Disciplinary problems with children at school
- Child suspended from school

- Child discovered taking drugs or stealing
- A family member arrested

Frequently, these stressors are out of one's control, which intensifies the level of frustration and helplessness. Even though public awareness has focused on ways to reduce stress if the initial causative factors cannot be wiped out, the stress factor will remain high.

Decision-Making Roles

A final factor which may create tension and pressure within a family unit is the existence of one party being the sole decision maker for the family. This includes situations where either the wife or the husband makes all the decisions and holds all the power. In these situations, the partner deemed powerless has no voice in the household management, and family communication is nonexistent. This portrays the partner with no voice in household management as weak, submissive, and vulnerable. This type of behavior encourages aggression on the part of the dominant mate and intensifies an already vicious cycle.

CONCLUDING THOUGHTS FOR EVALUATION AND ACTION

It is difficult to pinpoint precise causative factors leading to violence and aggression because each individual is just that—an individual responding and reacting in their own manner. However, common tendencies and patterns are valuable in determining yardsticks for measuring potential behavior.

One of the factors to be considered in this determination process is the realization that some families transmit to their children attitudes that accept violence. This may be transmitted through a lack of rejecting violent behavior as well as outward condonement.

The concept of behavior learned and accepted through observation and personal experience is sound. Children grow up viewing physical contact and verbal abuse as the only type of communication that receives a response. Even though individuals might not enjoy being the victim of physical abuse, they grow to accept it as a part of their life, a way of life.

Having patterned oneself in an already well-formed mold makes it very difficult to change behavior or attitude. This is evident even when the individual wants to change. All human behavior exists within the boundaries of a value and belief system. Violence is an expression of value and a specific human behavior. It evolves out of social interactions and existing conditions which, by the nature of its existence, give it meaning.

Attitudes, expectations, and daily occurrences are laced with violent behavior, some based on society's definition and others formed in self-identification. The incidence of violence has not morbidly increased, but the conscious awareness of violence and public attention to domestic violence has increased. This is noted in the recordings and research of behavioral scientists, the demand for intervention by the general public, and the enthusiastic response and focus by the media. This is evidenced by numerous trends as identified in Chapter Two.

Violence in our country is viewed as a means of coping— coping with the abundance of stressors which influence and impact our daily existence. This mechanism is seen as a means of socialization to which our children are exposed.

For example, youth are taught to be competitive, aggressive, highly individualistic, ambitious, self-reliant, and tolerant of losers. Youth are sent to war and honored for heroic feats of violence and battles of victory. Athletes are cheered for their display of power and aggression; children are rewarded with gifts of guns, knives, and weapons of destruction; law enforcement officers are encouraged to keep the peace with guns and billy clubs; and media heroes are acclaimed by their degree of toughness, meanness, and brutality. It is the lip service given by our society, the confusing, double messages issued to our youth, and the double standards developed for the rich and powerful that anger and confuse our society. Violence may be the only voice that is heard.

SUMMARY

It is the hope of society that changes will be made. These broad-based changes can occur only if society itself speaks out, establishes norms for acceptable behavior, advocates nonviolent methods of intervention, and portrays the violent person as the individual "out of style" and a social reject.

REFERENCES

1. Steele BF: Violence in our society. The Pharos of Alpha Omega Alpha, Vol. 33 No. 2, April 1970, p. 45
2. Steinmetz SK, Straus MA: The family as the training ground for societal violence. *In* Steinmetz SK, Straus MA: Violence in the Family. New York; Dodd, Mead and Company, 1975, p. 232
3. Steinmetz SK, Straus MA: The family as the training ground for societal violence. *In* Steinmetz SK, Straus MA: Violence in the Family. New York; Dodd, Mead and Company, 1975, p. 234
4. Straus MA, Gelles RJ, Steinmetz SK: Behind Closed Doors: Violence in the American Family. New York, Anchor Press, 1980, pp. 157-158
5. Straus MA, Gelles RJ, Steinmetz SK: Behind Closed Doors: Violence in the American Family. New York, Anchor Press, 1980, p. 163
6. Straus MA, Gelles RJ, Steinmetz SK: Behind Closed Doors: Violence in the American Family. New York, Anchor Press, 1980, p. 169
7. Straus MA, Gelles RJ, Steinmetz SK: Behind Closed Doors: Violence in the American Family. New York, Anchor Press, 1980, p. 177
8. Straus MA, Gelles RJ, Steinmetz SK: Behind Closed Doors: Violence in the American Family. New York, Anchor Press, 1980, pp. 180-181

II

IDENTIFYING THE PROBLEM

4 DOMESTIC VIOLENCE: ASSESSING THE PROBLEM

Ashley Walker-Hooper, BA

"Domestic violence," domestic disturbance," and "family violence" are all terms used to describe a victim, usually female, who is intimidated, threatened, and assaulted within the confines of her home, often within "plain view" of her children and within earshot of neighbors, family, and friends. The deliberate assault by men is perpetrated against women with whom they presently, or in the past, have had an intimate involvement, including financial and/or emotional support.

The problem of abuse against women has long remained hidden because of tacit approval given to the man to chastise his family and control its members through whatever means he deemed necessary. The world of battered women is lonely and terrifying. Most live in a state of constant anxiety. All attempts to modify their partners' behavior are met with inevitable failure. They are told that they are responsible for the violence. They are told by his family that they are his only hope, causing an underlying feeling of "failure" and responsibility for making the marriage work.

The stereotypical female and male roles force couples into situations in which the male's dominant role and "right" to use violence is never questioned. Many women see the role of wife as a submissive one and are socialized not to demand or expect a non-violent relationship. For women who grow up in violent homes, there sometimes is a connection made at an early age between violence and love. They see significant others fight and then kiss and make up. Children cannot discern the naunces of the relationship and sometimes think that if a person does not hit you, he or she does not love you. At the very least, hitting to express displeasure or to force compliance is seen as normal behavior. When it is seen and experienced again as an adult, it is met with hurt and fear, but not utter shock and disbelief.

Cultural values of this male-dominant society often approve of and encourage violence against women. The male is socialized to view himself as superior to "girls." By virtue of the numerous advantages sanctioned in our culture, men have been able to maintain their superiority. With the advent of the women's rights movement, the male's privileged position educationally, occupationally, and socially is being challenged. There is one area in which legislation will not change the outcome: men are physically larger and stronger than women. To challenge this physical superiority is usually to invite disaster. In his article "Sexual Inequality, Cultural Norms and Wife Beating," Murray A. Straus lists nine ways in which the male-dominant structure of society and the family" . . . create and maintain a high level of marital violence." These points are:

1. Defense of male authority.
2. Compulsive masculinity.
3. Economic constraints and discrimination which keep women dependent upon men for support of themselves and their children.
4. Burdens of child care without financial remuneration or assistance while she works.
5. Myth that the single-parent household is not a viable family unit.
6. Preeminence of the 'wife role' for women as the single most important role, while men have the option of investing as little or as much time in the 'father-husband role' as interest, time, or ability demands.
7. Negative self-image of women, especially in relation to achievement.
8. Women as children supported by legal statutes which give men rights over women, and the 'covert' moral right to use physical violence on wives and children.
9. Male orientation of the criminal justice system offers little and/or no protection and relief to battered women.[1]

Women are often the targets of hitting and are told that it is for their own good, or it is done because they are loved. Violence is so pervasive in this culture that no statistics are kept. There are estimates that 50 percent of all American wives experience some form of spouse-inflicted violence during their marriage, regardless of race or socio-economic status. These estimates were in a report prepared by the National League of Cities and the United States Conference of Mayors. A nationwide Louis Harris poll prepared for the National Commission on Causes and Prevention of Violence states that " . . . one-fifth of all Americans approve of slapping one's spouse on appropriate occasions. Surprisingly, approval of this practice increases with income and education." There was almost unanimous approval for use of physical punishment to discipline children.

WHY MEN BATTER–CHARACTERISTICS OF THE BATTERER

It is hoped that the reader will begin to view and understand the abuser as another victim of domestic violence. Batterers are casualties of a culture that forces them into a masculine stereotype. They must be strong and in control. They must make the rules and force compliance. They are expected to "own" a woman and family. They must be responsible to provide for that family at all costs. They are not to cry or express emotion. Within their framework, it is okay to hit as a way of making feelings known, displeasure felt, and maintaining control and power in most phases of their lives. In her book "The Battered Woman," Lenore Walker lists several characteristics of batterers. The batterer:

1. Has low self-esteem.
2. Believes all the myths about battering relationships.
3. Is a traditionalist believing in male supremacy and the stereotyped masculine sex role in the family.
4. Blames others for his actions.
5. Is pathologically jealous.
6. Presents a dual personality.
7. Has severe stress reactions, during which he uses drinking and wife battering to cope.
8. Frequently uses sex as an act of aggression to enhance self-esteem in view of waning virility; may be bisexual.
9. Does not believe his violent behavior should have negative consequences.[2]

Other characteristics of men who batter include:

10. Were abused as a child or saw significant other(s) abused, usually their mother by their father.
11. Have a preoccupation with weapons.
12. Have a high level of job dissatisfaction, underemployment, and/or unemployment.
13. Accepts violence as a viable method of problem solving.
14. Frequently abuses or threatens the safety of household pets.

15. Hunts for pleasure and not the sport of the kill.
16. Has a low frustration tolerance.

MEN WHO BATTER

Many batterers are the products of violent homes. Many more men than women in violent relationships saw their fathers beat their mothers. The sons, who were often the targets of abuse, identified with the parent who abused them and learned aggression as a viable means of dealing with emotions, life conflicts, and problems. These men bear the stigmatization of the battering home from which they came in that often, as a child, they did not have their needs met. They were powerless to control their environment. They were often frightened and deprived of a warm, supportive, nurturing home life. There was little chance to develop a healthy ego and sense of self-worth. Even in homes where violence was not present, the repressive cold environment and lack of nurturance provides the framework for the use of violence as an instrument of communication. The home did not provide effective role models for communication of needs or feelings nor of personal space and privacy. These men have never experienced real control and power, even over themselves. This ultimate sense of powerlessness leads to the projecting of one's failures, dislikes, feelings, and inability to cope onto others. The target least likely to resist is one's mate.

The low frustration tolerance level, external locus of control, and low impulse control make the behavior of battering men childlike. When not aggressive, many are dependent and passive. Many want to be nurtured and cared for, and see this as a "weakness" in themselves. They then express their anger about their dependence as a physical and/or verbal attack on women. The fear that they cannot do without women makes them more abusive.

Excessive jealousy and possessiveness are part of the pattern. The women are never able to convince the men that they are faithful and loyal, even though the men monitor their every movement. Checking and recording the odometer before they go to the market; reading their mail; listening in on their telephone calls; and even following them to the bathroom are not uncommon behaviors. Many women, at first, are flattered by all the "attention" their mates show to them. It is only later, when they cannot turn off the "faucet of jealousy," that they realize how pathological this behavior is. The men's dependency on women to make them feel whole and appear to others as a "real man" becomes blatant when the women attempt to leave. Men will often exhibit suicidal or homicidal rage.

The dual personality presented by batterers also keeps women hostage. For example, it is confusing to the woman to be beaten one day and brought flowers the next. It is difficult to make a clean break. The man who beat her up has been replaced by one so apologetic, repentive, attentive, and caring that she finds it hard to express her anger and hurt toward him. This is compounded because the facade of "loving husband and father" is often kept intact for friends, neighbors, family, and coworkers. The woman does not want to shatter this fragile, dreamlike existence, always hoping that the "man in public" will become the "man in private." She also faces the chance that she will not be believed by others who have never had to face this man when he is out of control and in a state of unrestrained rage.

Consumption of alcohol and drugs before, during, and after battering incidents is reported by many victims. It is not certain whether the intent of the drinking is to calm them down or to give them courage. The result of the consumption is that inhibitions are lowered, and there is a convenient scapegoat upon whom to project the blame. Traditionally, the use of alcohol and drugs is seen by the partners as the cause of the problem, for women rationalize and do not face the reality of the situation. Men either plead temporary loss of memory or "acceptable" loss of control. Also paramount is the fact that when drug use and alcohol consumption are reduced or eliminated, the violence still escalates.

Margaret Elbow, in "Theoretical Considerations of Violent Marriages," lists four personality types of abusers.

> The controller is a man used to getting his way, who sees people as objects to control. He tends to monitor his wife's activities, her money, friends and interests, and expects her to jump at his wishes. He can become violent when he does not get his own way, and believes his abuse to be justified. He opposes her leaving, because then he cannot control her and will often threaten retribution. He sees her as the parent who controlled him and feels that if he does not control her, she will control him. Women may be attracted to him because he seems so capable of handling things.
>
> The defender is also self-righteous, but wants not so much to control as to protect his wife in order to keep from facing his own need for protection. He encourages her to be dependent on him and likes to see himself as the sole bread-winner who can take care of his wife and family. He wants to give to her but not to receive, because that would be admitting he needs her. The basic anxiety that triggers his violence differs from the controller's in that while the controller fears being controlled, the defender fears being harmed.

The approval seeker has inappropriately high expectations of himself and, consequently, gets little satisfaction from his achievements. He gets depressed, needs constant approval and often goes out of his way to please others. He abuses when his self-esteem is especially low. He expects rejection from others because he sees himself as deserving it. His parents usually withdrew their love when he did not measure up, and he sees his wife the same way—he may hope she is accepting, but he expects her to reject him. He may instigate fights in order to test her love. Feelings of sexual inadequacy interfere with his ability to achieve sexual or emotional intimacy. This man does feel guilty for abusing his wife but is afraid to seek counseling because he is sure the counselor will put him down, confirming his own sense of worthlessness.

The incorporator is characteristically desperate to incorporate another's ego in order to make himself feel whole. He may use drugs or alcohol heavily, and he exhibits jealousy during courtship. He is insatiable in his need for support and comfort, and fearful that his wife will be taken away from him. He is frequently also a child abuser because he cannot differentiate between himself and others, and sees his kids as well as his wife as extensions of his ego.[3]

WHY WOMEN STAY/CHARACTERISTICS OF THE BATTERED WOMEN

It is not possible to determine who is or will become a battered woman on the basis of socio-economic, ethnic, cultural, religious, or age groups. An understanding of social and interpersonal conditions gives a clearer understanding of why women stay and endure violent, unhappy relationships for prolonged periods of time. Social approval is important. A person dependent upon others for feelings of self-worth will not readily do things that provoke societal disapproval. Failure in the role of wife and mother leaves many women with a poor sense of self-worth because they perceive these as the only viable roles available to them. Many personality characteristics and societal values and norms keep women in abusive relationships. Lenore Walker, in "Battered Women," outlines some commonalities of battered women.

1. Low self-esteem.
2. Believes all the myths about battering relationships.
3. Is a traditionalist about the home, strongly believes in family unity and the prescribed female sex-role stereotype.
4. Accepts responsibility for the batterer's actions.
5. Suffers from guilt, yet denies the terror and anger she feels.
6. Presents a passive face to the world, but has the strength to

       manipulate enough to prevent further violence and to pre-
       vent being killed.
7. Has severe stress reactions with psychophysical com-
    plaints.
8. Uses sex as a way to establish intimacy.
9. Believes that no one will be able to help her resolve her pre-
    dicament except herself.[4]

Fear of Loneliness, Loss of Sanity, and Reprisals

Forced and/or self-imposed isolation has left battered women with
only their partners to depend upon for an accurate reflection of their
mental states. There is little reason for batterers to attempt to boost
sagging egos or to reinforce the reality of situations. Many battered
women have had to develop a variety of coping strategies in order
to survive in a battering relationship.

    Uninformed observers, or those who view these behaviors in
isolation, perceive the women as being mentally ill. They label,
medicate, and alienate the women which reinforces the women's
own, often erroneous, misconceptions about themselves. Living
under constant fear and stress has physical as well as psychological effects on women. Hilberman and Munson found that:

> . . . agitation and anxiety bordering on panic was almost always
> present. . . . There was chronic apprehension of imminent doom, of
> something terrible always about to happen. Any symbolic or actual
> sign of potential danger resulted in increased activity, agitation,
> pacing, screaming and crying. They remained vigilant, unable to
> relax or sleep. Sleep, when it came, brought no relief. Nightmares
> were universal, with undisguised themes of violence and
> danger. . . . "
>   Somatic complaints, conversion symptoms, and
> psychophysiological reactions were abundant as evidenced by fre-
> quent clinic visits for headaches, choking sensations, hyperventila-
> tion, asthma, chest pain, gastrointestinal symptoms, pelvic pain, and
> allergic phenomena. Symptoms were connected to previous sites of
> battering.[5]

    The fear of being alone and sick is frightening to many battered
women. It has often been years since they have "felt well." Women,
over time, lose their physical and psychological strength and will.
They have become dependent upon a violent relationship which
was the precipitating factor in their illnesses, expecting it to take
care of them.

Compounding the fear of being alone, sick, unlovable, and unwanted is the constant threat by the mate that he will: kill her, prove she is an unfit mother and take the children, harm the children, or fix her so nobody else will want her. The women have ample evidence and precedents to believe that the threats are sincere, and that the partners are quite capable of carrying them out. More important is the fact that most women believe there is *nothing* they can do to stop him.

Economic Dependence/Lack of Resources

Economic self-sufficiency is probably the number one factor to consider when discussing why women stay. It is impossible to maintain an independent life style without adequate funds. The majority of battered women do not have *control* of the family earnings. Without money and a place to go, battered women do not have choices. Most abusers do not wish their partners to work outside the home because exposure to others makes it more difficult to maintain control over the woman's thoughts, movements, and actions. The relationship is based upon an unequal distribution of power and cannot be easily maintained if women work. In this culture, money is power. It is the golden rule: "He who has the gold makes the rule."

The relationship is sustained upon deprivation and isolation. Many skills are lost if not used. Battered women, through forced and/or self-imposed isolation, lose many of their survival skills and cannot easily be integrated into the mainstream of work without training. They are unfamiliar with many systems with which they must interact, such as counseling, employment, legal, medical, and financial assistance. If they leave battering relationships and are left unsupported and unassisted, they are very soon overwhelmed and intimidated. Their lack of self-confidence and self-esteem are soon reinforced and, out of fear, they seek at least the familiarity of their abusive relationships. Also important is the fact that the women re-enter the home during the "honeymoon period" of the violence cycle. The partners are usually attentive, repentent, and kind. They offer a stark contrast to the cold, cruel world of independence and freedom.

All battered women are not from one-paycheck families. Some women work and have substantial incomes; however, they do not have control of these incomes. Women who have access to money or whose partners have substantial wealth may stay because the loss of status and material goods is more than they are willing to give up. This is especially true if periodically they can escape or if there are children involved. They tell themselves that they do not wish to deny their children educational, social, and cultural opportunities that they could not afford to give them. In this case, the trade-offs become too great, and violence is tolerated in return for financial considerations.

Self-Blame, Guilt, and/or Embarrassment

Female children are socialized into three traditional sex roles which are integrally involved with "family" life: wife, mate, and mother. Society has allocated to women the responsibility of the emotional, physical, and psychological well-being of the family unit, and any malfunction becomes their direct responsibility. Dysfunction in the family, no matter how grotesque its manifestation, is covertly viewed by most people as the woman's fault. For women who have internalized this socialization, it is a natural progression that they blame themselves for the battering.

Anger that is felt in relation to the battering incidents may be directly expressed toward the partner (often with disastrous results), turned against people who intervene, or directed inward. This inward anger is often manifested as depression. The debilitating effects of depression makes these women less capable of performing day-to-day functions. Women who are beaten because (1) they did not clean the house or burned the meal (not a good wife); (2) did not change the baby's diaper (not a good mother); or (3) did not respond to their partners (not a good mate), forget the source of their diminished functioning and think that they indeed deserve the verbal abuse and beatings. Thus, the things that they are confronted with are true, and so they believe the incident is their fault.

Battered women may have left their relationships on other occasions, but have returned because of loneliness, financial insecurity, fear of physical reprisals, or any of a number of other reasons. They leave with the resolve never to return or to return only if their mates make concessions and promises about behavioral changes. With each return home, they lose another piece of self-respect and further blame themselves with each new episode. Battered women engage often in the "if only" syndrome. The end product of these "if only" statements is that they are the ones who are inadequate, incompetent, and incapable of fulfilling their obligations and roles.

Learned Helplessness

A psychological rationale for why women stay with abusers is the theory of "Learned Helplessness." Supportive data are available from tests done with dogs and rats subjected to random painful stimuli while under conditions of forced imprisonment. After repeated unsuccessful attempts to escape and avoid the shocks, the animals became and remained passive, did not actively avoid the painful stimuli, and did not seek to escape. The animals had acquired a sense of powerlessness that was not overcome even after it was clear that an escape route was available and shocks were discontinued.

The sense of powerlessness was generalized to other situations and, even when they were not powerless, the animals responded as if they were. The concept of belief of helplessness is important. Clearly, what a person believes to be true is true for them. Lenore E. Walker, Ph.D., in an article entitled "Battered Women and Learned Helplessness," states:

> This concept is important to understand why battered women do not attempt to gain their freedom from a battering relationship. They do not believe that they can escape from the batterer's domination. Often their perceptions are accurate, but they need not be for this theory to work.[6]

An anonymous battered woman, in response to an article in *Human Behavior Magazine* (September 1977), states: " . . . consider that an abusive marriage situation is behavior modification—we become what we become to survive."[7] In her attempts to avoid the painful stimuli of the relationship, she tried the acceptable escape mechanisms:

> 1. Counseling and therapy: "To make my decision to get out, it was pointed out to me that if I stayed in it, I would die. If I tried to get out, I had one chance in a thousand that I would make it. They weren't much for odds.[8]
> 2. Friends and neighbors: "Something that was not touched were caring neighbors. I use the term loosely. My next-door neighbor often asked me to go to church with her. Yet her husband stood not 15 feet away and watched my husband drag me into the house by the hair."[9]
> 3. The police: "I was told by the police that they could not come if a beating had not taken place, but was anticipated (I understand this). However, I was also told that if he starts beating me up, to give them a call. I still have trouble understanding that."[10]
> 4. Lawyers: "I had a lawyer explain restraining orders to me. I could not see how a piece of paper was going to keep someone from

breaking a door down. I have since been informed that restraining orders don't really keep someone out, but a woman has legal recourse after he breaks in and beats her. She can charge him with contempt of court, but a judge rarely puts a man in jail because he is a bread-winner." [11]

Battered women have tried numerous times to elicit assistance and support without success. Their feelings that they are alone and unable to escape are frequently reinforced by agencies, policies, and procedures.

The following table (4.1) by Boyd and Klingbell [12] compares and contrasts behavior characteristics of the *victims* of domestic violence (see page 58).

THE CRISIS STATE

When in a crisis state, a person's emotional-feeling level is extremely high in proportion to his or her rational, thinking, reasoning level. One goal of crisis intervention is to bring these two dimensions into equilibrium. It is necessary to consider the person's third dimension—that of conscience or parent. This dimension contains the "shoulds," "oughts," values, prejudices, and rules that punish and reward the person. The self-image of the batterer and the victim must be understood if some effective interaction is to take place. Acceptance of blame by the woman; the element of right to chastise and ownership by the batterer; feelings of loss of control by both parties; feelings of helplessness, guilt, fear, anger, and embarrassment by the woman; and the frustration, anger, and rage by the man are interrelated and integral parts of the battering relationship.

In the battering relationship there is continuing conflict. In the beginning, problems are resolved or continuously set aside by some action by one of the mates. The abuse escalates to a "crises" state when either partner is unable to resolve or accept the resolution by the other partner. It is important to focus on the precipitating event. For domestic violence participants, the precipitating event often seems to be insignificant and small ("I wouldn't turn the radio off"), but it represents the "straw that broke the camel's back." Gary A. Crow states in *Crisis Intervention: A Social Interaction Approach* that " . . . crisis is always preceded by a relatively definable and observable precipitating event." [13] He feels that a crisis has two components.

Table 4.1. Behavioral Characteristics of Domestic Violence

Abuser	Abused Partner	Children
Evident at all socio-economic levels; all educational, racial, age groups.	Evident in all socio-economic levels; all educational, racial, age groups.	Evident in all socio-economic levels; education, racial, and age groups.
Characterized by poor impulse control; explosive temper; limited tolerance of frustration.	Characterized by long suffering, martyr-like endurance of frustration.	Manifests a combination of limited tolerance, poor impulse control, and martyr-like long suffering.
Hidden symptoms of characterologic dysfunction; sophistication of symptoms and success at masking dysfunction vary with level of social/educational sophistication.	Obvious depressive and/or hysterical symptoms; stress disorders and psychosomatic complaints.	Depression, much stress and psychosomatizing, absences from school—hidden symptoms of characterological dysfunction.
Emotional dependency—subject to secret depressions known only to family.	Economic/emotional dependence—subject to depression, high risk for secret drugs and alcohol, home accidents.	Economic/emotional dependent, high risk for alcohol/drugs, sexual acting out, running away, isolation, loneliness, fear.

Table 4.1. *Behavioral Characteristics of Domestic Violence* (continued).

Abuser	Abused Partner	Children
Reduced capacity for delayed-reinforcement—very "now" oriented.	Unlimited patience for discovery of what is needed to solve marital and battering problems—can "travel miles" on tiny bits of reinforcement.	Combination of poor impulse control and continual hopefulness that situation will improve.
Insatiable ego needs—has quality of childlike narcissicism (not generally detectable to people outside family group).	Unsure of own ego needs—defines self in terms of family, job, and others.	Very unstable definition of self-grappling with childlike responses of parents for modeling—poor definition of self.
Low self-esteem—perceived unachieved ideals and goals for self; disappointment in career even if successful by others' standards.	Low self-esteem; continued faith and hope abusing mate will get "lucky" break.	Low self-esteem.
Qualities which suggest great potential for change and improvement; such as frequent "promises" for the future.	Unrealistic hope that change is imminent; belief in "promises."	Mixture of hope/depression that there is no way out; peer group can be more important contact, if available.

Table 4.1. Behavioral Characteristics of Domestic Violence (continued).

Abuser	Abused Partner	Children
Convinced self to have poor social skills; describes relationship with mate as closest he has ever known; remains in contact with own family.	Gradually increasing social isolation, including loss of contact with own family.	Increased social isolation; increased peer isolation.
Accusations—jealousy—voices great fear of being abandoned or "cheated on."	Unable to convince partner of loyalty; futilely guards against accusations of "seductive" behavior toward other men.	Manifests bargaining behavior with parents; gets into proving self as does mother.
Contains mate and uses spy tactics against her (for example, checks mileage and times errands); cleverness depends on level of sophistication.	Permits containment or confinement/restriction; interprets as sign that partner "cares."	Develops deceptiveness: lying, excuse for outings, and more.

Table 4.1. Behavioral Characteristics of Domestic Violence (continued).

Abuser	Abused Partner	Children
No sense of violating others' personal boundaries; accepts no blame for failures (marital, familial, or occupational) or violence.	Gradually loses sight of personal boundaries for self and children (unable to assess danger accurately); accepts all blame.	Poor definition of personal boundaries; violation of others' personal boundaries.
Believes forcible behavior is aimed at securing the family nucleus (for the good of the family).	Believes transient acceptance of violent behavior will ultimately lead to long-term resolution of family problems.	Has little or no understanding of dynamics of violence (often assumes violence to be the norm).
Often reports not feeling guilt on emotional level even after intellectual recognition.	Emotionally accepts guilt for mate's behavior; thinks mate "can't help it;" considers own behavior provocative.	Blames self (depending on age) for family feuding, separations, divorce, and more; internal conflicts.
Generational history of family violence.	Generational history of family violence.	Continues pattern of family violence in own adulthood.

Table 4.1. Behavioral Characteristics of Domestic Violence (continued).

Abuser	Abused Partner	Children
Participates in pecking-order abusing.	Participates in pecking-order abusing.	Pecking-order abusing—kills animals, abuses younger siblings (and some times parents in later years).
Abusive skills improve with age and experience, but danger potential and lethality risks also rise.	Learns which behavioral events will either divert or precipitate partner's violence but level of carelessness increases; judgment of lethality potential deteriorates over time.	Uses violence as problem-solving technique in school, with peers, with family.
Demanding and oftentimes assaultive in sexual activities; sometimes punishes with abstinence; at times experiences impotence.	Poor sexual self-image; assumes role is to accept totally partner's sexual behavior; attempts to punish partner with abstinence resulting in abuse.	Poor sexual image; unclear about appropriate behavior; confuses model identification.
Controls by threatening homicide and/or suicide; often attempts one or both when partner separates; known to complete either or both.	Frequently contemplates suicide—history of minor attempts; occasionally completes either suicide or homicide of partner.	Heightened suicide attempts; increased thoughts of doing away with self and/or murdering parents; prone to negligence and carelessness.

"The 'now potential' is high and the 'self-resolution' factor is low. The 'now' in the now potential refers to the immediacy or emergency quality of the crisis; 'potential' refers to what might or could happen. The 'self-resolution' factor obviously refers to the person's ability to resolve his own problem without intervention."[14]

CRISIS FOCUS

In dealing with violent couples, it is necessary to develop a crisis focus and to maintain it. The focus is by nature a narrow one which concentrates in a laser-like fashion on the crisis itself. The crisis focus, according to Crow, can be tested by answering these questions:

1. Specifically, what is likely to get worse?
2. How bad might it get?
3. If things get worse, what is the potential effect and on whom?
4. Why do we think the individual or someone else in the crisis will not be able to deal with it?

Adequate answering of these questions and the establishment and maintenance of the focus increases effectiveness of crisis intervention.

INTERVENTION IN THE CRISIS STATE BY FIRST RESPONDERS

The mood or effect of the person in crisis is important. Anger may be the prevailing mood. It is important to remember that anger is not always expressed by tension, loud verbal expression, or exaggerated physical movement. Anger is observable in quiet, calm-like states through nonverbal behavior and from verbal remarks whose meaning and overtone are indignant and hostile. Anger is debilitating, and the fear that the person will explode and destroy are real. It is necessary to reduce the anger to the degree that the person can verbally express his or her displeasure and not have to act it out. The intervener engaged with an angry person must be careful not to increase the anger or to mirror it. Calmness must be stressed. One needs to acknowledge that the person is angry, but not reinforce it. It is essential to focus on the problem in a laser-like fashion, and not be swayed into tangential issues. By helping the person achieve some verbal expression, you increase the ability to deal with his or her crisis.

For many counselors on crisis hotlines, the most difficult call is the depressed person. It is physically exhausting to even hear what the person is saying. It takes every fiber of their being just to concentrate and keep the person on the line. The voice is usually very soft, and the speech is very slow and often slurred. It can be assumed that the person is under the influence of drugs or alcohol.

Keeping the person talking and attempting to change his mood by giving positive feedback is necessary. Although it is difficult to give the person a reason to continue, if left disconnected and alienated from his surrounding, suicide is often the result. Sometimes the crisis worker becomes angry at the caller because of the uncomfortable position of being responsible for a life.

The majority of interactions with battered women over the telephone or in person shows women who are confused, anxious, and desperate. Police and crisis workers often encounter women who are crying, upset, and cannot get the "story straight." They are frightened and nervous and want desperately to be rescued. It is necessary to help women focus on their problems. Acknowledgement and discussion of their feelings are important. The skilled crisis worker does not move from general to specific until the woman is able to focus in on one problem and possible resolutions. By slowly asking questions and repeating the same question until an answer is forthcoming, the worker encourages the woman to calm down and to think clearly. Deliberate repetition of the same question assists the woman in quieting down and moving toward resolution of the problem.

How the crisis intervener responds often determines the outcome for the person in trouble. It is important to remain calm, concerned, and objective. The worker should acknowledge the person's mood, but not become a part of it. Voice and mannerisms are important as they convey as much as the spoken words. The issue is to help the woman define her problem, be able to discuss it in a clear, coherent manner, and to develop some plan of action for its resolution.

Questions should have a precise purpose and lead the person in a clear direction. A rational approach to solving the problem should begin to emerge. An additional issue in counseling battered women is that some of the calls demand immediate action because the woman is in physical danger. In this situation it is necessary to handle the immediate crisis without processing the victim to the point of reaching the decision herself. When this is the case, continued contact with the victim is indicated so that she will understand the dynamics of her situation and not become dependent on the rescue aspect of the previous interaction. She must quickly be given back the responsibility for her own safety and problem resolution. The woman must be made to feel that the problem is manageable and that she can arrive at a solution.

The goal of crisis intervention is not to solve the long-standing problems that the woman is experiencing. The goal is to help the person through the crisis. A great deal of frustration is felt by crisis interveners because they do not properly perceive their role. It is not the role of medical personnel, the crisis counselor, or the police officer to cure the dysfunctional family interaction, make the victim assertive, or make the batterer nonviolent. It is the purpose of intervention to focus on the crisis, calm the participants down, and to help them deal with their feelings. Providing emergency services, referrals, and information necessary to help the battering couple formulate a plan of action will help prevent the crisis state from reappearing. Long-term involvement and resolution of problems are not the goals of crisis intervention.

The Police Role in Domestic Violence Intervention

The importance of police as first responders in domestic violence incidents cannot be overstated. Usually when things are getting out of hand, people cannot think of anyone else to call. The old adage is appropriate: "For many, calling the police is like taking castor oil—you take it because you have no other options, but you still hate it and it doesn't make it taste any better." Police are necessary in these incidents because they are the only agency that has the legal sanction to stop the violence. No other agent in our culture can cause cessation of violence by its presence. Police are respected and feared by some batterers as a force greater than themselves, and their response is crucial for man and woman alike. Police need to act quickly, and must avoid exceeding their authority, increasing tension in the relationship, and, most of all, overreacting. The officers must communicate in a fashion that calms and slows people down, starts a thought process, and helps them formulate a plan of action. The crisis nature of police work does not lend itself to solving the long-standing and multifaceted problems of domestic relationships. This should not be an expectation or a goal.

Restoring the peace, protecting the victim, making appropriate legal decisions, information giving (referrals), and, if possible, emergency transportation are a tall order and enough for the law enforcement officer to be concerned with. Psychological and sociological aspects of the problem are more appropriately handled by those with specific training and adequate time.

In Training Key Number 246, the "Investigation of Wife Beating," published by the International Association of Police Chiefs, a complete procedure is outlined for the handling of wife abuse cases from initial response to the arrest.[15] The basic components of that Key are indicated below.

Receiving Complaint

Dispatcher should: (A) get information from the victim; (B) keep the phone line open; (C) check for repeats; (D) ascertain the extent of injuries, use of weapons, and location of alleged assailant; (E) listen for background noises; and (F) if danger is ascertained, ask the victim to meet officers outside (if her husband will let her out).

Arriving at Scene

- Approach from vicinity that offers most protection.
- Be observant, view inside if possible to determine activity of the moment before announcing your presence. The "plain view" doctrine can be used to establish probable cause that a crime was committed.

Gaining Entry

- Introduce yourself, giving reasons why you are on the premises. If denied entry, calmly explain that you need assurance that there is no serious trouble inside.
- Force entry if there is reason to believe that the victim is in danger (cries for help, weapons displayed, obvious signs of struggle, eye witnesses).

Establishing Control

- Locate all parties, determine if there are weapons, and determine extent of injury.

- Separate the parties so both can be seen by you, but not heard by each other.
- Avoid the kitchen, as it is a natural source of weapons.
- Remove witnesses to avoid compromising their status at hearing(s).
- Voluntary statements should be stopped when the alleged assailant begins to incriminate himself and should be advised of his rights.

Protecting the Victim

- Victim should be protected from further battery and administered first aid.
- Injuries are frequently internal—stomach, breast area, portions of head covered by hair, and back; pregnant women in the stomach.
- Determine if the wife is rational, injury is obvious, and victim is unable to care for herself. The officer is responsible for obtaining medical attention even if the victim protests.

Interviewing the Victim

- Display concern for physical and psychological well-being of victim.
- Permit the victim to wash and care for herself.
- Allow 'ventilation' periods; stress and trauma of event distort her self-image—she may talk and act helpless.
- The officer's verbal and/or nonverbal communication builds or destroys confidence. Eye contact, slight nods, head and facial movements, and neutral terminology such as "Yes" and "Oh, I see" encourage communication.

Interviewing Witnesses

- Interview as soon as possible.
- Evaluate for inconsistencies.
- May need to check with neighbors for prior and chronic abuse; physical evidence, observation, and hearing are important.

Interviewing Assailant

- General on-the-scene questioning, fact-finding, and inter-rogation (if to elicit incriminating information) of assailant as criminal suspect.
- Be aware of "threshold confessions" made at the beginning when assailant is asked, "What's going on here?" If the hus-band becomes a criminal suspect, he must be advised of his rights.
- Importance of nonverbal communication, shifting in seat, outburst of anger, shifting subject of conversation.

Gathering Evidence

- Evidentiary articles—photographs, victim accounts, and physician's reports—should be collected as in all investiga-tions.
- Injuries to victim(s).
- Crime scene—photographs or written report about scene—necessary to state that assailant was advised of rights.

Arrest

- With strong physical evidence and strong circumstantial evidence in felony cases, an investigation can take place and an arrest made without wife's cooperation (probable cause).
- In misdemeanor cases (officer not present during assault), victim must secure an arrest warrant or make citizen's ar-rest.[16]

The Advocate/Escort

The advocate/escort is an important person in the assistance of bat-tered women. This person offers much needed emotional support and information to battered women who are facing large bureau-cracies and anxiety-provoking situations, such as the hospital, police department, lawyer's office, and courtroom. In many in-stances, the advocate is the eyes and ears of battered women. When trauma and chaos occur, it is an impossible expectation that women will remember all the information given to, or requests made of, her. Two days later, many women do not remember any details of the visit to the hospital or attorney's office. It is necessary to remember that advocates are entering into systems that were not designed to accommodate this role. They are often seen as intruders, nuisances, or adversaries. To be supportive of the victim without interfering with the mechanics of the system is the prime directive.

The following protocols for advocates were developed by the Marital Abuse Project of Delaware County, Pennsylvania.[17]

Victim Relations

1. Remember that all information is confidential.
2. Do not make judgments.
3. All victims are different; treat each one as such. *Don't assume* you know what she will say or what she is thinking.
4. Do not write anything down! Wait until you get home or in your car.
5. If the victim is in the waiting room, introduce yourself, give her a card. Eye contact is very important. Help her to feel you are there for her—and her alone. Ask her if she would like you to stay with her.
6. If she is already in the examining room, get permission at the desk, knock on the door, enter and introduce yourself, and again ask if she would like company.
7. A good opener would be: "How do you feel?" Then, "Would you like me to explain the purpose of the hospital report?" She may want to hold your hand—offer it.
8. If she asks for something to drink, ask the nurse if it is okay.
9. Be a good listener.
10. Do not tell a woman what she ought to do. Offer alternatives and let her make her own decision.
11. Crisis will cause a person to become confused. She may not make sense when she tells you what happened. Listen. Do not make judgments. She probably has not gotten her thoughts together yet.
12. She is probably feeling guilty. "Why me?" is a question indicating guilt. Explore this and try to say, "It's not your fault." Whatever she may have done in the marriage, it does not justify violence.
13. If you sense she is feeling something but not saying it, you

could say, "You sound like you are more concerned about your husband than yourself," or "You sound like you think you should have done more in the situation." Get those feelings out and help her to clarify them.

14. Find out who brought her. If family members are there, offer to talk to them while she gets dressed to let them know she is okay.
15. Tell her, as soon as she can, to write everything down and keep it. She may need to know the order of events later.
16. Always make sure that you tell her about your services and make plans to follow through on whatever support and services she wants. Be sure she has the hotline number, if nothing else. If she wants nothing more from you now, be sure to ask whether you can call her back later to see how she is.
17. Do not feel useless. Just being there helps.

Though the battered woman and her advocate must evaluate each situation separately in deciding how to proceed, these useful general principles for hospital and police accompaniment, developed by the Marital Abuse Project, Delaware County, Pennsylvania, should be kept in mind.

Hospital Protocol

1. When on call for hospital accompaniment, be prepared to come to any hospital if notified by the victim, or by the hospital or police, with the permission of the victim.
2. Introduce yourself to the Emergency Department person as a volunteer from your organization, then introduce yourself to the victim and to anyone who has accompanied her to the Emergency Department (family, friends, or police).
3. Remain with the victim in a supportive role in the examining room—only one volunteer. Assist the physician and nurse during the examination if requested. Handle no evidence! Do not take samples to the lab, even if asked by the hospital staff. Politely explain that you cannot.
4. Have change in your pocket and offer to get coffee, or other refreshment for the victim. (No coffee in the examining room.)
5. Do not attempt to elicit information about the abuse from the victim if she is not inclined to talk about it, but act as an attentive and supportive listener if she does want to talk.

6. Answer any questions she has about her options, and explain to her the importance of having a hospital report of her injuries. Encourage her to be sure that the cause of her injuries is written on the hospital report.
7. Find out if the police have been notified, and request that this be done if the victim wants them. Explain that a police report may also be valuable.
8. Remember the importance of privacy—answer immediate questions, but suggest holding more detailed discussion of her situation until later when there is more privacy and she is less upset. Do not fill out any intake or other forms in the Emergency Department.
9. Tell the victim about your services and give her a brochure. (If it is not safe for her to take this with her, try to be sure she has the hotline number at least.) Discuss her immediate safety and arrange for follow-up.
10. If the victim wants no further assistance or follow-up, ask her to write her name and telephone number for you.
11. Give her a card with a name on it, and tell her to refer to this number when she calls the office, in order to ensure confidentiality.

Police Protocol

1. Introduce yourself at the desk as a volunteer from your organization and ask to see the victim.
2. Knock if the door is closed and wait for an invitation to enter.
3. If you are asked to sit in on the interrogation, explain that you can do so with permission of the victim, but you cannot participate in the questioning. Explain that your role is emotional support of the victim.
4. If the police are talking to the victim, ask her if she would like you to stay. If she wants you there, stay as her friend. Also ask police if you may stay.
5. They may ask if she told you anything about the assault. Explain that your role is emotional support, and do not repeat what she has told you. Encourage her to make a complete report to police. If there is a difference between what she told you and what she tells the police, discuss this with her later in private.
6. Do not write anything down in the presence of police or the

victim. Arrange for her to give you her telephone number.

7. Be familiar with the remedies available to police and suggest to the woman that she ask them to use these remedies if appropriate. What they are *willing* to do will differ from district to district. Be sure to report to the office about your interaction with the police.

8. If decisions need to be made about what she should do next, ask if there is a place where you can talk to her alone. Perhaps you could go out to your car if there is no private place in the police station. Discuss her options and her safety, decide whether to go to the hospital for a hospital report, tell her about your services, and decide on the next step.

9. Be sure she has a brochure (or at least the hotline number) and give her a card with a number on it. Tell her to refer to the number to insure her confidentiality when she calls the office.

10. Try to get the police to drive her to wherever she is going next.

11. If the police are taking her to her house to get her things or are going to her house for any other reason, make it clear that you are not allowed to go to the house and to arrange for them to meet you nearby, out of sight of the house.

12. If the victim wants no further assistance of follow-up, ask if you may call her in a few days to see if she is okay. If she agrees, ask her to write her name and telephone number for you.

Relating to Police and Hospital Personnel

1. Listen carefully to everything that is going on.

2. Learn the names of the people you are dealing with. You may see them again. Let the office know which people were helpful in the situation and which were uncooperative.

3. When you identify yourself, do it quietly. Do not draw attention to the victim in the Emergency Deaprtment or the police station.

4. Try not to get in the way in the Emergency Department or the police station. Everybody is busy with their own job. You are only one of many.

5. Do not argue with police or hospital personnel. Be diplo-

matic and polite, while keeping the victim's best interests in mind.

6. Do not let anyone draw you into making judgments about the case. Someone may say, "I don't know about this woman—she was drinking," "I don't think she was really hurt," "She's a hysterical type." Just smile and be noncommittal, or say something like "I don't understand."

7. You may have suggestions the police or hospital may take in behalf of the victim. Usually, you should suggest this to her, and let her suggest it to the police or hospital.

8. If the victim is going into emergency housing, she may use your organization's office address as her mailing address while she is there. Her home address will still be on police and hospital records also, but her future address should be the office, not the actual place where she will be staying.

9. You are there for support of the victim. Avoid using the time for social conversations. You may be asked questions about the services. Be open to this and give the information asked for, but try not to spend more time than necessary. It will take your time away from the victim.

10. If you discover people on the staff who are unaware of your services, or if you feel in general the staff is a problem make a note of it in your report.

11. Compliment the hospital staff and police officers when a job is well done.

12. Do not talk to reporters. Refer them to the office.

CRISIS INTERVENTION TECHNIQUES

Law Enforcement: Decision to Arrest[18]

1. Officers should determine if there is a protective order or any other civil order. If such an order is in effect, officers should follow appropriate enforcement procedures.[19]

One of the problems encountered by police officers working with domestic dispute cases is their own feelings of futility. These are the same feelings shared by the victims after risking life and limb, and spending a great deal of time and money getting an order of protection. Although these women do not fit the stereotype of women unwilling to change, their treatment by law enforcement officers is, in many instances, the same. When police do not enforce orders of protection, even though they are appropriate, the women's sense of isolation and belief of helplessness are reinforced. The officer then becomes part of the societal pressure to keep women in the dangerous and abusive relationships.

2. Arrest is appropriate when injury and the assailant are present, or when serious injury (apparent or nonapparent) has been confirmed by medical authorities, whether or not such injury results in hospitalization.[20]

Since many injuries sustained by the victims are internal, it is frequently necessary to seek medical attention. Injuries to the stomach, breast area, portions of the head covered by hair, and the back are not readily viewed by the officer. The need for medical care should be determined by the officer if women are obviously unable to care for themselves or are not lucid enough to make the decision.

If the assailant is present and injuries are confirmed, it is appropriate for the officer to treat the incident in the same manner as "stranger to stranger" violence. Training Key #246 of the International Association of Police Chiefs states:

> *Despite the many complications that surround wife beating cases, one fact should always remain clear and should be the basis for police action. The wife has been physically assaulted and must be treated as the victim of a crime. The husband is a violent lawbreaker who should not be shielded from legal action.*[21]

3. Officers should not substitute their judgment about the *value* of arrest for that of the victim when arrest is legally justified.[22]

The following issues may be in the conscious thought process of the officer, but should not be used to dissuade victims from filing a complaint if the evidence is clear: (A) Victims cannot *afford* to have the men arrested because they will lose economic support. The greater issue is whether they can *afford* to lose their lives. (B) The culture and ethnicity of the victims accept violent behavior and it is a waste of time to arrest. By calling the police and asking to have the men arrested, the women are saying, in the only means available, that the violence is *not* acceptable. Seeking assistance represents a clear change in women's behavior. (C) The action will only serve to anger the men, and they will return and really "give it to her." (D) Prosecutors will do nothing with the case or will be too lenient. (E) Officers have been through all this before with these two, and feel the woman will never follow through.

Police action usually consists of three components: circumstances, personal inclination, and experience. If the circumstances justify an arrest, your personal inclination should shift to the victim. Police experience may well corroborate the issues discussed previously, but it also corroborates the fact that (A) violence escalates; (B) unless there is active intervention by the criminal justice system and social service agencies, no changes in the level of violence will occur; (C) Almost 25 percent of all murders are intrafamilial and over 50 percent are one spouse killing another (FBI Uniform Crime Statistics, 1975). In a substantial number of cases, the husband's violence escalates to murder, and the wife's need to protect herself leads to the death of the husband; (D) Complaints are filed and charges later dropped in many other kinds of cases, but it is unheard of to refuse to process a complaint because someone else did not follow through. Each case should be judged on its own merit and not on precedents. Only criminal aspects are the domain of the policeman, not psychological or sociological aspects.

4. When officers are in doubt as to whether a victim has actually suffered injury, the victim should be transported to an Emergency Department for documentation of injuries and treatment.[23] The reasons for this are discussed above.

5. When an arrest is appropriate but the victim refuses to cooperate, police should respect her opposition in the majority of cases. Occasionally, in a severe case, a felony can be pursued if there exists strong evidence (circumstantial and physical). In a few cases, there may be eye witnesses to the assault. Based upon available evidence, the officer may be able to make a probable-cause arrest in a felony case regardless of the wife's cooperation.[24]

If there have been repeated calls to that address and it is clear that the violence is escalating, the officer's decision to arrest may be valid despite the fact the victims often accept an assailant's apology or assume blame for the incident. If there is possession or use of a weapon, serious injury, or the probability of repeated incidents or serious harm, arrest gives women minimal time to leave and/or allows some distance and a "cooling off" period.

6. Officers should avoid the use of physical force.[25] The manner in which the officer carries out his or her peacekeeping duties is crucial. Police are called to restore order and decrease the violence. When violence is used against the assailant, it reinforces his or her values about the use of violence and its appropriateness. ("You use it when you want compliance.")

The use of violence in minority communities takes on more serious implications. It is difficult to ask someone from the dominant white middle-class culture to intervene in any dispute. But in minority families, it is considered the ultimate in disloyalty and treachery. Most minorities (black, Hispanic, Pan-Asian, and Native American) prefer "handling" their own problems because the advent of the police brings with it white middle-class values, and the use and abuse of power. The policeman is seen as the keeper and protector of the alien status quo.

When violence is used against the loved ones that women only wished protection from, their allegiance shifts quickly and automatically to the partner. The need to protect mates is usually stronger than the need to be protected from them. Because police are viewed as the enemy even before the encounter begins, it is mandatory to observe all formalities which are overt indications of respect.

> *Pride and dignity are often involved in these volatile operations, which require delicate handling by policemen who should refrain from using blunt and provocative approaches such as abusive language and threats of abuse, let alone unnecessary violence.* [26]

Whether or not an antagonistic relationship exists between the couple and police, culturally and/or socio-economically, projection of anger away from themselves to a new common enemy is not uncommon. It affords the couple at least a temporary reconciliation at the expense of the officer.

7. Officers should refrain from any action that might provoke violence from either spouse.

As discussed above, victims may attack the police officer in an attempt to protect their mates. Many officers moralistically indict the life style of the victims through language as well as nonverbal behavior. There are numerous ways of showing disapproval and disinterest which are obvious to both victims and assailants.

Many police respond to these calls with preconceived attitudes of dislike or fear.

> *. . . family disturbances constitute the largest single category of police calls. . . . The police dislike and fear family conflict calls for several reasons. First, this type of call lacks the glamour, prestige and public appreciation of a crime fighting summons. Most important, such calls are extremely dangerous. Many a policeman coming to the aid of a wife who has been beaten by her husband has had a chair or a bottle thrown at him or has been stabbed or shot by the wife who suddenly becomes fearful of what is going to happen to her husband and who abruptly transfers her rage from her husband to the policeman. Twenty-two percent of all police fatalities occur during investigations of altercations between husband and wife or parent and child.* [27]

Bent also states that fear for their personal safety has led to two general types of police behavior patterns. The first is avoidance and overlooking of certain crimes and proceeding with extreme caution. The second is fear-induced and manifests itself by overly aggressive behavior. The hostile nature of victims is often difficult for police officers to understand. They need to become familiar with the psychology of battering. For the first time, women may feel safe and protected enough to release their anger and hostility. They perceive police as safe targets who will not retaliate. If it is understood that women do this because they feel safe, the police response may not be as negative.

8. When making a decision regarding whether or not to arrest, the desires and needs of the victim should be taken into consideration.[28]

9. Officers should make note of or gather evidence including:[29]

Statements of witnesses	Bloody clothing
Injuries	General disarray
Broken furniture	Weapons

The above categories (1 through 9) were taken verbatim from *Stopping Wife Abuse* by Jennifer Daker Flemming (Garden City, New York: Anchor Books, 1979). The discussion which follows each category is original.

When Arrest is Inappropriate

A. In misdemeanor cases that do not occur in the officer's presence, the victim should be informed that she will have to follow through with the legal process if she wants to prosecute. She should be informed, where appropriate, of her right to make a citizen's arrest so that she can weigh her own circumstances.

B. Victim should be advised of available prosecution procedures. She should be given addresses, telephone numbers, names, etc., where appropriate.

C. She should be advised to gather names and addresses of witnesses to this and prior assaults to provide to the prosecutor.

D. She should be advised as to whether she will have to pay a fee to file a complaint with the prosecutor.

E. She should be advised to seek medical treatment as documentation of her injuries.

F. She should be advised of available civil procedures.

G. Officers should offer to transfer victim to a place of safety and provide protection while she gathers up children, clothing, identification, etc.

H. The victim should be advised of medical services: medical, legal, advocates or victim/witness unit of prosecutor's office.

I. Officers should encourage victim to avail herself of appropriate resources to counteract her feeling of helplessness and isolation.

J. Officers should make appropriate referrals as discreetly as possible, in addition to and not in place of appropriate law enforcement action, unless the victim specifically indicates desire to use services referred to instead of criminal or civil action.

K. Officers should encourage victims to file a complaint when appropriate.

L. If assailant is on probation or parole, victim should be advised to contact assailant's probation officer immediately.

M. Officers should examine the limitations and responsibilities of police in providing police protection.

N. Officers should give referral cards and leaflets with appropriate information to victim.[30]

CRISIS-HOTLINE COUNSELING

One of the fastest growing and more important intervention techniques for working with battered women is the twenty-four hour, seven-day-a-week crisis hotline. Hotlines offer battered women immediate access to the outside. It is often the first step for women attempting to come to grips with their violent life styles. Often women call several times and hang up without identifying themselves because they have not yet accepted the label of "battered woman." Hotline services include one-to-one peer counseling, information, advocacy, and referrals. The importance of these services cannot be underestimated because they reduce isolation for women and help them become more aware of their options. In isolation, women would not be able to plan strategies or gather this essential information. A large percentage of women will call "just to talk," but each encounter helps boost their positive feelings about themselves and should be viewed as a concrete step toward the eventual assertiveness necessary to end the violence and/or the relationship.

Barbara Cooper discusses the care of the crisis counselor and of the client as an ongoing process. She embarks on a common-sense approach to crisis counseling:

A common hazard of cirsis intervention work is a tendency for counselors to expect too much of themselves. Client problems can be overwhelming to the client, but they should NEVER be overwhelming to the counselor. The client's problems may be of many years' standing, involving many other persons. They may be part of a life situation which is inadequate to meet basic physical and emotional needs. Faced with a crisis, the client frequently communicates a sense of panic, fear, and urgency. Clients may tell themselves and the counselor that they need an immediate and effective solution to their problems, and it is needed now. This is unrealistic, but clients are often so frightened and overwhelmed that they are willing to give up responsibility for themselves and their problems.

The message from the client is often "Rescue me, take care of me." These clients, however, need more than temporary rescue. What they do need is a supportive listener who believes in the client's own ability to cope with the problem. A listener should convey the belief that the client has inner strength to draw on. A listener/counselor can communicate firmly and supportively that the client's problems can be solved, that the client can get help in solving those problems, but that a final solution may not be reached immediately. The counselor should offer alternative solutions and access to resources; however, it is always the client's responsibility to make decisions concerning her life.

It is sometimes difficult for counselors to maintain their belief in a client's strengths and ability to cope with the problem. As helping persons concerned with the well-being of their clients, counselors may accept responsibility for their clients. Counselors may expect immediate improvements in their client's behavior. Often, a counselor becomes disappointed after investing time, energy, and faith in a client, only to realize that the client has slipped back into old patterns and behaviors. It is important to realize that no one is capable of performing miracles with another person's life. If a counselor expects the client to respond immediately with initiative and motivation to the counselor's assessment of her situation, and to the counselor's proposed solutions, she may soon become discouraged.

If and when a client refuses to cooperate with a counselor's suggested solutions, the counselor may naturally get angry at either herself or the client. It is important for a counselor to acknowledge and express that anger to a supervisor or fellow counselor. This anger should not be internalized, nor should it be overtly directed at the client (although a counselor may directly express her disappointment and feelings of frustration to the client). . . . A client in a crisis stating extreme intolerance for her situation and making desperate resolutions about change should not be expected to follow through on any or all statements. Alternatively, a client who appears unable to make any plans or is paralyzed by fear or ambivalence should not be expected to respond immediately to a counselor's efforts to help her, to organize information, and select alternatives.

On-call counselors are expected only to assess immediate needs, and to help the client list available alternatives and solutions. This includes helping the client recognize her inherent abilities and strengths. *The client may or may not be willing to recognize these or accept the help her counselor has to offer, but the choice is up to the client.* Counselors must protect themselves and their clients by clarifying expectations of the counselor and the limitations of the project. Remember, even an assault victim is responsible for herself—all the counselor can do is to help her define the problem, and to explore ways of responding to the problem.

Crisis work is difficult to do. It requires a cool head. It usually requires a counselor to expend a lot of emotional energy in a short space of time. A little attention to yourself can go a long way to assure you have the resources you need to make working with your clients rewarding.

To prepare yourself for crisis intervention with assaulted women, take a few minutes to recall situations from your own life in which you felt either in a crisis or dead-end, trapped situation. Did it take you some time to decide the situation was intolerable and to resolve to take action? Did you slip back several times into known unsatisfactory solutions, even after resolving to make positive changes? If you are female, have you ever been frightened at the prospect of terminating emotional and/or financial dependence on men in your life? What happened to your self-esteem?

If you have had these experiences, recall your attempts at problem solving. Perhaps you will remember temporary paralysis or high states of anxiety. Were there other obstacles to problem solving which you experienced? Think about how you handle crisis now—perhaps you turn to trusted friends, withdraw for a while, or resort temporarily to some less-than-mature behaviors. A friend who accepts your anxiety and your need to talk and who does not respond to your panic, but maintains a firm belief in you and your ability to cope is a valuable ally.

In your work with wife-assault victims, learn to expect and accept fear concerning major changes in clients' lives. Expect grief reactions if the client has chosen to leave her husband or boyfriend to begin a new life. These moves represent significant losses and frightening independence. Learn to expect a victim's fear of being judged by you. If clients are judging themselves harshly, they will assume the same reactions from you.[31]

MEDICAL

For many battered women, the medical community is the first contact with a system or agency after a battering incident. The comprehensiveness and sensitivity of care given to victims are often determining factors in whether they obtain and maintain contact with legal, social service, and health care agencies. It is understood that the contact that medical personnel (private physicians, nursing units, dentists, medical clinics, Emergency Departments)

have with battered women is limited. In recognizing time constraints, it is found that good care can still be given to victims. The
primary emphasis, of course, is medical in nature. However, the
incident cannot be treated in a vacuum; victims should be given
accurate referrals and information about filing a complaint. Notifi-
cation of police should not be left to women's discretion in cases of
serious injury. Minimally, in the Emergency Department, victims
should receive a referral to the social service department of the
hospital or, from private practitioners, referrals to community-
based social service agencies.

Medical Considerations for Battered Women

Immediate treatment of acute injuries. Many battered women make
frequent trips to seek medical attention. Typical complaints are:

> Somatic complaints, conversion symptoms, and psychophysiolog-
> ical reactions . . . as evidenced by frequent clinic visits for
> headaches, choking sensations, hyperventilation, asthma, chest
> pains, gastrointestinal symptoms, pelvic pain, back pain and allergic
> phenomena. . . . Most had been treated, either intermittently or
> chronically, with sedative hypnotics, tranquilizers and/or antidepres-
> sants. [32]

A number of injuries are to the stomach, breast area, portions
of the head covered by hair, and the back. These areas are not easily seen. A complete examination of victims is often necessary to
ascertain the extent of injuries. Physicians must concern themselves with the cause of the injuries as well as the cure. Often, victims are sent home with numerous drugs to treat the physical
symptoms *even without acknowledgement* of spousal assault.

Reduction of trauma and emotional upset. It is important to acknowledge the presence of the battered woman immediately upon
entrance into the waiting room of either the Emergency Department, clinic, or office. This is stressed because the psychological
state of these women differs from that of other emergency patients.
Victims often feel unworthy, even of treatment for injuries. To allow
them to sit in isolation without acknowledgement reinforces their
sense of worthlessness.

Nonverbal behavior of medical personnel is important. Many
battered women have reported hostility from nurses and physicians which made them feel undeserving of medical attention. This
was especially true if they had been seen in the Emergency De-

partment on several occasions. This disdain was clearly evidenced by short, curt answers; physical distance, lack of eye contact, and demeaning facial expressions. Staff need to examine their personal attitudes and values about women and battering. If women are made to feel that they must be worthy or justify their visit to the physician, they will be understandably reticent to share any unsolicited personal information. The nurse's wish to spare the physician "wasted" time often leaves battered women without information or support from the medical profession that is not strictly treatment oriented. It is the nurse's personal feelings and prevailing attitudes that women do not deserve any "special" treatment because they either indirectly cause their injuries by not being a "good" wife or they like being beaten.

Information should be gathered as privately as possible, and women should be placed in a quiet waiting area immediately. The nature of the medical room setup separates patient from caretaker and it is this loss of privacy, many women say, that keeps them from giving information to the nurses. The embarrassment of stating with many people watching, "My husband beat me," is too humiliating and debasing. Embarrassment is one of the primary reasons battered women stay in abusive relationships, and it is crucial not to discount this factor.

In as quiet and nonthreatening a manner as possible, the following information should be gathered in addition to general medical background.

- If there are children, where are they now?
- Are the children safe?
- Where is the assailant? (Notice the fear level of the victim.)
- Who accompanied the victim to seek help?
    1. If police, they will usually take responsibility for informing victims of the legal process if they wish to prosecute. If they do not, medical personnel should be knowledgeable enough to do so.
    2. If friend or relative, ascertain the mental state of the person. Determine if their presence is helpful or detrimental to the victim's. If they are not calm and tend only to add stress to the situation, do not allow them to accompany victim to the examining room.
    3. If an advocate/escort is present and of comfort to the victim, allow them entrance.
- Where will she go after treatment is completed?

It is not appropriate to discuss the dynamics of the relationship, but it is necessary to stress that the woman is not responsible for the beatings and that *no one deserves to be beaten*. The acknowledgement that the incident indeed occurred and expression of concern for the safety of the women and their children reduces the anxiety and stress levels, making them more cooperative patients.

Documentation of injuries in the case record. Many women will not tell physicians where they got their injuries. On the other hand, many physicians never ask. The fear of involvement in domestic cases and loss of time attending court hearings, often to no avail, make many physicians shy away from meaningful interaction with victims. For the sake of victims, it is necessary to make clear chart notations because these records may well end up in a courtroom. In addition to vital medical history and treatment, the general emotional state and physical appearance of victims should be noted. Photographs should be taken and made a permanent part of case records. Information relevant to the photograph also should be noted (who took the photo, who is in the photo, and the day, date, and time are important). In hospitals, these notations take on an added dimension because personnel experience shift and station changes, and only the record is available to alert new staff of a recurring visit.

Consistent referral information and assistance. It would be helpful if all medical personnel had at least a rudimentary acquaintance with community resources that are valuable to battered women. If only one referral can be made in hospitals, it should be to the social service department of that hospital. Ideally, an on-call social worker would then assist victims with crisis counseling and temporary housing. If this is not the case, referral should still be made to the social service department. Emergency Department personnnel should make immediate referrals to crisis hotlines, emergency shelters, and the police. Making a referral should not entail simply giving women a series of telephone numbers, but, whenever possible, making initial contact on behalf of the victim. The physical and psychological exhaustion of victims often leaves them with little energy to begin the process. Making this contact connects the victims to services and shows them that there *are* systems which respond to their need for assistance. For abused women, a busy telephone often says that "it is useless."

For private physicians and clinic personnel, knowledge of community resources for battered women is crucial. Many women are unfamiliar with resources and are told by their partners that no one will help them. They see the physician as their only link to the "outside" and trust his/her judgment. The physician's office may be the only place the battered woman is "allowed" to go without suspicion. Because of the prominence of the physician in the life of many battered women, precise and relevant information can often save them from years of physical and psychological abuse.

Community Linkages

Extensive knowledge of, or access to, information cannot be overemphasized in work with battered women. The women have many decisions to make. Knowledge of community resources by the counselor/medical personnel/police officer is directly related to the number of options the victims perceive themselves as having. It is not the responsibility nor the right of interveners to force information or actions upon victims. However, people who have been isolated from individual and/or agency contact for long periods of time need precise, relevant information. A great deal of time and impetus are lost when victims receive false, inappropriate, and inaccurate information. In extreme circumstances, this information can lead to increased physical and mental harm.

Dr. Hilberman, in the report "Sixty Battered Women," presents an excellent synopsis of community resource knowledge needed by the "help" professionals who deal with battered women.

Some, if not all, of the following resources will need to be mobilized:

- Medical institutions for birth control, abortions, tubal ligations, good medical, and mental health care for herself and her children.
- Social service agencies for financial aid for herself and children, child protective services, food stamps, clothing, day care, housing, and emergency shelter.
- Criminal justice agencies for protection against further violence.
- Legal aid for assistance with warrants, court procedures, separation, and divorce agreements.
- Vocational rehabilitation agencies for financial assistance and information about educational pursuits, job training, and employment counseling.
- Women's groups for information, support, and shelter.[33]

SUMMARY

An understanding of the psychodynamics of battering increases the effectiveness of all who interact with the dysfunctional family as a unit or as individuals. It is important that the rescue mentality be abandoned. All victims must be assisted in acknowledging their problems and accepting responsibility for making the changes they desire.

Counselors, physicians, law enforcement, and others have a unique assistance role, but the ultimate mechanism for changing a battering situation rests with the victims themselves. As first responders we must know what our role is, give realistic truthful information to the victims, make appropriate referrals, and remain available to assist as often as is necessary for changes to be made.

Dealing with victims of domestic violence is time consuming, relatively thankless, and frustrating. To assist the victim and remain effective as a helper, expectations of one's self and the victim must be within the realm of possibility.

REFERENCES

1. Straus MA: Sexual inequality, cultural norms and wife beating. Victimology: An International Journal, 2, Spring 1976, pp. 552-555
2. Walker LE: The Battered Woman. New York, Harper and Row, 1979, p. 30
3. Elbow M: Theoretical considerations of violent marriages. Social Casework, November 1977
4. Walker LE: The Battered Woman. New York, Harper and Row, 1979, p. 26
5. Hilberman E, Munson K: Sixty battered women: A preliminary report. Unpublished paper prepared for a special session of the American Psychiatric Association Meetings on Battered Women: Culture As Destiny, Toronto, 1977
6. Walker LE: Battered women and learned helplessness. Victimology: An International Journal, 2, 1977-1978
7. Anonymous: The love that kills. Human Behavior, September 1977:7
8. Anonymous: The love that kills. Human Behavior, September 1977:7
9. Anonymous: The love that kills. Human Behavior, September 1977:7
10. Anonymous: The love that kills. Human Behavior, September 1977:7
11. Anonymous: The love that kills. Human Behavior, September 1977:7
12. Boyd V, Klingbell K: Behavioral characteristics of domestic violence. Seattle, unpublished, 1978
13. Crow GA: Crisis Intervention: A Social Interaction Approach. New York, Association Press, 1977, pp. 28-29
14. Crow GA: Crisis Intervention: A Social Interaction Approach. New York, Association Press, 1977, pp. 28-29
15. Training Key #246: Investigating Wife Beating. Police Management and Operations Divisions of the International Association of Chiefs of Police, Inc., Gaithersburg, MD; 1976, pp. 1-5

16. Training Key #246: Investigating Wife Beating. Police Management and Operations Divisions of the International Association of Chiefs of Police, Inc., Gaithersburg, MD; 1976, pp. 1-5
17. Marital Abuse Project of Delaware County, Pennsylvania: "Victim Relations," "Hospital Protocol," "Police Protocol," and "Relating to Police and Hospital Personnel."
18. Fleming JB: Stopping Wife Abuse. New York, Anchor Press-Doubleday, 1979, p. 183
19. Fleming JB: Stopping Wife Abuse. New York, Anchor Press-Doubleday, 1979, p. 183
20. Fleming JB: Stopping Wife Abuse. New York, Anchor Press-Doubleday, 1979, p. 183
21. Training Key #246: Investigating Wife Beating. Police Management and Operations Divisions of the International Associations of Chiefs of Police, Inc., Gaithersburg, MD; 1976, p. 1
22. Fleming JB: Stopping Wife Abuse. New York, Anchor Press-Doubleday, 1979, p. 183
23. Fleming JB: Stopping Wife Abuse. New York, Anchor Press-Doubleday, 1979, p. 183
24. Fleming JB: Stopping Wife Abuse, New York, Anchor Press-Doubleday, 1979, p. 183
25. Fleming JB: Stopping Wife Abuse. New York, Anchor Press-Doubleday, 1979, p. 183
26. Bent AE: Police, Criminal Justice and the Community. New York, Harper and Row, 1976, p. 26
27. Bent AE: Police, Criminal Justice and the Community. New York, Harper and Row, 1976, pp. 26-27
28. Fleming JB: Stopping Wife Abuse. New York, Anchor Press-Doubleday, 1979, p. 183
29. Fleming JB: Stopping Wife Abuse, New York, Anchor Press-Doubleday, 1979, p. 183
30. Fleming JB: Stopping Wife Abuse. New York, Anchor Press-Doubleday, 1979, p. 183
31. Cooper B: Counselor Training Manual #2. Domestic Violence Project, .Ann Arbor NOW, 1976
32. Hilberman E, Munson K: Sixty battered women: A preliminary report. Unpublished paper prepared for a special session of the American Psychiatric Association Meetings on Battered Women: Culture As Destiny, Toronto, 1977
33. Hilberman E, Munson K: Sixty battered women: A preliminary report. Unpublished paper prepared for a special session of the American Psychiatric Association Meetings on Battered Women: Culture As Destiny, Toronto, 1977

BIBLIOGRAPHY

Anonymous: The love that kills. Human Behavior, September 1977:7
Bent AE: Police, Criminal Justice and the Community. New York, Harper and Row, 1976

Boyd V, Klingbell K: Behavioral characteristics of domestic violence. Seattle, unpublished, 1978

Cooper B: Counselor Training Manual #2. Domestic Violence Project, Ann Arbor NOW, 1976

Crow GA: Crisis Intervention: A Social Interaction Approach. New York, Association Press, 1977

Elbow M: Theoretical considerations of violent marriages. Social Casework, November 1977

Fleming JB: Stopping Wife Abuse. New York, Anchor Press-Doubleday, 1979

Hilberman E. Munson K: Sixty battered women: A preliminary report. Unpublished paper prepared for a special session of the American Psychiatric Association Meetings on Battered Women: Culture As Destiny, 1977

Marital Abuse Project of Delaware County, Pennsylvania: "Victim Relations," "Hospital Protocol," "Police Protocol," and "Relating to Police and Hospital Personnel."

Straus MA: Sexual inequality, cultural norms and wife beating. Victimology: An International Journal, 1, Spring 1976

Training Key #246: Investigation of Wife Beating. Police Management and Operations Divisions of the International Association of Chiefs of Police, Inc., Gaithersburg, MD; 1976

Walker LE: The Battered Woman. New York, Harper and Row, 1979

Walker LE: Battered women and learned helplessness. Victimology: An International Journal, 2, 1977-1978

5 CHILD ABUSE: DYNAMICS OF THE CURRENT PROBLEM

Kathleen Collins, RN, MSN

Child abuse and neglect affects over one million children in the United States. Countless others are touched by the problem to some degree, either as family members, friends, or by virtue of being a concerned member of a community. Prevention, identification, investigation, and treatment of those affected by child abuse and neglect may involve professionals of varying roles and levels of expertise. However, anyone who has contact with children and families may be confronted with the responsibilities of being the first responder in a case of child neglect or abuse. Likely first responders may include educators, medical and emergency transport personnel, mental health workers, social workers, and police officers.

To provide information appropriate to the expertise and role of all first responders is beyond the scope of this chapter. However, general information needed by all first responders will be covered. Readers are strongly encouraged to make occasional perusals of current literature appropriate to their professional roles in order to keep abreast with current practices, trends, and research in the area of child abuse and neglect. They must also be aware of legislation, reporting procedures, and practices within their state and community.

The ultimate effect of child abuse or neglect is death of a child. Therefore, in most cases, the first response should be viewed as prevention. Prevention occurs on three levels: primary, secondary, and tertiary. Ideally, in terms of the health and welfare of our society, all first responses should be on the primary level—that is, education of all adults in effective parenting and adult-child interactions. However, in reality, a child abuse problem exists. Therefore, first responses also occur on the secondary (identification of at-risk families and intervention aimed at preventing potential abuse and neglect) and tertiary (recognition and treatment of abuse and neglect) levels.

Any first response presupposes an understanding of the problem. Secondary and tertiary responses require knowledge of factors which have been found to place a family in the high-risk category, and the ability to recognize indicators of child abuse and neglect. Equipped with an understanding of the problem and with information needed for identification, the first responder has three responsibilities in cases of abuse and neglect: (1) obtaining necessary information, (2) submitting appropriate reports, and (3) rendering appropriate treatment and/or referral. The degree of responsibility of individual first responders is dependent on their particular professional role and level of expertise. This chapter will help prepare the first responder to effectively carry out those basic responsibilities common to all first responses.

DEFINITION

Defining child abuse and neglect is a difficult task and has been a point of controversy among those involved with the problem. A definition which is comprehensive enough to be useful to all professionals from the many disciplines involved in the prevention and treatment of the problem (sociology, psychology, medicine, nursing, and others) and one which takes into consideration the myriad of educational levels, value systems, and cultures of all families in our society may never be developed. Because of the difference in backgrounds, what may be considered by one to be child abuse, another may believe to be discipline required to rear a child into a socially competent adult. However, for the purposes of this chapter, the definition of child abuse and neglect found in the Model Child Protective Services Act will be used (see Table 5.1). Essentially, this definition says: "An 'abused or neglected child' means a child whose physical or mental health or welfare is harmed or threatened with harm by acts or omissions of his or her parent or other person responsible for his or her welfare."

Child abuse is usually categorized according to the actions or omissions involved. Physical abuse involves physical harm sustained by a child, whereas neglect implies threatened harm. Sexual acts committed against a child fall into the category of sexual abuse. Those acts or omissions which harm or threaten to harm the mental or emotional health of a child are considered as emotional maltreatment.

Child abuse and neglect occur on a continuum. There are varying degrees in all four categories and, although some cases are obvious, most require a great extent of subjectivity in identification because of the lack of a clear-cut definition. In assessing situations for possible child abuse, the professional must have knowledge of

Table 5.1. Excerpt From the Draft Model Child Protective Services Act.

SECTION 4. DEFINITIONS

When used in this Act and unless the specific context indicates otherwise:

(A) "Child" means a person under the age of 18.

(B) An "abused or neglected child" means a child whose physical or mental health or welfare is harmed or threatened with harm by the acts or omissions of his parent or other person responsible for his welfare.

(C) "Harm" to a child's health or welfare can occur when the parent or other person responsible for his welfare:

    (I) Inflicts, or allows to be inflicted, upon the child, physical or mental injury, including injuries sustained as a result of excessive corporal punishment; or

    (II) Commits, or allows to be committed, against the child, a sexual offense, as defined by State law; or

    (III) Fails to supply the child with adequate food, clothing, shelter, education (as defined by State law), or health care, though financially able to do so or offered financial or other reasonable means to do so; for the purposes of this Act, "adequate health care" includes any medical or nonmedical health care permitted or authorized under State law; or

    (IV) Abandons the child, as defined by State law; or

    (V) Fails to provide the child with adequate care, supervision or guardianship by specific acts or omissions of a similarly serious nature requiring the intervention of the child protective service or a court.

(D) "Threatened harm" means a substantial risk of harm.

(E) "A person responsible for a child's welfare" includes the child's parent, guardian, foster parent, an employee of a public or private residential home, institution or agency, or other person responsible for the child's welfare.

(F) "Physical injury" means death, disfigurement or the impairment of any bodily organ.

(G) "Mental injury" means an injury to the intellectual or psychological capacity of a child as evidenced by an observable and substantial impairment in his ability to function within a normal range of performance and behavior, with due regard to his culture.

and consider the cultural and community values and standards of parenting, as well as the specific characteristics of the particular parent and family. The first responder should not use his or her own personal family background as the criteria for determining whether or not another family has a problem.

INCIDENCE

Given the difficulties with defining and detecting child abuse and neglect, it follows that determining the actual incidence is difficult, to say the least. Because of problems with defining abuse and neglect, the differences in legislation and reporting practices from state to state, and the neglect of professionals to report identified cases to the proper agency, any national statistics are only estimates of the problem. However, the National Center on Child Abuse and Neglect, after studying a number of surveys, concluded that 200,000 cases of physical abuse, 800,000 cases of neglect, and approximately 60,000 cases of sexual abuse and molestation represent a conservative middle ground estimate of the national incidence. To that total, which already is over one million, also can be added an unestimated number of emotional neglect and abuse cases, as well as the unestimated number who are exploited economically for commercial interests and those exploited in the child pornography market. Tragically, two thousand or more children may die each year as a result of abuse or neglect.

These numbers have far-reaching implications for society. Just as language is learned, so is behavior. Much of the manner of how an individual interacts within a society is learned in the home. Victims of child abuse and neglect are affected in many ways, but the increasing incidence of juvenile delinquency, violent crime, and mental illness may be merely reflecting the increasing incidence of child abuse and neglect. Also, the child who receives ineffective parenting learns ineffective parenting, and usually raises his or her children in the same manner. Thus, the problem multiplies with each generation.

PARENTAL CHARACTERISTICS

Unfortunately, there is no exact set of circumstances which indicate in which families abuse and neglect will occur. Cases of abuse and neglect are found in all socio-economic levels. The parents vary in intelligence and educational levels from very low to very high, and are from all ethnic and religious backgrounds. They represent a cross section of the general population rather than any particular stereotype.

There also is no psychological profile that is descriptive of the parent who abuses his or her child. However, there are characteristics which have been identified in abusing parents which may be present singularly or in combination. Because parents who do or have the potential to abuse or neglect children represent a cross section of society in their characteristics, the following list is by no means exhaustive, but may serve as a general guideline.

- A history of abuse, neglect, or emotional deprivation as a child.
- Low self-esteem, feelings of worthlessness, depression.
- Poor coping skills.
- Lack of impulse control.
- Social isolation (may be evidenced by having few or no close friends, lack of transportation, few involvements in social or community activities).
- Facing a crisis situation (unemployment, financial difficulties, divorce, and other problems); frequent crises may indicate a life pattern of crisis.
- Rigid, unrealistic expectations of child's behavior.
- Frequently uses and/or defends the use of harsh punishment.
- History of mental illness (however, less than 10 percent are considered psychotic[1]).
- History of criminal offenses.
- Violent temper outbursts (may be evidenced by spousal abuse occurring in the same family).
- Looks to the child for satisfaction of needs for love, support, and reassurance.
- Project the blame onto the child for their "troubles."
- Lack effective parenting skills.
- Inability to seek help from others.
- Perceives the child as bad or evil.
- History of drug and/or alcohol abuse.
- Feels little or no control over life.
- Low toleration for frustration.

Abuse and/or neglect may occur on a chronic or episodic basis. Episodic abuse may occur at times when the parent finds his or her coping skills insufficient for dealing with periods of increased stress or crisis. At other times, adequate parenting skills may be observed.

It is not uncommon for one child in the family to be singled out as the recipient of all parental hostility, or "scapegoated." In this situation, all other children may be well cared for and receive adequate parenting. It may be the child who the parent most identifies with or who reminds the parent of a hated spouse or parent that is abused. Occasionally, the child is different from the other children in some way. The reason a parent has for scapegoating a particular child may have no rational basis, but there are some factors which identify at-risk children:

- A child who is a product of an unwanted or unplanned pregnancy. This may be evidenced prenatally by attempts to conceal the pregnancy, failure to obtain early prenatal medical care, absence of home preparation for the coming baby.
- Early prolonged parent-child separation as may be the case in premature birth or prolonged illness of the child requiring hospitalization.
- Low birth weight babies.
- Sickly, deformed, or retarded children.
- A child that is difficult to care for, such as a colicky baby or hyperactive child.

INDICATORS OF ABUSE AND NEGLECT

There are certain physical and behavioral clues that indicate child abuse and neglect. They may be overt or very subtle and present singularly or in combination. However, anyone having contact with children or families should be aware of them, and the presence of just one should raise questions and indicate the need for more information.

Any physical injury of a child, especially of infants and children under three, is an indication of suspect abuse. If a child is a victim of abuse, the parents are frequently vague as to the cause of the injury or attempt to conceal it. Their story may change from time to time or when repeated to different people. They may disagree as to how the injury occurred, even though both claim to have been present, or they may try to protect the person responsible. The history of the injury as related by the parent may be incongruent with the injury or developmental level of the child. Frequently, the blame may be placed with the child, a sibling, or a relative. Abusing parents may comment on the clumsiness of the child or on how easily the child bruises. In cases of abuse, parents frequently delay or fail to seek medical care. When they are questioned about the child's illness or injury, they show agitation or irritation. Parents who abuse or neglect their child may appear unconcerned about them, give no indication of remorse concerning the child's condition, and constantly or inappropriately criticize the child.

Bruises or welts may indicate physical abuse, especially if found in varying stages of healing, in unusual patterns, or in areas not typical of accidental injuries. For example, small bruises in clusters may represent marks from fingertips which can result from grabbing, slapping, or choking. Unusual patterns of bruises may reflect human bites or the pattern of an instrument, such as a strap or stick. Any bruises on an infant and injuries to the face, genitalia, or posterior side of a child should alert professionals to the possibility of child abuse.

Burns are frequently found on abused children. Doughnut-shaped burns of the buttocks and genitalia and glove-like burns on the arms and legs indicate a child has been dunked in hot liquid. Small, circular marks, frequently found on hands, feet, and buttocks of some abused children, may be cigarette or cigar burns. Patterned burns resembling electric burners or irons and rope burns on arms, legs, or necks are all highly suspicious of nonaccidental injuries.

Particular types of skeletal injuries are commonly seen in battered children. Twisting or pulling of arms or legs may cause spiral fractures, metaphyseal fractures, epiphyseal separations, periosteal elevation, and/or joint dislocations. An abused child may have several fractures in varying stages of healing, not only of the long bones, but also of the skull, face, and ribs. Any fracture in a child under two years of age is rare, except in cases of abuse.

Abdominal injuries are a common cause of death in battered children. Hitting or kicking a child in the abdomen can cause bleeding or rupture of the spleen, liver, stomach, bowel, or bladder. Indication of an intraabdominal injury may include distention of the abdomen and recurrent vomiting.

Child neglect is the chronic failure of a parent to provide a child with the necessary physical and emotional support. Making the diagnosis of neglect is usually a more subjective judgment than diagnosing physical abuse; however, there are certain indicators which signal neglect. The most obvious is either total abandonment or episodic abandonment over long periods of time. Lack of supervision may be evidenced by very young children being left unattended, left in the care of other children too young to adequately protect them, children left for long periods of time, or when engaged in dangerous activities with inadequate supervision. Inadequate dress for the weather and chronically dirty and unbathed children indicate neglectful parents. Persistent illness or skin disorders, excessive exposure such as frostbite and sunburn, and severe diaper rash indicate parental neglect of the physical needs of the child. Frequently, parents who chronically neglect their children will fail to seek adequate medical care, such as childhood immunizations or dental care for their children. A lack of adequate nutrition may be indicated by the child who consistently complains of hunger, who rummages for food, or who gives evidence of severe developmental lags. For those who have the opportunity to assess the home environment, inadequate heating, unsafe conditions in the home such as exposed wiring or broken windows, and unsanitary conditions are considered indications of neglect. Professionals, such as teachers, who observe children over a period of time may see indications of child neglect in chronic absence from school, constantly falling asleep in class, coming to school very early and leaving very late, or addiction to drugs or alcohol.

Parental acts or omissions which result in mental injury to the child are considered to be emotional maltreatment. In the Model Child Protective Services Act, mental injury is defined as: "Injury to the intellectual or psychological capacity of the child as evidenced by an observable and substantial impairment in his ability to function within a normal range of performance and behavior, with due regard to his culture." Key concepts in identification of emotional maltreatment are that the parent's behavior has an effect on the child which is long-lasting, that the effect can be observed in the child's abnormal performance and behavior, and that the effects constitute a handicap to the child. Emotionally maltreated and emotionally disturbed children exhibit similar behavior; however, parental behavior may help distinguish between the two. Parents of emotionally disturbed children accept that there is a problem and actively seek help. Parents of emotionally deprived children may deny that a problem exists, blame the child, and/or fail to seek recommended help.

Abused and neglected children display certain behavioral characteristics which can be observed by the sensitive professional. They demonstrate extremes in behavior, such as extreme aggressiveness or extreme withdrawal, excessive or minimal crying, or great fear or no fear of adults. They are frequently wary of physical contact and may shrink at the touch or approach of an adult. An abused child may exhibit extremely adult behavior evidenced by overconcern for the emotional and/or physical needs of the parent, or extremely dependent behavior inappropriate to the developmental level of the child. Physical or emotional abuse may result in developmental lags where the child falls below the norm for their age in physical development, motor skills, socialization, and/or language development.* A discussion of behavioral indicators of emotional maltreatment is beyond the scope of this text; however, Table 5.2 will provide a good overview.

GATHERING INFORMATION

The presence of one or more of the indicators should signal the professional to seek more information from a parent and/or child. Specific information gathered by the first responder is dependent on their professional role and expertise, and on the resources available to the professional. The goal in information gathering is to determine whether child abuse or neglect should be suspected and reported to the appropriate agency and to obtain needed information for reporting.

Table 5.2. Indicators of Emotional Maltreatment of Children.

CHILD BEHAVIOR		PARENT BEHAVIOR
TOO LITTLE	TOO MUCH	ABUSIVE IF CONSISTENT GROSS FAILURES TO PROVIDE
1. Psycho-social dwarfism, poor self-esteem, self-destructive behavior, apathy, depression, withdrawn	Passive, sheltered, naive, "over-self-esteem"	1. Love (empathy), Praise (acceptance, self-worth)
2. Academic failure, pseudo-mental retardation, developmental delays, withdrawn	Hyperactivity, driven	2. Stimulation (emotional/cognitive) (talking-feeling-touching)

*For further information regarding physical development, motor skills, socialization, and language development refer to:
1. Denver Development Screening Test
2. Girls and Boys Physical Growth NCHS Percentile Charts, Ross Laboratories, Columbus, Ohio, 43216

Table 5.2. Indicators of Emotional Maltreatment of Children (continued).

CHILD BEHAVIOR		PARENT BEHAVIOR
TOO LITTLE	TOO MUCH	ABUSIVE IF CONSISTENT GROSS FAILURES TO PROVIDE
3. Symbiotic, stranger and separation anxiety	Pseudo-maturity	3. Individuation
4. Lack of integrative ability, disorganization, lack of trust	Rigid-compulsive	4. Stability/permanence/continuity of care
5. Feelings of inadequacy, passive-dependent, poor self-esteem	Pseudo-maturity, role reversal	5. Opportunities and rewards for learning and mastering
6. Autistic, delusional, excessive fantasy, primary process, private (unshared) reality, paranoia	Lack of fantasy, play	6. Adequate standard of reality
7. Tantrums, impulsivity, testing behavior, defiance, antisocial behavior, conduct disorder	Fearful, hyperalert, passive, lack of creativity and exploration	7. Limits, (moral) guidance, consequences for behavior (socialization)
8. Impulsivity, inappropriate aggressive behavior, defiance, sadomasochistic behavior	Passive-aggressive, lack of awareness of anger in self/others	8. Control for/of aggression

Table 5.2. Indicators of Emotional Maltreatment of Children (continued).

CHILD BEHAVIOR		PARENT BEHAVIOR
TOO LITTLE	TOO MUCH	ABUSIVE IF CONSISTENT GROSS FAILURES TO PROVIDE
9. Interpersonal difficulty (peer/adults), developmental lags, stranger anxiety	Lack of familial attachment, excessive peer dependence	9. Opportunity for extrafamilial experience
10. Poor peer relations, role diffusion, (deviant behavior, depending on behavior modeled)	Stereotyping rigidity, lack of creativity	10. Appropriate (behavior) model
11. Gender confusion, poor peer relations, poor self-esteem	Rigid, stereotyping	11. Gender (sexual) identity model
12. Night terrors, anxiety, excessive fears	Oblivious to hazards and risks, naive	12. (Sense of) (Provision of) security/safety
ABUSIVE IF PRESENT TO A SEVERE DEGREE		
1.	Poor self-esteem, depression	1. Scapegoating, ridicule, denigration
2. Rigidity	Lack of purpose, determination, disorganization	2. Ambivalence
3. Poor self-esteem, passivity	Pseudomaturity	3. Inappropriate expectation for behavior/performance

Table 5.2. Indicators of Emotional Maltreatment of Children (continued).*

CHILD BEHAVIOR		PARENT BEHAVIOR
TOO LITTLE	TOO MUCH	ABUSIVE IF CONSISTENT GROSS FAILURES TO PROVIDE
4. (Depends on behavior while intoxicated)		4. Substance abuse
5. (Depends on behavior/type frequency)		5. Psychosis
6. Not Applicable	Night terrors, anxiety excessive fears	6. Threats to safety/health
7. Not Applicable	Sadomasochistic behavior, low self-esteem, anxiety, passivity, anti-social behavior, self-destructive dangerous behavior	7. Physical abuse
8. Not Applicable	Anxiety, excessive fear, dependency	8. Threatened withdrawal of love

Interviewing the child, parents, and other involved individuals (including other professionals involved with the family) is important in order to obtain or clarify information. Because the first responder is in a position to set the tone for future relationships of the family with other professionals, they must be particularly cautious to conduct their interview in a nonjudgmental and nonblaming manner so as not to alienate those involved (see Chapters Ten, Eleven, and Thirteen for specifics in interviewing). The first responder must be particularly alert to discrepancies in explanations and ac-

---

*Ira S. Laurie, MD and Lorraine Tafano, "On Defining Emotional Abuse: Results of an NIMH/NCCAN Workshop."

counts inconsistent with observable data. Knowledge of the high risk factors previously discussed may act as a guideline for information the professional may want to seek.

The first responder must also be alert for particular observable data, both physical and behavioral. Physical observations include general physical appearance of the parent and child, looking for signs of physical abuse or neglect in the child, and the possible existence of a substance abuse problem in the parent. Physical surroundings in the home environment must be observed for adequacies in space, heating, ventilation, safety, cleanliness, and presence of adequate food and water. Behavioral data to be observed for are those indicators of abuse and neglect already discussed, nonverbal behavior (particularly those suggesting love and support or anger, distrust, and rejection), and family interaction. Again, discrepancies in information given verbally and behaviorable observations should indicate that suspicion of child abuse is appropriate.

A source of information, which may be useful but which may not be available to the first responder, is a check of previous records. The police department, juvenile court, juvenile probation, or department of social services may show past or active files as a result of previous incidents of abuse or neglect. Some areas maintain central registers where all reports of suspected abuse or neglect are filed. Hospital records may show repeated admissions of a child for injuries or consistent illnesses. Although such information is helpful, if it is not found when records are checked, the possibility of current abuse should not be ruled out.

When child abuse or neglect is suspected, the first responder must make additional assessments. Most critical is determination of the child's immediate safety. If the child appears to be in immediate danger of injury, steps must be taken appropriate to the professional role of the first responder and to community procedures to insure that child's safety. If this determination is beyond the scope of the first responder's expertise, a professional or team of professionals who can make that determination must be consulted. Some general guidelines which can be used to aid in making the decision of whether or not immediate intervention is needed for the child's protection are:

- The parents refusal to obtain medical and/or psychiatric care for the child in immediate need of such care.
- The physical environment of the home indicates an immediate threat to the safety of the child.
- The parent or parents are so out of touch with reality as a

result of psychiatric illness or substance abuse that they are unable to provide for the basic needs of the child.

- The family has a prior history of abuse, neglect incidents, or allegations.
- The parents refuse to cooperate by providing information or by maintaining contact with any social agency.
- There are any indications that the parent may direct his or her anger or fear toward the child in the form of physical abuse.

The next responsibility of the first responder is to report the suspected child abuse or neglect using protocols appropriate to specific reporting laws of the state and professional role. Reporting laws vary from state to state in regard to who must report, the types of abuse and neglect that must be reported, to whom the reports are made, when they must be made, what information is to be reported, and the criminal penalties and civil liabilities for failure to report. Every state reporting law contains a provision for immunity to the reporter for all reports of child neglect and abuse that are made in good faith. All states require "suspected" cases of child abuse and neglect to be reported. The key word "suspected" means that the reporter need not be certain abuse or neglect has occurred, but she or he must only have reason to believe or have reasonable cause to suspect that abuse and neglect have occurred. Although state laws do not mandate all people to report suspected child abuse or neglect, any person may report and many have a professional responsibility to do so.

A responsibility of the first responder, regardless of his or her professional role, is to share the information gathered with other professionals involved with the family. The first responder may have valuable information which could be helpful or essential in investigation, assessment and/or treatment of the family, and duplication of professional efforts should be avoided. The mechanism for sharing the information will vary according to procedures used in particular areas, but it may be written and/or verbal, in person, by telephone or in team conferences.

The first responder, regardless of her or his professional capacity, is involved in treatment by virtue of being the first contact the family has with the professional world, or by virtue of having identified the problem. As stated earlier, this first contact is crucial in that it may set the tone for the professional relationships that follow. This first contact should be nonjudgmental and create a helping atmosphere, rather than one of criticism and blame. Because nonverbal behavior, as well as verbal, conveys certain messages to the family, the first responder must recognize her or his feelings about child abuse and neglect and put those feelings in perspective. Doing so will help to respond constructively and appropriately to the situation and to prevent or slow professional exhaustion or "burnout." The following are particular areas which provoke intense feelings in the professional and should be personally explored in continual self-examination.

- The nature of the problem.
- The compelling identification with the injured child.
- The need to identify with and understand abusive and neglectful parents.
- The use of childhood experiences as an evaluation tool.
- The possibility of making mistakes and the potential price of a mistake.
- Unconscious sensual feelings.
- Having to confront parents with suspicions of child abuse or neglect.[2]

The first responder also must be prepared with at least the basics of crisis intervention skills (see Chapter Nine) and recognize the crisis nature of child abuse in terms of the particular incident or as a result of discovery.

Further responsibilities of the first responder will vary according to his or her professional role. While the paramedic may be responsible for transporting the child to a medical facility, the social worker may be involved in ongoing treatment of the family, and the police officer may be responsible for conducting an investigation and determining the disposition of the case.

MULTIDISCIPLINARY TEAMS

Obviously, child abuse and neglect is a very complex problem and can present the first responder with situations she or he may feel overwhelmed by and inadequate to deal with singularly. Many decisions about child neglect and abuse cases involve life and death issues and should not be made by any one discipline. Recognition of such has led to the development of multidisciplinary child protection teams which function to effectively diagnose and treat child abuse and neglect, and to coordinate efforts of the many professionals involved.

A multidisciplinary approach has many benefits for the first responder. The burden of total responsibility for decision making is taken off one person, thus minimizing the chance for a wrong decision being made. Having others available to discuss child abuse and neglect cases is a learning opportunity and also a means of exploring and ventilating one's own feelings.

Hospital based teams are perhaps the most common child protection teams currently in existence. Members of the team vary according to the facility, but may include physicians, nurses, social workers, and mental health workers. Members from the team are available to evaluate possible cases of child abuse and neglect; to provide consultation to other professionals regarding diagnosis and treatment; to provide treatment and/or referral; to review identification and treatment effectiveness within the facility; and to educate those affiliated with the facility and the community in the area of child abuse and neglect.

Teams have been established within other agencies such as social service and mental health agencies, and within the criminal justice system. For example, the San Diego Police Department's Juvenile Division utilizes two full-time social workers. They act as consultants to detectives and work to aid coordination, communication, and cooperation between the Juvenile Division of the Police Department and their clients and agencies in the area.

Interagency teams have also been developed. Such teams share information so a comprehensive data base can be compiled to be used in the formulation of a diagnosis and a treatment approach. They review and evaluate cases and make the necessary revisions in the treatment program to insure the effectiveness of case management. The opportunity for sharing information between agencies that such a team provides can lead to a more appropriate disposition of cases and better utilization of services available. With such a program, a police officer who responds to a report and can find no reason for police involvement, but does identify at-risk characteristics, may suggest the family seek help from a particular family service agency before police involvement becomes necessary. Such action may be particularly effective if the officer then communicates his or her referral to the agency along with any information which has been gathered.

Setting up a multidisciplinary team requires careful planning. Particular needs within the community should be identified and the team purpose should be designed to meet those needs. Decisions must be made as to whom the appropriate members of the team are to be and their roles clearly identified. Policies and procedures should be agreed upon by all members and written to be certain of the quality and availability of information to all team members. Regular team meetings should be held in which all cases are discussed and evaluated.

Child protective teams are not only valuable as a mechanism for sharing information and expertise. They are also a means for identifying the needs for services within the community and for insuring a continuity of response. Community knowledge of the existence of a child protective team also may lead to improved reporting and an increase of primary and secondary responses.

CONCLUSION

Child abuse and neglect does not only involve mortality figures—it also has immeasurable morbidity implication. Ineffective parenting, as evidenced by abuse or neglect, is learned and can be passed down from generation to generation. Thus, the problem is multiplied with each abused or neglected child. Prevention and early identification are essential if the chain is to be broken and the incidence of child abuse and neglect is to decrease rather than increase. Potential first responders must realize the impact they can have, not only on the child and the family, but also on the social welfare of the community, state, and society as a whole.

REFERENCES
1. Schmitt BD: The Child Protection Team Handbook. New York, Garland STPM Press, 1978, p.3
2. National Center on Child Abuse and Neglect: A Curriculum on Child Abuse and Neglect. Washington, DC; US Government Printing Office, 1979, p. 113

BIBLIOGRAPHY

Broadhurst D, Knoeller J: The Role of Law Enforcement in Treatment of Child Abuse and Neglect. Washington, DC; US Government Printing Office, 1979

Ebeling NB, Hill DA: Child Abuse: Intervention and Treatment. Massachusetts, Publishing Sciences Group, Inc., 1975

Fontana V, Bisharvo D: The Maltreated Child: The Maltreatment Syndrome In Children. A Medical, Legal and Social Guide 3rd ed. Springfield, IL; Charles C. Thomas, 1977

Kempe CH, Helfer R: The Battered Child, 2nd ed. Chicago, University of Chicago Press, 1974

Kempe CH, Helfer R: Child Abuse and Neglect: The Family and the Community. Cambridge, MA; Ballinger Press, 1976

Kempe CH, Helfer R: Helping the Battered Child and His Family. Philadelphia, J.B. Lippincott, 1972

Martin HP: The Abused Child: A Multidisciplinary Approach to Issues and Treatment. Cambridge, MA; Ballinger Press, 1975

McNeese M, Hebeler JJ: The abused child: A clinical approach to identification and management. Ciba Clinical Symposia 29:5, 1977

National Center on Child Abuse and Neglect: A Curriculum on Child Abuse and Neglect. Washington, DC; US Government Printing Office, 1979

Polansky NA: Profile of Neglect. Washington, DC; US Government Printing Office, 1976

Schmitt BD: The Child Protection Team Handbook. New York, Garland STPM Press, 1978

Smith S: The Battered Child Syndrome. Woburn, MA; Butterworth, 1975

Susman A, Cohen S: Reporting Child Abuse and Neglect: Guidelines for Legislation. Cambridge, MA; Ballinger Press, 1975

6   RAPE AND ITS CONSEQUENCES

Carmen Germaine Warner, RN, PHN

The devastation, the trauma, and the ugliness of rape can only be fully understood by those who have fallen victim to one of the most hostile, violent, aggressive, selfish acts one human can enact on another. Even when a family member or close friend has been victimized, realizing the pain, anguish, embarrassment, fear, and desertion one experiences cannot be fully appreciated. The ability to understand how totally distraught a victim feels is not possible until it becomes a personal experience. Then—and only then—can one say, "Yes, I know how frightened you felt. Yes, I know that feeling of total destruction. Yes, I know it is worse than one could ever possibly imagine."

Considering the vast numbers and diversification of emergencies attended to by first responders, rape victims require the greatest degrees of empathy, sensitive listening, and patience. This is a challenge as it demands the full, uninterrupted attention of the first responder, the ability to view the situation realistically, and the talent to calm and support a distraught human being. In no other emergency can the initial contact have such a formative impression than with victims of rape. The ability of the victim to trust, to open up to others, to begin to release pent up feelings is created or destroyed in those first few moments with the initial contact person. In fact, the immediate support and kindness displayed by the first responder may be the single most important aspect of the entire intervention process.

RAPE: ITS LEGAL AND WORKING DEFINITION

Despite the varying state statutes and their personal interpretation of rape, the original source of definition stemmed from English Common Law. This definition clarified rape as carnal knowledge of a woman by force and without her consent. Even though all states had originally accepted this definition as uniform, varying changes and adaptations have been made in each state over the past several decades.

State statutes have included in their definition considerations of the following:

- Criminal circumstances like sexual penetration accomplished through the use of a weapon.
- Sexual penetration of a victim under a certain age or of a specific mental state.
- Using the word "sexual battery" or "criminal sexual conduct" in place of rape.
- An offense against the member of either sex.
- The act of rape committed by a husband against his wife.

First responders should familiarize themselves with the particular statutes in their jurisdiction and respect their judicial implications. The legal definition is important for the law enforcement and judicial systems, and should be thoroughly understood. However, an awareness of the working definition of rape is equally as important.

This working definition portrays rape in its realistic, humanistic aspect. As quoted by Burgess, "Every rape has elements of anger and power in it. It helps the rapist to deny a fear of women and to discharge his impulse to violence."[1]

The victim experiences a disruption in his or her physical, psychological, social, and sexual level of wellness and life style which may exist the remainder of one's life.

A physical injury like a laceration or broken bone is repaired, leaving minimal impairment as a reminder of the incident. Rape, unfortunately, disrupts and even destroys self-respect, family units, trusting capabilities, job security, feelings of safety, social and recreational habits, and optimism toward the future.

In essence, rape is a devastating, ruthless, ugly, traumatic form of violence, aggression, and hostility which impacts the person as a holistic being, as well as their significant others.

RATE OF OCCURRENCE

It is a well known and a widely accepted fact that incidents of rape are grossly underreported. The Federal Bureau of Investigation indicates rape to be the fastest growing crime in the United States, with an estimated count of one assault every nine minutes, or a calculated total of 160 each day and 58,400 annually. The unfortunate fact is that only approximately 25 percent of rape incidents are reported annually.[2] Should the total number of incidents be accounted for, the figure would soar to over 233,600 cases of rape each year.

Upon further examination of recorded data concerning rape assault cases, the following commonalities have been noted.[3]

Victims

- Usually young with over one-half the victims being 20 years of age or younger.
- One-quarter to one-third of the victims are under 25 years of age.
- Less than 15 percent of the rapes reported are over the age of 30 years.

Offenders

- Most offenders are in their twenties, with an average age four to five years senior to their victims.
- In approximately 60 percent of the *cases reported*, the offender is unknown to the victim.
- In 25 percent of the reported assaults, the victims are acquaintances.
- In 10 to 15 percent of reported rape attacks, the victim is a close friend or relative.

These percentages must be recognized as those associated with reported rapes. It is understandable that a victim would be much more willing to report if he or she did not know the offender— thus, the reason for the 60 percent being a stranger to the victim. As previously noted, about 75 percent of rape incidents go unreported. Recorded data are understandable recognizing the increased amount of difficulty one might have when the offender is known to the victim.

Initial Contact

- Attacks occurred most commonly in the victim's home or on the street.
- In 50 percent of the cases, the use of force was noted.
- In 33 percent of the cases, the victim reported being with the perpetrator for less than 60 minutes when the attack occurred.
- Less than 15 percent of the rapes occurred due to hitchhiking.

Weapons, Force, and Threats

- In 50 percent of the cases, weapons were used, primarily knives or guns.
- In 75 percent of the attacks, some form of strong-arm force was used against the victim.
- In 60 percent of the cases, threats were made against the victim's life.

Resistance

- In 33 percent of the rapes, the victims were unable to employ any form of resistance.
- In 50 percent of the instances, the victims fought with their assailants. Of this figure, one-third noted their resistance had no effect, and most of them realized their physical resistance actually increased the violent behavior in the offender.

Injuries

- In 50 percent of the reported rapes, physical injuries were present, with very few being serious.
- Of the injured victims, 50 percent noted their resistance precipitated further injury, and 80 percent commented that further injuries would have occurred had additional resistance been applied.

It is to be reiterated that these figures are based *only* on the rapes that are reported, which represents approximately 25 percent of all rape attacks. The profile could change considerably were data known on every instance of rape. It is critical for first responders to keep in mind that each case is unique and has individualized needs.

MYTHS AND MISINFORMATION

Despite the fact that considerable information has been disseminated regarding the reality of rape, tendencies for doubt and blame exist with respect to the victim's role. In an attempt to reinforce the facts concerning this act of violence, the following myths are identified and discussed.[4]

1. Perhaps the most common myth is the widely held belief that a rapist is a sexually unfulfilled man carried away by a sudden uncontrollable surge of sexual desire. *The actual facts*: 90 percent of group rapes were planned in advance, and 50 percent of the rapes committed by a single man were planned. Generally, rape is not a crime of impulse. As to the myth that rapists are sexually unfulfilled, Dr. William Prendergast of the New Jersey State Prison states that *all* the rapists he has studied had available sexual relationships. Sixty percent of the men in Dr. Amir's study were, in fact, married and led normal sexual lives at home.

2. A second myth is that all rapists are pathologically sick and perverted men. Evidence does not support this view of the rapist. Men convicted of rape were found to have normal sexual personalities differing from the norm only in their greater tendency to express violence and rape. *Sex, therefore, is not the motivating factor in rape*—it is merely the chosen mode of expression. Alan Tayor, a parole officer who has worked with rapists in the prison facilities at San Luis Obispo, California, said about the men, "Those men were the most normal men there."

3. Another popular myth is that most rapes occur in dark alleys or to women who hitchhike. Some people feel the only solution to rape is for women to spend their lives staying at home. Over *one-third of all rapes are committed by a man who forces his way into the victim's home!* Over half of all rapes committed occur in a residence.

4. Most people believe that the typical rapist is a stranger to the victim. This is not so. Women cannot even trust the men they are acquainted with. A full *48 percent of the rapists* in Dr. Amir's study *were known to the victims*. Some were merely casual friends, others were close relatives.

5. The age-old myth that black men rape white women at every opportunity is still perpetuated, even though Dr. Amir reports that *in 93.2 percent of rape cases, both the man and woman are of the same race*. In fact, white men attack black women more often than black men attack white women (3.6 percent compared to 3.3 percent respectively).

6. Many people are inclined to believe that a raped woman was at fault somehow—that she probably provoked the attack. This provocation, considered a mitigating factor in a

courtroom, may consist of only a gesture or a way of dressing. Even using this extreme scale, *the Federal Commission on Crimes of Violence reports that only 4 percent of reported rapes involved any precipitative behavior on the part of the woman*. In some cases *precipitative behavior* is nothing more than walking or dressing in a way that is *socially defined as attractive*. Our society lauds women who are sexy—but those unlucky enough to be raped are dismissed as tramps.

7. Some persons really believe that rape is impossible without consent, that a normal man cannot rape a normal woman unless he has assistance. Unfortunately, it is simply not true that a woman who does not want to be raped can always prevent it. *She may be knocked unconscious, or may submit because she fears for her life if she struggles.* Most men are physically stronger than most women, and the attacker has the advantage of surprise. There have been instances where experienced policewomen, trained in self-defense and emergency situations, have been raped despite all their efforts at resistance. There are many men, especially in American prisons, who are attacked and sexually assaulted by their fellow men—despite their superior strength.

8. Another myth, upheld even by the law in some states, is that *a woman cannot be raped by her husband*. This legal fallacy is a direct result of the age-old concept that a woman is the property of her husband. Any act of sexual intercourse to which the woman does not consent is rape. *This law applies even in cases of annulment, divorce dissolution, or legal separation.*

9. The common belief that women, in fact, enjoy rape when it occurs would be hilarious if it was not such a tragic and destructive myth. The very idea that a woman could enjoy being attacked by a man to whom she is not attracted, that she could enjoy being exposed to injury or death, that she could enjoy being treated in a humiliating and brutal fashion is preposterous.

It is commonly stated that only attractive, young women get raped. It is becoming common knowledge that *all* individuals are potential victims: the male and female infant of four months, the elderly woman of 85 years, the married and unmarried male of all ages. These are people who daily become victims of the aggressive act of rape.

It is essential that first responders understand the concept of rape and the traditional public image it carries. Only with the aid of compassionate, sensitive professionals can victims develop the element of trust that is the foundation for recovery.

As myths have been dispelled through public and professional education, higher standards of medical care have been established. Along with this, professionals in the psychiatric field also reflect attitudinal change. It is valuable for first responders to realize this developmental change and note the increased awareness many professionals are experiencing.

The following survey appeared in a professional journal a few years ago. A questionnaire was mailed to psychiatrists throughout the country by the journal "Medical Aspects of Human Sexuality." The data presented was tabulated following the return of the first 500 questionnaires. In some instances, not all questions were answered, multiple answers were provided, or uncertainty was noted.

Sexual Survey #11[5]

1. Is the possibility of rape a more pervasive fear of many women than the fear of robbery or murder?

Yes	68%
No	30%

2. Do most rape victims have psychiatric symptoms afterward?

Yes	80%
No	16%

3. Do most husbands of rape victims have ambivalent feelings toward their wives as a result of the rape?

Yes	69%
No	24%

4. Should all rape victims receive psychiatric counseling?

Yes	71%
No	26%

5. Do most men have rape impulses?

Yes	35%
No	61%

6. Some contend rape is an outgrowth of our male-dominated culture. Do you agree?

Yes	27%
No	71%

7. Are people with other sexual disorders such as voyeurism, exhibitionism, and making obscene telephone calls likely to become rapists?

Yes	10%
No	88%

8. What is the predominant motive of rapists?

Sexual release	3%
Psychopathic lack of restraints	19%
Anger toward women	51%
Feelings of sexual inadequacy	19%

THE MALE RAPE VICTIM

The statutes in many jurisdictions have limited their scope of victim identification to the female adult. The incidence of homosexual rape and its psychological effects are uncertain,[6,7] but it is reasonable to assume that like other instances of rape, it is grossly underreported. Despite these uncertainties, several generalities have been noted.[8]

- Most male rapes reported to medical and law enforcement authorities involve children and early adolescents.
- Rapes occurring in jails and prisons go unreported unless the victim is otherwise critically injured.
- Male rapes by fathers or stepfathers are rarely reported.
- Rapes committed on young boys by men generally do not manifest extensive physical harm.
- The use of force is more common in homosexual rapes.
- In the majority of cases, where the victim is an adult male, the victim and perpetrator are cohabitants in a setting which provided a minimal heterosexual release of emotions.

The initial contact with the male victim is similar in the psychological, medical, and legal aspects to that of the female victim.[9] The anatomical and physiological differences should be considered by first responders with respect to proper collection of evidence and preservation of venue.

Commencing with the initial contact, and continuing throughout the subsequent stages of intervention, the following considerations should be addressed:

- The age of the victim and the assault's impact on his identity and self-image.
- The beliefs, attitudes, and dynamics evident in the family unit.
- The potential existence of family sexual abuse.
- The victim's personal feelings about the assault.
- The availability of community resources for follow-up and ongoing intervention.
- The ultimate well-being of the victim following his medical discharge.

THE ELDERLY RAPE VICTIM

Relatively few elderly women report an incident of rape, but occasionally complaints from women in their eighties and nineties will be received.[10] Davis records that with estimated rates of 45 percent to 95 percent of rapes going unreported among women over 50 years of age, the rate could be as high as 19 or as low as two per 1,000 women per year.[11]

The physical, psychological, and social characteristics of the elderly compound the problems associated with rape victims. Their age in particular makes elderly women especially vulnerable. Other factors unique to the older victim include:

- The emotional impact of the assault becomes more pronounced in the elderly.
- Their sense of recall for specific facts is less acute.
- The feelings of fear which develop following the incident are devastating.
- The disruption of their physical environment and their security is overwhelming, as moving is virtually impossible for the elderly.
- The thought of the news media, medical personnel, and law enforcement officers invading her home is too much to bear and isolation is sought.

First responders, when relating to elderly victims, must apply additional intervention techniques. The basic means of responding to and assessing rape of the elderly are modified to include some of the following:

- Speak clearly, loudly, and slowly, recognizing the possible loss of hearing.
- Sit beside the victim rather than standing over them to

minimize the overwhelming nature of the event.
- Alter the normal vocabulary to facilitate a greater level of comfort and understanding by the victim.
- Apply crisis intervention techniques in an orderly, slow process.
- Assist the victim in contacting family, a neighbor, close friend, or church member to aid in the process.
- Respect the limitations of accurate visual recall and query other means of securing identifying information.

CHILD AND ADOLESCENT VICTIMS

In respect to the fact that child and adolescent assault and abuse are more common than that of the male or elderly female, this subject is dealt with separately in Chapters Five, Seven, and Fifteen.

IMPACT ON FAMILY MEMBERS

The increased openness regarding rape, its reporting and intervention has precipitated an additional concern—that of family and friends. As victims seek professional assistance, they bring with them the added worries, concerns, and fears of significant others. This poses an additional burden on the victims as they are often concerned about the well-being of their family or friends, and frequently the victim becomes the focus of the personal reactions of others.

Research has just begun to identify certain factors as they concern males related to victims of rape.[12] The two most common immediate reactions experienced by males who are closely related to rape victims include shock and hostility. Shock occurs as a result of disbelief—how could this traumatic event actually happen to them? The hostility constitutes an eruption of emotions directed toward the perpetrator, the professional involved, and the victim him/herself. The feelings of helplessness, confusion, disruption, anger, disbelief, and remorse mold into one force which emits hostile reactions everywhere.

Some of the actions commonly displayed by males closely related to the victims include:
- Overprotection of the victim.
- Constant attempts at comforting and supporting the victim.
- Attempts at ascertaining information regarding the assault.

- Assuming full responsibility for household duties.
- Outbursts of crying and sobbing.
- Attempts at suicide.
- Inability to sleep for three and four weeks following the rape.
- Developing an acute interest in target shooting.
- Indicating signs of intense stress.
- Inability to concentrate for up to two months after the assault.

The thought process of the involved male demonstrates a wide range which includes:

- Suspicious of others—males and females included.
- Contemplating carrying a firearm.
- Focus on ones role as the "protector."
- Constant rehashing of "If only I had. . . . ," or "If only I hadn't. . . . " thoughts.
- Manifesting frequent thoughts regarding fear of the environment and other males.
- Thinking the assault was a dishonor and disgrace to him and the family.

Closely related to the thought process are the expressed feelings of the involved males. These include:

- Total disbelief of the situation.
- Fear of one's safety.
- Anger at all men.
- Anxiety in general.
- Rage at the rapist.
- Overwhelmed with the situation.
- Helplessness regarding where to begin rebuilding.
- Powerlessness over the defiant act.
- Rage fantasies regarding what they would do to torture the rapist if he were caught.

Professionals working with these men have found their trauma to be intense and warranting intervention. One common pattern discovered during the recovery process was that the males resolved their feelings about the incident much more quickly than the victim. Once the males have resolved the incident in their own mind, they become very impatient with the victim whose resolution was much slower and more painful.

These factors are important considerations to be respected by first responders throughout their intervention process. Recognizing the broad-based effect rape has on all those involved will aid professionals in their holistic and total approach toward reassessment, regrowth, and recovery.

PREHOSPITAL INTERVENTION

Attitudes and intervention techniques have changed considerably during the past decade. This is valuable not only for the well-being of the victim and his or her family, but also for the effectiveness and thoroughness of the initial responder.

There are several reasons for this improved level of care:
- Increased public awareness regarding the reality of rape.
- Demands made by men and women who have identified areas of need.
- Greater emphasis on law enforcement, EMT, and paramedic training to include the concept of victims of violence.
- Changes in attitude regarding victims, their needs, and a standardized level of care.
- Design and implementation of protocols for management of rape victims and their families.

In discussing the intervention responsibilities for first responders, it is important to remember that each situation is unique. Circumstances will vary, immediate reactions by victims will differ, and the stage in which the victim initially contacts the first responder will depend upon their own unique case. First responders should incorporate the following points in their standard intervention process.

Incorporation of Medical Triage Procedures

It is imperative that a thorough assessment be made of the physical injuries. Due to the possible reluctance of the victim to discuss the situation and the possibility of internal injuries, a sensitive thorough, pertinent, relevant questioning process must be conducted to insure that safe and proper medical attention is provided.

Involvement with Law Enforcement Officials

If the first responder is a law enforcement official answering the victim's call, an obvious decision has been made to report the incident. Should the first responder be a paramedic, police or sheriff involvement must be dealt with. Each state has its own laws regarding involvement of the law in cases of rape, and these must be respected. In some states, California as an example, a law now exists which allows victims not to contact law enforcement agencies. In situations like this, it is critical that victims be totally informed of the potential situation with and without law enforcement involvement. This information must be presented as realistically and completely as possible to assist the victim in making his or her decision. Under *no* circumstances should the victim ever be forced into a decision or made to feel guilty regarding personal feeling or the final decision.

Preservation of Evidence

Evidence must be preserved by all first responders, regardless of the involvement of law enforcement agencies. This is an integral part of the physical examination and an essential link in the prosecuting process. After securing the victim's consent, he or she should fully understand the importance of not:
- Changing clothes
- Gargling
- Taking a shower
- Urinating or defecating
- Drinking fluids or eating solids
- Delaying medical intervention

The reasoning behind these restrictions may have to be repeated several times to make the victim understand that evidence should be preserved. Any of these actions would destroy the evidence, along with a possible conviction.

Sensitive, Supportive, On-the-Scene Conflict Intervention

In essence, the entire intervention process, which may continue for months and even years, is critically influenced by the first responder. Sensitive, supportive, gentle listening, and comprehensive initial intervention will ease the entire process. Abrupt, judgmental, abrasive, and nonconcerned interaction may retard, disrupt, and virtually destroy all hopes for regrowth and recovery. Special considerations for first responders dealing with victims of rape include:

- Avoid influencing any additional physical or emotional pain. Victims are extremely vulnerable following a rape attack.
- Make sure the victim NEVER is left alone. The feeling of isolation or abandonment is frightening.
- Refrain from careless talk such as giving advice to the victim concerning how the attack could have been avoided. Do not make personal judgments concerning the attack. This includes both verbal and nonverbal communication.
- Aid the victim in making decisions. Encourage personal involvement throughout the intervention process.
- Encourage the victim to express his/her feelings of fear, anger, and remorse.
- Verbalize that you realize this is a very difficult time, but do not state you understand how they feel unless you have actually been a rape victim yourself.
- Let the victim know that certain aftereffects are normal. These include:
  1. Inability to sleep
  2. Onset of nightmares
  3. Fear of being alone
  4. Loss of appetite
  5. Inability to go to school or work
  6. Development of self-blame and guilt
  7. Onset of physical illnesses
  8. Development of foolish child-like behaviors
- Maintain open lines of communication listening very carefully to what is said as well as what is not said.

Continuity of Care

First responders, as previously noted, are the critical link between successful and unsuccessful care. The concept of trust developed in the early stages of intervention will afford an ideal mechanism for bridging the gaps between professionals. If the victim has had the benefit of concerned empathetic first responders, they will be more willing to communicate with medical, social service, and other agency personnel. In addition, the transfer of information concerning the victim will aid in maintaining and transferring the established level of care. This will minimize the trauma of care that, at best, is fragmented and splintered.

Crisis counseling, according to Schloss,[13] that has no time constraints must begin at the scene of the assault and continue as needed. Should first responders receive another call, all attempts should be made to secure backup assistance, thus encouraging continuity of care and a continued development of trust. The emotional factors of rape and the accompanying intervention techniques are addressed in Chapter Fourteen.

SUMMARY

Rape is a brutal act of violence that is just beginning to be fully understood. Its traumatic consequences are finally being recognized by first responders. Rape victims demand more sensitive interaction and compassionate listening than any other emergency or nonemergency situation.

   Developing a working level of comfort when seeing rape victims is a slow, yet necessary process. The role of first responders that represents an entrance into the medical and legal systems carries with it the responsibility for the ultimate success or failure of the intervention process. Unless first responders can provide quality care and sensitive counseling, the victim will continue to be "raped" as he or she proceeds through the medical/legal system. It is the challenge of all first responders to establish and maintain quality care and a uniform standard of excellence.

REFERENCES
1. Burgess A: Power, anger: Primary motives in rape. Cambridge, MA; International Medical News Service, November 1, 1977
2. Federal Bureau of Investigation: Uniform Crime Report for the United States. Washington, DC; United States Government Printing Office, 1976
3. National Institute of Law Enforcement and Criminal Justice: Forcible Rape: Police Administrative and Policy Issues. United States Department of Justice, Law Enforcement Assistance Administration, March 1978
4. Amir M: Patterns of Forcible Rape. Chicago, University of Chicago Press, 1971
5. Sexual Survey#11: Current Thinking on Rape. Medical Aspects of Human Sexuality, June 1978, pp. 125-127
6. Raybin JB: Homosexual incest. Journal of Nervous Mental Disorders, 148:169, pp. 105-109
7. Dixon KN, Arnold LD, Calestro K: Father-son incest: Underreported psychiatric problem? American Journal of Psychiatry, 135, 1978, pp. 835-838
8. Braen GR: The male rape victim: examination and management. In Warner CG (ed): Rape and Sexual Assault: Management and Interven-

tion. Germantown, MD; Aspen Systems Corporation, 1980

9. Josephson GW: The male rape victim: Evaluation and treatment. JACEP, Vol. 8 No. 1, January 1979, pp. 13-15

10. Hayman CR: Sexual assaults on women and girls. Annals of Internal Medicine, Vol. 72 No. 2, 1970, p. 277

11. Davis LJ: Rape and older women. In Warner CG (ed): Rape and Sexual Assault: Management and Intervention. Germantown, MD; Aspen Systems Corporation, 1980

12. Strachan M: Psychological reactions of males related to victims of rape. Unpublished masters thesis presented at California State Coalition of Rape Crisis Centers, Sacramento, California, May 9-10, 1980

13. Schloss BJ: Sexual assault. Emergency, Vol 11 No. 2, February 1979, pp. 47-49

7 THE DILEMMA OF SEXUAL ABUSE IN CHILDREN

Carmen Germaine Warner, RN, PHN

First responders are frequently confronted with incest and sexual abuse of children in a nonemergent, after-the-fact situation. Of all the calls respondents deal with, sexual abuse cases, like rape, demand the ultimate in sensitive interaction. Due to the delicacy and controversy regarding this issue, it is imperative that first responders establish a concrete protocol for intervention. Recognizing that there exists a broad spectrum of varying points of view surrounding sexual abuse—its identification, verification, and intervention—it is critical that a thorough understanding be developed not only of the conflict, but the responder's view of the situation as well.

EXISTENCE OF INCEST

Incest as a distinct and individualized form of sexual abuse requires a great deal of specialized knowledge and understanding. Clinically, incest is defined as inappropriate sexual behavior among family or surrogate family members.[1] Legally, although varying from state to state, it refers to inappropriate sexual contact including fondling, fellatio, intercourse, and other forms of contact from an adult to a child.[2]

The prevalence of incest or sexual abuse still remains unknown due to sketchy reporting patterns. However, according to Forward and Buck, there are undoubtedly more than ten million Americans who have been involved in incest. Up to one of every four women in the United States is a victim of sexual abuse by the age of 18, and in children, girls outnumber boys by seven to one.[3] These statistics, although derived from invalidated research, do indicate that the problem exists and must be dealt with appropriately.

Other data recorded by Weber note that only one-quarter of all sexual abuse cases are committed by strangers. Only 2 percent take place in cars, 5 percent in abandoned buildings, and 34 percent occur in the victim's home.[4]

The Queens Bench Foundation, in its "Rape Victimization Study," reported that approximately 39 percent of rape victims were under the age of 18, and about 10 percent were 13 years of age or younger.[5] These figures do not take into account that 20 to 50 percent of all sexual abuse cases are never reported.[6]

Numerous studies and researchers portray differing statistics. The exact numbers are irrelevant. The critical issue is how best to relate to those involved in sexually abusive relationships.

A PROFILE OF THE VICTIM*

Identifying the profile of victims of sexual abuse is important primarily as a consciousness-raising tool. Responders well acquainted with the broad picture will be able to recognize and understand the mechanism of the situation better. Certain characteristics of these victims include:

- The median age of child victims is 11.65 years of age.
- Approximately one-third of the children **involved are between** seven and ten years of age.
- One-half are between the ages of 13 and 15.
- Seven girls are abused for every one boy.
- An age and sex correlation appears consistent throughout several studies:
  —*Involving female victims:* 63 percent are usually under 12 years of age and 37 percent are adolescents.
  —*Involving male victims:* 36 percent are under 12 years of age and 64 percent are in the adolescent group.
- Victims of sexual abuse represent a cross-section of the total population.

Victims of sexual abuse can be broadly identified as falling into one of three categories:

1. Coerced victims: individuals who were physically forced by the offender.
2. Passive victims: children experiencing only one noncoercive sexual experience where they did not initiate the contact.
3. Participant victims: children having more than one sexual

---

* Statistics taken from reference number 7.

experience with the offender. The experience, of nonsexual activity, is rewarding to them, where sexual activities are unpleasant.

First responders should be aware that most children are vulnerable and not capable of true consent. However, psychological consent focusing on the motivations of the child represents another factor. Children may invite participation as a means of gratifying emotional needs, or they may encourage it as a response to initial approaches of the offender. In addition, it is not uncommon to view abused children as having a history of disturbed parent-child relationships, predisposing them to seek attention and affection from others. The affection and attention they seek is of a nonsexual nature, even though sexual involvement appears to be the common result.

Children also may be pressured into sexual activity by a person representing the power figure in their lives. The offender, who may be any combination of nuclear or extended family members, frequently uses the position of power to take advantage of a child's ambivalence and nonexistent decision-making power. Thus, it is not surprising that children respond as directed.

THE ABUSIVE NATURE

Family sexual abuse poses a situation very complex in etiology, assessment, and intervention. Involved parties have long-term and complex relationships that affect all family members. Sexual abuse is unique in that it does not represent an isolated incident. It usually begins when the child is in the latency or even preschool years and continues for several years. Manifested behavior originates with prolonged kissing and fondling of the genitalia, and later develops into genitalia sexuality.

As this pattern emerges, it is not infrequent for the victim, in most cases the daughter, to feel that the individual and collective happiness of the family; the degree of personalized attention; and the existence of the family as a unit depends on her continued willingness to participate and her continuing silence. Unlike other forms of sexual abuse, the victim often experiences considerable feelings of confusion and ambiguity. These reactions constitute mixed emotions of some sexual pleasure and feelings of power and importance, laced with negative feelings rooted in sexual displeasure, pain and guilt. These reactions become intensified with the psychological and emotional development of other family members.

THE HOME: WHERE IT ALL BEGINS

Sexual abuse among family members occurs in every social, economic, and ethnic background and involves such behavior as fondling, fellatio, cunnilingus, sodomy, and intercourse.

As a child grows older and recognizes the implications of this behavior, the element of position and authority by the offender plays a significant role. Accompanying threats, should disclosure be considered, prevents the victim from seeking outside help.

If the victim chooses to seek help, he/she often finds/him/herself alone as other family members may remain loyal to the offender for reasons of finance, social position, or a fear of public embarrassment. Even the mother may refuse to admit its occurrence. Recognizing this pattern, first responders aware of the phenomenon will not automatically disbelieve the child, but attempt to maintain an open mind and objective perspective.

Residential homes for disturbed children and drug abusers report that many residents relate to being sexually abused while living at home. Sexual promiscuity and prostitution may become a way of life for many sexual abuse victims, if they have grown up with the belief that they are good for nothing except sex.

The existence of fear, lack of trust, and the desire for a close male-female relationship, along with a lack of self-love and respect, require meaningful intervention and support. Due to the lack of emphasis on victims of violence, first responders have some difficulty in identifying and assessing sexual abuse. They frequently lack the knowledge relating to the dynamics, interview process, proper identification, referral procedures, and specific intervention techniques. Personal feelings and bias must be isolated and dealt with prior to attempting to work with sexual abuse families. Increased awareness of the problem and techniques for specific intervention will help in relieving this situation.

MANIFESTED DISTURBANCES OF SEXUAL ABUSE VICTIMS

It is not uncommon for professionals to identify certain behaviors which may result from sexual abuse or any other form of traumatic injury. As first responders, it is helpful to recognize and identify some of these behaviors that will assist in meaningful intervention.

Removal

Children often remove themselves from painful and confusing experiences. Sexually-abused children learn this early in life and frequently detach their minds from their bodies. They may appear asleep in an attempt to block what is happening, or they may inflict self-pain through pinching or biting rather than deal with the sexual abuse.

Regression

Young children under the age of six will often regress to behavioral acts which remind them of a safer period in their life. Actions such as thumb sucking, bed wetting, reclaiming a favorite blanket or toy, baby talk, fear of the dark, whining, clinging, and crying when mother leaves are indicators of this behavior.

Developing Other Symptoms

School-age children may manifest such behaviors as continuous nightmares, phobias, acting out sexually with toys and animals, or even development of physical symptoms such as abdominal pain, sore throat, or anal or vaginal pain.

Newly-Found Behaviors

Adolescents who have been abused sexually tend to move forward toward unexplored ventures rather than regressing. Such behaviors as becoming overly emotional or acting out sexually toward others are characteristic. Other actions might constitute running away from home, suicide attempts, drug and alcohol abuse, stealing, lying, and delinquency. They seek affection and attention outside the family that may make them vulnerable to other assaults. Overeating, undereating, and poor performance in school are other strong indicators of behavioral changes.

Each of these behaviors represents a real and significant call for help from those too afraid to speak the truth. Through a greater level of knowledge regarding sexual abuse and an understanding of its ramifications, first responders can begin to uncover the complex maze of hidden fears and feelings. Responders can then begin meaningful intervention.

FAMILY IDENTIFICATION

Sexual abuse does not constitute a primary diagnosis by itself. It is a related symptom to other existing dysfunctional patterns within the family. In an attempt to understand the pathology of total behavior, certain common identifiable features may contribute to the overall pattern.

- The mother physically, emotionally, and socially withdraws from the home. Her activities do not include other family members.
- The daughter, due to the mother's absence, experiences a change in her role, emerging as the primary figure in the home.
- Sexual incompatibility is existent and intimacy is rare, if ever.
- The father usually is insecure in his own role and self-image and refrains from leaving home for companionship. He turns to his daughter for affection instead.

Family psychodynamic patterns vary, thus influencing initial and long-term intervention strategies. In an attempt for first responders to better understand certain common characteristic behaviors, the following profiles are outlined.

Mother's characteristics.
- Dependent on a marital relationship for financial support.
- Dependent to a lesser degree on a marital relationship for emotional support.
- Frequently aware of the existence of some family problems, but will emphatically deny the prevalence of sexual abuse.
- Often is accepting of and encourages a role reversal between mother and daughter.
- Participates in the act of offering the daughter.
- Frequently were victims of child abuse themselves.
- Unable to identify their role in the relationship due to denial.

Father's characteristics.
- Generally passive and dependent.

- Lacks self-esteem and self-respect.
- Fearful and frequently becomes angry over little things.
- Able to relate to little girls better than adult women.
- Frequently were victims of sexual abuse as children.
- Seeking companionship and love.

Family characteristics.
- Rigid, with unbending rules and role relationships.
- Do not adapt to daily upsets.
- Lack problem-solving skills.
- Minimal open communication.
- Nonverbal communication and double messages are the only forms of communication utilized.
- Direct messages become threatening.
- Role relationships are rigid and confusing to the children.
- Produces a loud and clear message that these family activities must *NEVER* be discussed.

Specific family identification is provided for easier assessment purposes. Techniques for intervention are outlined in Chapters Nine and Fifteen.

SUMMARY

Sexual abuse traditionally has been a family secret kept behind closed doors. Only within the past decade have professionals extended an understanding heart and a supportive hand, and assisted families in dealing with this concern. Recognizing the sensitivity of this abuse, it is imperative that first responders be well informed, nonjudgmental, and afford the foundation upon which intervention can begin. Unless that initial element of trust is established, families might shut themselves off to ongoing assistance. This compounds the problem and delays or permanently blocks counseling and assistance. Thus, it is critical that first responders respect their role and the influence they have on families experiencing sexual abuse.

REFERENCES
1. Gottlieb B: Incest: therapeutic intervention in a unique form of sexual abuse. *In* Warner CG (ed): Rape and Sexual Assault: Assessment and Intervention. Germantown, MD; Aspen Systems Corporation, 1980
2. Gottlieb BG: Incest: therapeutic intervention in a unique form of sexual

abuse. *In* Warner CG (ed): Rape and Sexual Assault: Assessment and Intervention. Germantown, MD; Aspen Systems Corporation, 1980, p. 121

3. Forward S, Buck C: Betrayal of Innocence. Los Angeles, CA; J. P. Tarcher, Inc., 1978, pp. 2-3
4. Weber E: Incest: Sexual abuse begins at home. Ms. Magazine, April 1977, pp. 64-67
5. Queen's Bench Foundation: Sexual abuse of children. San Francisco, 1976, p. 3
6. Biderman A: Surveys of population samples for estimating crime incidence. Annals of the American Academy of Political and Social Science, 1967, pp. 374, 16ff
7. Queen's Bench Foundation: Sexual abuse of children. San Francisco, 1976, pp. 5-6

8 INFREQUENTLY IDENTIFIED FORMS OF VIOLENCE

Carmen Germaine Warner, RN, PHN

The increasing amount of literature focusing on violence and violent behavior has stressed the adult-to-adult or adult-to-child interaction. Very little has attempted to focus on the child-to-adult or child-to-child forms of violence. This type of behavior exists by the mere nature of violence-ridden families. Professionals working in the area of domestic violence are just beginning to research, evaluate, and design intervention for the multifaceted existence of family violence. First responders must realize that abusive interaction may exist between and among any combination of members within the family network.

THE AGGRESSIVE CHILD

It is difficult to believe that a small child, eight years of age and under, could conceivably be the aggressor in situations of violent behavior, even death. In fact, the situation does exist—the victims of these child aggressors are usually infants less than one year old. Vulnerability of the infant victim is based on the nature of their existing physical stature. The delicacy of the infant's head, with its soft and bony structure, is the primary reason these infant victims are susceptible to traumatic and lethal abuse.

Literature identifies very little data establishing trends, commonalities, or contributing factors. This dearth of research, investigation, or discussion does not reflect the lack of its existence—only the minimal attention directed toward this abusive syndrome.

Adelson, in 1972, cited five case studies in his practice as Cuyohoga County (Cleveland, Ohio's county) coroner over a period of three and one-half years. The summary of his pertinent data is outlined in Table 8.1.[1] Even though the data is miniscule, it is presented in the hopes of identifying certain trigger points which may be valuable for first responders in recognizing and identifying potential cases of abuse. Some of the commonalities identified are as follows:

- All victims were eight months old or less.
- All died of chronic cerebral trauma, supporting the vulnerability of the infant's head to blunt injury.
- None of the infants showed evidence of previous neglect or abuse.
- All infants were clean and well nourished.
- X-rays revealed no previous fractures, tissue damage, or dislocations.

Contributing factors to the assailant's behavior, due to the age factor, are considerably different from those of adolescent and preadolescent children who kill. The primary reason for a child eight years and younger to express the death wish is jealousy because of the maternal attention received. Adelson notes through follow up conversations with the child and parents that the tiny child who kills is motivated because killing represents the most thorough form of retaliation he or she knows, and it implies the complete removal of the unwanted infant.[2] The assailant, however, is incapable of grasping or produces extreme difficulty in coping with the aspect of death as permanent and irreversible.

It is recorded as probable by Adelson that in young child-infant assault, the initial impact is a result of the assailant's deep-seated impulse. The following blows represent an attempt to quiet the victim. The first responder should recognize that this automatic response to quiet a crying infant is a natural response by the child assailant, and repeatedly is one of the recorded reasons why adults abuse their children.

Identifying, analyzing, and treating the crying child—physical trauma response syndrome—could outline many commonalities in the human response to crying, regardless of the age.

Strategies identified and applied toward the coping and intervention skills of humans dealing with the crying child could greatly reduce the "loss of control" response. Certain actions which might serve as a prevention link important for the first responders to communicate include:

- Foresee the child's needs and intervene before crying starts.
- Do not increase the child's frustration by losing control.
- Learn to talk to the child during these crying spells. This will reduce your anxiety and help to calm the child.

SIBLING ABUSE

From the beginning of biblical times, violence has been noted, as recorded in the sibling interaction between Cain and Abel: " . . .

Table 8.1. Five Abuse Case Studies.

Age and Sex of Victim	Age and Sex of Assailant	Assailant's Relationship to Victim	Causes of Death
3 months, 16 days male	8 years, female	Aunt	Manual assault and dropped on floor.
1 month, 21 days male	5 years, male	Son of babysitter	Manual assault and dropped on floor.
4 months female	2½ years, male	Cousin	Assaulted with metal toy.
8 months male	5 and 2 years, males	Neighbor's sons	Assaulted with women's shoes; dropped on floor.
7 weeks female	7 years, male	Brother	Assaulted with leg of spinning wheel and beaten.

and Cain talks with Abel his brother: and it came to pass, when they were in the field that Cain rose up against Abel his brother, and slew him."[3] It is a normal reaction to expect siblings to engage in squabbles as they are growing older. The difficulty arises in the frequency and severity of these conflicts, and identifying at what time they are recognized as cases of sibling abuse. Straus et al identify violence between siblings as the most prevalent form of family violence.[4]

Children are not born with violent behavior. However, children learn very quickly that physical force is an effective means of resolving conflicts. A perfect role model for this learning process is through observing how their parents resolve marital conflicts and their own experiences with discipline.

It is interesting to note that even though families may be reluctant to discuss aspects of spouse abuse or child abuse, they openly discuss sibling violence as a matter of normal growth and development. Certain factors appear to contribute to the potential sibling-sibling violent interchange. These include:

- Violence between and among siblings occurs more frequently than any form of parent-child or spouse abuse.
- As children grow older, much of this abusive interaction diminishes, reiterating the fact of sibling abuse to be more prevalent among younger siblings.
- Boys tend to be more violent than girls.
- The highest incidence of violence occurs when all children are males.

A recent study conducted by Straus et al gathered data from 2,143 families, of which 733 had two or more children. Some interesting data evolved from this research, as noted (see Table 8.2).[5] This classically demonstrates the fact that four out of every five children in this country, ages three through 17, have a sibling living at home who perpetrates at least one violent act in any given year. Based on that data, 36.3 million children fall into this age category, with over 29 million children in this country participating in at least one act of physical violence annually.

For reasons such as unfamiliarity of parents with total sibling behavior and poor recollection of physical contact among siblings, these figures are quite conservative.

First responders must keep in mind that sibling conflict is frequently the foundation for future adult violence toward their spouse, their children, or an outsider. Early recognition of this existing pattern may assist in developing nonviolent methods of

Table 8.2. Existence of Sibling Violence.

Specific Behavior	Percent of violent children of families studied
Any form of violence	82
Sibling was pushed or shoved	74
Sibling was slapped	48
Sibling had things thrown at them	43
Sibling was punched, bit, or kicked	42
Sibling was hit with an object	40
Sibling was physically beaten	16
Sibling was threatened with a knife or gun	0.8
Weapon used was a knife or gun	0.3

dealing with siblings—thus, a greater tendency for nonviolent behavior in general.

Factors which might assist in recognizing the existence of sibling violence include:

- The rate of violence decreases as the child increases in age.
- Boys tend to be more physical in their abuse, while girls engage in more verbal abuse.
- If there are more boys in a family, their nature toward increased physical violence is felt, compared with the verbal abuse demonstrated by a more female-dominated family.
- Families with only male children experience more sibling abuse than those with only female children.

ADOLESCENTS INVOLVED IN VIOLENCE

Juvenile violence is increasing similar to other forms of violence. It has been recorded that more individuals who commit acts of homicide, rape, assault, and robbery fall into the age groups of 15 to 17 and 18 to 24 years than any other age group.[6]

Early detection of potentially violent behavior is noted in the family unit. First responders working with families in crisis may become familiarized with some of these manifestations during a time when preventive interaction is possible. Some of the common factors displayed by these youth are:

- A close, almost symbiotic, emotional bonding with one parent.
- An indirect, almost uninvolved, relationship with the other parent.

- Hidden and open marital disturbances usually are present in the family constellation.
- Separation from the family with increasing autonomy from the parents.
- Parents are struggling with middle-age life crises, declining health, and identity confusion.
- Inconsistency in values, limits, and restrictions as set forth by the parents concerning the youth.
- Youth feeling intense hostility on one side and guilt and shame on the other due to this separation.
- Parents and other sibling stress results from the youth's separation.[7]

It is not infrequent to visualize self-destructive behavior as a result of existing guilt following separation from the home. These feelings, along with the psychopathology of the parents, the inability of parents to resolve marital problems, and the poor self-esteem of both parents and youth climax in an atmosphere in which severe disruptive behavior may occur. The inability of the youth to set limits, based on a home environment where the same thing occurs, can prove to be very harmful and potentially dangerous. The youth may exploit the parents' shame which develops from their own feelings of failure. As a result, parents will fear the youth's violence and withdraw from confronting the youth's behavior.

EARLY SIGNS OF HOMICIDAL AGGRESSION

Factors used to help identify a sequence of events leading to a homicidal act have been outlined by a number of clinicians. Their intent is to alert practitioners to various patterns which, if broken, may attempt to abort a possible homicide. Malmquist feels there are certain warning signs which occur prior to a homicidal act.[8] Specific contributing factors are indicated in Figure 8.1. It is hoped that first responders will recognize these factors and serve as a factor in preventing these youth from potentially committing a homicide.

Behavioral Changes

Specific changes related to mood shifts with an emphasis on a deep pessimism concerning themselves start to develop. They begin to

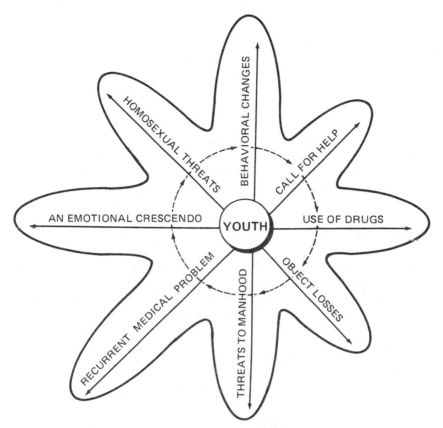

Figure 8.1.   Warning signs prior to a homicidal act.

brood and compound an already self-critical attitude. Self-hate becomes an open expression among peers.

Call for Help

Specific calls for help were often muted and not recognized by family members or friends. Even when a behavioral change was noted, denial existed among family members. They felt that since mood changes had not resulted in a violent act previously, it would not occur now.

Use of Drugs

Those individuals on barbiturates and tranquilizers still manifested impulsive behavior and apparently had increased the dosages of the drugs on their own initiative. Others were involved significantly with amphetamines and drugs which induce a psychotic-like state.

Object Losses

The symbolic loss of someone close, usually a mother or a lover, was a precipitating factor which ties into a complex relationship. The youth usually was placed in a position of trying to help the mother or lover with a difficult problem and was unable to do so. This places the youth in a guilt-ridden situation.

Threats to Manhcod

Encouragement by females to be strong and aggressive may result in unsuccessful attempts to accomplish a specific task. When this occurs, the youth may become aggressive toward the female and either beat her up, kill her, or injure someone close to her.

Recurrent Medical Problems

Most complaints were of a chronic, recurring nature and consisted primarily of such symptoms as headaches of an increasing severity, persistent physical aches, and somatic concerns.

An Emotional Crescendo

Such appearances as an increased buildup of agitation and energy, motor restlessness, and disturbed sleeping and eating patterns were common. Restless pacing, talking incomprehensibly to themselves, manifesting periods of acute anxiety, panic or catatonic excitement were clinically present. Frequent breakdowns in ego control evidenced themselves in crying and sobbing spells.

Homosexual Threats

Incidents of either overt or covert acts resulted in an increase of homicide in youth.

In addition to the previously outlined contributing factors, Duncan identified certain factors[9] which would assist first responders in evaluating a youth's potential for dangerous behavior. These include:

- The intensity of the youth's hostile, destructive impulses expressed verbally, behaviorally, or through a psychomatic test.
- The youth's knowledge of, and ability, to pursue realistic alternatives to a violent resolution.
- The provocativeness of the intended victim.
- The degree of helplessness in the intended victim.
- The availability of weapons.
- The homicidal hints or threats which warrant serious concern.

The ultimate point at which a youth may reach a crucial breaking point is identified by Halleck as an overwhelming feeling of helplessness and hopelessness which culminates in an act of violence.[10] This appears to be irrevocably compounded by a state of mourning, identified by Malmquist to be the point of no return.[11] The mourning may not necessarily include a loss but involves such things as academic or vocational failures, social disappointments, failure in any form of love relationship, or the feeling that someone has been dishonest to them.

These indications and cries for help are important for first responders to identify, evaluate, and manage. Even though the initial family crisis might focus around spousal unrest, reverberations of this trauma may be activating a pre-violent crisis in some of the youth of the family. Consequently, the role of prevention remains integrally laced with that of specific intervention.

BATTERED PARENTS

The spectrum of battered parents is as broad-based in its scope as that of children, reflecting both physical attacks, verbal and nonverbal threats, and emotional battering. However, only the physical aspect of battering will be addressed here.

The extent of abuse of parents focuses primarily on repetitive or threatened attacks ranging from threatening behavior, such as destroying furniture, verbally assaulting them, and attacking them physically, seriously enough to require hospitalization.

It is commonly noted that the precipitating factor evolves from a disagreement between parent and youth. The parents usually will have committed some act, either disciplinary or behaviorally, that was upsetting to the youth. A frequent response by the parent was an indirect reward of giving in to the child or changing their pre-established position on an issue.

Harbin and Madden in recent studies have begun to identify certain clinical manifestations which could be valuable to first responders in assessing the dynamics of family behavior.[12]

These manifestations include:

- Outwardly the family does not appear to be acutely stressed.
- Disturbance in the authority hierarchy is noted.
- One or both parents have abdicated the executive position or considerable covert competition exists, so neither parent rules.
- Parents and youth exist in an environment where the youth is identified as being in charge.
- Parents in these situations shy away from stating that they establish the family rules.
- Parents are nonspecific in either blaming or condoning the youth following physical abuse.
- In certain decision-making processes, youth of assessed cognitive limitations are granted the final say.
- The abdication of authority is noted to be granted to the youth due to their dictatorial or bossy personality.
- Parents often appear threatened by the youth.
- Parents recall that the youth possessed hostile personalities even at an early age.
- Physical characteristics of the parents or youth may contribute to aggressive behavior—for example, the youth is much larger than the parent.
- Youth may attempt to replace their ineffective parents.
- Youth may attempt to punish their parents who may have exploited them through permissiveness and lack of leadership.
- Youth act like know-it-alls with a grandiose sense of self.

FAMILY PERSONAL REACTIONS

Denial is as prevalent a concept in parent battering as in child and spouse abuse. Immediately following an aggressive episode, parents might be able to admit its existence, but very shortly afterward, the denial process occurs again.

Harbin has noted that parents will take considerable effort to protect their children.[13] This denial and protection are displayed in several ways:

- Avoid any recognition or discussion of the violent action.
- Attempt to minimize the seriousness of the violent action.
- Avoid punishing aggressive behavior.
- Refuse to seek outside help and assistance.

These behaviors are taken in the hopes of protecting their child, with concomitant protection being sought for their own self-image. Recognition of the problem admits failure as a parent, and their goal is to maintain the image of family solidarity and harmony at all costs.

If parents were to admit their child had attempted to kill them, this would disrupt the family system and create an environment of fear, anxiety, and depression. Consequently, these families begin to sanction the youth's behavior, feed existing feelings of helplessness, and destroy any potential for intervention.

Despite destructive, aggressive behavior and hostility of the youth toward a weak parent, the youth will avoid family separation at all costs. This compounds and feeds into the feelings of dependency.

MANAGEMENT OF AN AGGRESSIVE CHILD

Patterson and Cobb have hypothesized that aggressive behavior in youth is influenced and controlled by positive and negative reinforcement.[14] The existence of aggressive behavior toward or by another family member encourages behavior of the same by other family members. These abusive behaviors establish a set for violence and encourage its existence in the family unit. This ongoing syndrome reinforces the continuance of aggressive behavior and frequently condones it.

Patterson et al completed research that outlines the impact of social environment on aggressive youth.[15] They attempted to establish a situation where parents were trained and utilized as behavior managers. The method used was one where children were reinforced for performance well within their reach, and their behavior was not addressed at all. The concluding results supported Patterson's belief that impacting the social environment rather than the deviant youth was a much more appropriate and effective means of intervention. Specific techniques for intervention are dealt with in Section Three.

SUMMARY

The nature and dynamics of violent interchange among family members is diverse. Its complexity lies in the network of potential abuse between and among family members. Even though the traditional focus of assessment and intervention has evolved around child abuse and, more recently, spouse abuse, first responders must be alerted to the potential for any and all forms of violence involving the family unit. Early recognition, intervention, and attempted change in role behavior is a critical first step in reducing the general acceptance and practice of violence as a way of life.

REFERENCES

 1. Adelson L: The battering child. JAMA Vol. 222 No. 2, October 9, 1972
 2. Adelson L: The battering child. JAMA Vol. 222 No. 2, October 9, 1972, p. 161
 3. Holy Bible, King James version, Genesis 4:8
 4. Straus MA, Gelles RF, Steinmetz SK: Behind Closed Doors. New York, Anchor Press, 1980, p. 77
 5. Straus MA, Gelles RJ, Steinmetz SK: Behind Closed Doors. New York, Anchor Press, 1980, p. 81
 6. Mulvihill DJ, Tumin MM (eds): Crimes of Violence. Washington, DC; US Government Printing Office, 1969, pp. 603-637
 7. Harbin HT: Episodic dyscontrol and family dynamics. American Journal of Psychiatry, Vol. 134 No. 10, October 1977
 8. Malmquist CP: Premonitory signs of homicidal aggression in juveniles. American Journal of Psychiatry, Vol. 128 No. 4, October 1971, pp. 93-97
 9. Duncan JW, Duncan GM: Murder in the family. American Journal of Psychiatry, Vol. 127 No. 11, May 1971, pp. 74-78
10. Halleck S: Psychiatry and the Dilemmas of Crime. New York, Harper and Row, 1967
11. Straus MA, Gelles RJ, Steinmetz SK: Behind Closed Doors. New York, Anchor Press, 1980, p. 97
12. Harbin HT, Madden DJ: Battered parents: New syndrome. American Journal of Psychiatry, Vol. 136 No. 10, October 1979
13. Duncan JW, Duncan GM: Murder in the family. American Journal of Psychiatry, Vol. 127 No. 11, May 1971, p. 1290
14. Patterson GR, Cobb JA: A dyadic analysis of aggressive behavior: An additional step toward a theory of aggression.Proceedings of the Fifth

Minnesota Symposium on Child Psychology, University of Minnesota, pp. 72-109, 1972

15. Patterson GR, Cobb JA, Ray RS: Training parents to control an aggressive child. *In* Steinmetz S, Straus M (eds): Violence in the Family. New York; Dodd, Mead and Company, 1974

III

APPROACHES TO INTERVENTION

9 TECHNIQUES IN CONFLICT INTERVENTION

Carmen Germaine Warner, RN, PHN

Conflict, stress, crisis—these are terms common to most people in their daily lives. The pressures of work or possible unemployment; the escalating costs of living or the inability to afford daily necessities; the overwhelming cost of health maintenance or the struggle to pay for medical care; the pressures to achieve prominence and security, or the failure to accept and love oneself are common examples.

These situations exist in the personal lives of first responders, as well as those individuals requiring their services. Intervention in conflict, or crisis situations, related to social and domestic violence provides a bold and innovative holistic approach to preventive health maintenance for individuals and families who are victims of abuse, assault, and related trauma.

Conflict can be defined for the purpose of this text as a clash between opposing concepts, ideas, or beliefs. It can serve as a mechanism for reassessment and change or it can impose irreconcilable pressures which may lead to events of violence. The way a person feels about a particular situation, accompanied by his or her ability to cope with that situation, contributes to the design and formation of a conflict situation.

PRELIMINARIES OF CONFLICT SITUATIONS

In most instances, the first responder sees a family only after an act of abuse or violence has occurred. These situations force the responder to focus on an act already committed. However, in an attempt to minimize further conflict, or when reacting with potential situations of abuse or violence, one must understand some of the precipitating factors leading to crisis or conflict.[1]

Step 1. The perpetrator of the abuse or assault is faced with a stressful and conflicting situation.

Step 2. He or she attempts to deal or cope with the situation and experiences failure.

147

Step 3. The resulting frustration produces anger and/or depression.

Step 4. The uncontrollable frustration causes the perpetrator to lose equilibrium and control.

Step 5. An act of abuse or assault is committed. See Figure 9.1.

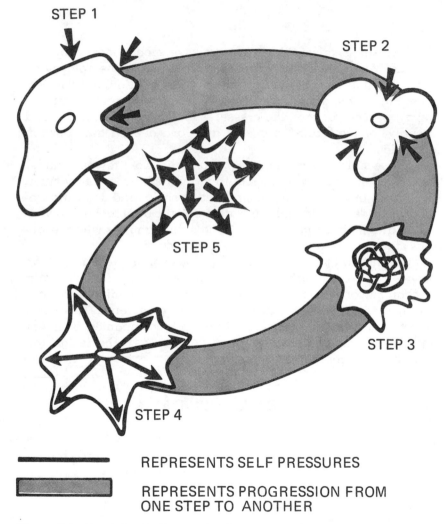

REPRESENTS SELF PRESSURES

REPRESENTS PROGRESSION FROM ONE STEP TO ANOTHER

Figure 9.1   Precipitating factors leading to a conflict.

The first responder will find that an assessment of the situation may help in determining whether a crisis conflict and the tendency for violence exist. Specific considerations when making this assessment include:[2]

- Investigate unusual behavior.
- Look for a triggering event.
- Determine how involved the person is with the existing conflict.
- Assess existing balancing factors. This includes the perception of the event, available emotional support, and intact coping mechanisms. If all three factors exist, conflict will be handled adequately. If two of the three factors are present, some difficulty may exist, and with only one factor in balance, a conflict situation is likely.

Once a careful and accurate assessment is made by the first responder, assistance can be provided to victims and families. This intervention cannot only abort potential life-threatening situations but can offer first responders a chance to demonstrate their concern for victims of situational crisis as well as imparting the potential for change in behavior and circumstances. As noted by Katz, it is important for first responders to become adequately educated to function effectively in this role because:[3]

- First responders are presently engaged in a number of service functions and mental health activities with insufficient technical and attitudinal training.
- Family disputes and other abuse and assault cases are some of the most common cases dealt with by first responders.
- Family conflict situations are characterized by a high rate of relapse into criminal behavior.
- Responders can provide direct assistance to persons in distress.
- Intervention depends solely on individual powers and inner resources.
- Success in first responders handling situations of abuse and assault improves their image in the eyes of the community.
- Intervention with family abuse and social assault victims is very frustrating. This attitude must be dealt with.
- Family and social conflict intervention requires new knowledge, skills, and attitudes which are transferrable to other interactions and lead to a general upgrading in personnel.

Therefore, it is of the utmost importance for greater emphasis to be placed on continuing education directed toward conflict intervention.

CONFLICT INTERVENTION FOR RAPE VICTIMS

Rape, being a situational crisis, produces an overwhelming environment of fear, psychologic trauma, guilt, physical mutilation, and even death. This agony frequently prevents the victim from seeking help. It is essential that the first responder establish a supportive base of trust and understanding with the victim. Some of the steps to be taken during the initial intervention to accomplish this goal are outlined in Table 9.1.

Table 9.1. Steps in Conflict Intervention.

Do not intensify the situation through your behavior or comments.
Remain calm yet concerned.
Encourage the victim to talk about the rape attack.
Practice active listening skills.
Take what the victim says seriously.
Do not criticize the victim.
Recognize that an unusually calm person may be hiding extreme stress.

The victim, frequently in shock, may manifest certain behaviors which are normal. Some of these behaviors include:[4]

1. Inconsistencies in the story
2. Incoherent speech
3. Confusion about numbers
4. Inability to determine time intervals
5. Crying, with periods of uncontrollable sobbing
6. Restlessness or tenseness
7. Inappropriate smiling and laughing
8. Extreme anger accompanied by wishes for revenge

No matter what the existing behavior, the victim should always be taken seriously.

Establishing Trust

Developing relationships of trust is probably one of the most important steps the first responder can accomplish. Unless a firm foundation is established, the victim's future may be filled with constant fear and shame.

Reassurance should be offered to the victim that you will stay throughout the initial process. Assessing the victim's level of

understanding and using words appropriate to that level are imperative. If the victim responds in a hostile, belligerent manner, consider the following as possible causative factors:[5]
- What occurred during the assault?
- What is the victim's perception of the rape?
- What coping mechanism is the victim using?
- Does the victim feel he or she is to blame?
- What support mechanisms are intact?
- What type of support is the victim receiving from first responders and other personnel?
- Is the victim's dignity being preserved at all costs?

Communication Skills

As a first responder, it is essential to represent the victim's primary support system. The victim should not be left alone for any reason. Encouragement must be given to talk about feelings, and an environment of comfort must be provided. Guidelines for conversation to assist in this intervention are found in Table 9.2.[6] Once the victim feels less frightened and begins to communicate personal fears, it is apparent that she or he does not have to proceed alone.

CONFLICT INTERVENTION FOR CHILD ABUSE VICTIMS

Victims of abuse and assault present a challenge that differs from other medical emergencies. They include many of the same physical injuries as other trauma related situations, but the associated emotional factors are intensified. This is particularly true in cases of reported child abuse. It is critical that the first responder view the situation solely on existing facts and not personal feelings. A careful and accurate assessment of the case is to the benefit of all. Certain factors to consider when responding to an abuse call which include:
- Provide prompt assessment and intervention to existing physical injuries.
- Secure as much information as possible regarding the alleged incident.
- Discuss the situation with the parents and note any discrepancies in the story.
- Note whether the parents are quick to blame others for the incident.

- Question an illogical explanation for an injury. Do not automatically assume it is a lie. (Observe how a child and parent interact. Note things like flinching, nervous behavior, and fear of parents.)
- Note behavior that suggests role reversal, like parents seeking adult protectiveness from the child by acting helpless.

Communication Skills

First responders should explore all cases suspect of violence by encouraging communication on the part of both parent and child. In communicating with the child, an initial process must be used to develop rapport and openness between responder and child. Some of the following techniques might be helpful:
- Utilize extreme gentleness.
- Inquire what happened, but do not force an answer.
- Do not expect that a child will perceive abuse as abnormal or undeserved.
- Do not use words which might be interpreted as consolation or in support of the parent's action.
- Question the child to uncover everything that happened prior to the incident.

Specific skills for communicating with parents are equally as important. Certain questioning considerations are outlined in Table 9.3.[7] Parents must not receive the impression they are being criticized, evaluated, or encouraged to accept the responder's personal beliefs. The only way both parent and child will be able to constructively deal with the problem is for the first responder to demonstrate understanding, patience, and openness. The best way to deal with the problem on this basis is to gather as much data as possible. Certain points to be addressed are:
- How the parent disciplines the child?
- What are the parents' personal feelings following disciplinary action?
- What are the parents' reactions to soiled diapers?
- How do the parents handle a crying child?
- What do the parents do if the child does not sleep?
- Do the parents think the child is misbehaving on purpose?
- Who do the parents talk to when they become upset?

Any information obtained during this initial interview should

Table 9.2. Verbal Interchange.*

General Guidelines	When Victim Says	Negative Response	Positive Response
Refrain from making threatening statements.	"I've been raped. Should I go to the hospital?"	"Absolutely! You have to be checked for VD."	"I'll accompany you. Ms. Jones works in the Emergency Department and is very supportive. She will assist with your exam."
Empathize, don't sympathize.	"It was horrible! I feel so ashamed and dirty."	"I really feel sorry for you. It must have been horrible."	"You've had a frightening experience. Would you like to talk about it?"
Encourage the victim to verbalize his or her fears.	"I don't want to talk about it."	"Well, if that's how you feel. I have to go now."	"It sounds like you're trying to forget the rape, but it is important that you share your feelings and resolve it. Let's talk."

*Table modified for this text.

be shared with personnel continuing work on the case. Continuity is imperative not only for process purposes, but to minimize repeat questioning.

CONFLICT INTERVENTION FOR SEXUAL ABUSE IN CHILDREN

Sexual abuse occurs in boys and girls of all ages, beginning with infancy. A child may not be able to complain of the trauma associated with child molestation. However, once he or she is old enough to communicate, complaints must be taken seriously. The reporting of such trauma may not come from the parents, as family members frequently experience shock and disbelief. Thus, it is essential that the case be thoroughly investigated to clarify all suspicions.

In some cases parents, family members, or friends are responsible for the assault. As a first responder, one must never presume anyone to be guilty, but must focus primarily on the well-being of the child.

Steps necessary to fulfill this include:
- Offer personal support.
- Stress genuine concern for the child.
- Clarify terminology used by the child when signifying body parts.
- Inquire about family members, friends, and neighbors.
- Determine those responsible for child care.
- Assess family sleeping patterns and arrangements.
- Determine if the child fears a certain location; for example, a routine path to school or the store.
- Are behavioral problems manifested?
- Are nightmares a recent occurrence?

These questions will provide part of the data essential in determining proper intervention. Additional input must be gathered through interviewing the child directly. Specific questions identified for this purpose include:
- "Does anyone get into bed with you at night?"
- "Does anyone ever take off your pajamas or underpants?"
- "Does anyone take their pants off in front of you?"
- "Has anyone ever put their finger or other object between your legs?"

Table 9.3. *Verbal Interchange with Parents and Guardians.* *

General Guidelines	When Parent Says	Negative Response	Positive Response
Refrain from scapegoating.	"If my husband were here he could help me with the children."	"I can understand."	"Have you talked to him about it?"
Avoid negative feelings.	"I can't tolerate this child anymore."	"Come now—it can't be that bad."	"What seems to annoy you the most?"
Emphasize the positive.	"I wish I were a good mother."	"How did your mother treat you as a child?"	"You can be and will be with some help from people who care about you."
Accept the family as they are.	"I need help."	"We'll talk about that later."	"I will help you locate the people who can help."

*Table modified for this text.

The first responder must keep all personal feelings hidden or it will affect both the child's and parent's response, and might even dissolve communication.

CONFLICT INTERVENTION WITH SPOUSE ABUSE VICTIMS

As previously noted, first responders answering calls of domestic violence face a very volatile and hostile situation. Growing anxieties, fears, and frustrations on the part of both parties may be redirected at an uninvolved, nonfamily third party. Physical harm and even death may result, so utmost care must be taken when approaching and assessing the situation. Possible steps in the intervention process include:

- Separate the two parties so appropriate intervention can begin.
- Address the needs of the woman while her partner is calming down.
- Allow only one person to speak at a time.[8]
- Switch first responders so the stories can be verified.[8]
- In listening to the stories, try to determine what each individual contributed to the conflict.[8]
- Assess whether each disputant perceives the situation realistically.
- If one of the disputants holds him or herself to blame, identify in what ways the other shares the blame.[8]
- Ask questions in order to gather clear details.[8]
- Determine whether or not there has been a history of this type of behavior.[8]
- Investigate whether the history goes back prior to marriage or other relationships.[8]
- Give each person the opportunity to speak.[8]
- Point out similarities and discrepancies in the stories.[8]
- Get a reaction from both parties regarding how the first responder perceives the situation.[8]
- Ask the couple what they plan to do.[8]
- If the first responder disagrees with the choice of action, suggest they seek professional help.[8]
- Assess existing coping or stabilizing mechanisms.
- Encourage the woman to talk about her feelings of fear, frustration, guilt, anger, or shame.
- Assist the couple in making decisions regarding immediate action.

- Prior to departure make sure she or he has your name and telephone number.
- Discuss alternatives such as:
  1. Seeking help from friends and relatives.
  2. Having the husband or boyfriend seek help from friends and relatives.
  3. Getting the husband or boyfriend to seek professional help.
  4. Take the children and go to a temporary shelter.
  5. Seek assistance from community social service or crisis center agencies.
  6. Indicate options for legal recourse.
  7. Explain the concept of citizen's arrest and restraining orders.
  8. Provide the couple with a list of resources available to them.
  9. Take the woman to a hospital if injuries require medical attention.

Even though the victim may not indicate an interest in any of the alternatives beyond medical attention, she should be given a comprehensive referral list for future consideration and use.

CONFLICT INTERVENTION FOR SUICIDE VICTIMS

Suicide is the final option for anyone in stress, and any first responder confronting such a situation must recognize that this might be that final option. In an attempt to assess the situation accurately, the following signals should be observed and dealt with.

- Has this individual threatened suicide in the past?
- Has he or she hinted or joked about it with friends or family?
- Has an attempt or half-hearted attempt been made in the past?
- Does the individual appear depressed?
- Is there a manifested behavior of recklessness or does the individual appear accident prone?
- Has a change in behavior or personality been noted?
- Is the individual relinquishing treasured materials and personal belongings?

Conflict intervention is critical in this area and must be handled with precision and total awareness of the situation. Certain conversational skills may prove invaluable when facing a potential suicide victim. Specific guidelines are outlined in Table 9.4.[9] First responders can help by recognizing suicide's danger signs early, initiating appropriate intervention, and making a rapid referral. Suicide is a tragic alternative to living, but a greater tragedy is when someone indicates their intent to kill themself and no one listens.

GENERAL CONSIDERATIONS IN CONFLICT INTERVENTION

There are several principles of conflict intervention which can be applied to all victims of violence. They include:

- Help the victim to identify their problem and break it down into segments they can handle one at a time.
- Promote task mastery by helping the victim select alternative actions, then guide him or her to select the best one.
- Encourage the victim to face and deal with their crisis.
- Do not promote false reassurance.
- Support those in crisis in face of uncertain outcome while providing concern, optimism, and confidence.
- Discourage scapegoating and blaming others.
- Attempt to maintain an element of hope.
- Discourage meaningless activities.
- Prevent involvement with previous personal problems by encouraging recognition of the here and now.
- Support and encourage victims to secure outside assistance.
- Encourage use of informal systems such as significant others (friends, family, and neighbors).
- Aid people in crisis to be honest with their feelings. Tears and expressions of anger are appropriate.
- The most appropriate time for conflict intervention is during the crisis.
- Intervention contacts should be short and frequent.
- Dependency during a crisis with appropriate resolution may decrease long term dependency.
- Direct victims to individuals who have resolved a crisis successfully themselves.
- Help victims to secure adequate sleep without heavy sedation.
- Discourage the use of pills and alcohol as a means of resolving crisis.

Table 9.4. The Suicidal Patient.

General Guidelines	When He or She Says	Negative Response	Positive Response
Take all suicide threats seriously.	"Sometimes I think it would be better if I were dead, but I'd never really kill myself."	"You'll feel better soon."	"What's troubling you? Why do you feel so desperate?"
Discuss suicide openly.	"I think about death a lot."	"Don't talk that way. Look what you have to live for."	"How long have you felt like this? Have you thought about how you'd kill yourself? Have you made any plans?"
Don't be judgmental.	"I did it because my parents don't care about me."	"That's a terrible thing to say about your family. Think how they feel."	"Why do you feel that way?"
Don't belittle his or her feelings.	"I'll feel so embarrassed at home. People will watch me to see if I'll try it again."	"You're right—what did you expect?"	"Why do you think you'll be embarrassed? Do you feel you might try again?"
Don't encourage false pity.	"When my wife left me, I knew it would be impossible."	"I see why you're so unhappy."	"When did your wife leave you? How did you feel when you were alone?"
Don't make unrealistic promises or remarks.	"I can't stand being depressed any longer."	"Don't worry. There are many ways to cure depression."	"There's lots of help available from people who specialize in your problem."

These principles are provided as guidelines for conflict intervention. Special considerations must be given for each individual situation.

SUMMARY

The most significant phase of assessment and intervention is initiated by the first responder. Without establishing an initial strong, supportive foundation of trust, emergency management and ongoing follow-up become shallow, weak, and ineffective.

Unless the victim and family members can communicate with a nonbiased, open, empathetic individual, the desire and cooperation for appropriate intervention becomes nonexistent, and the established pattern of abuse or assault is likely to continue.

REFERENCES

1. Johnson R: Recognizing people in crisis. In Using Crisis Intervention Wisely. Horsham, PA; Nursing 79, Books Intermed Communications, Inc., 1979, p. 16
2. Johnson R: Recognizing people in crisis. In Using Crisis Intervention Wisely. Horsham, PA; Nursing 79, Books Intermed Communications, Inc., 1979, pp. 18-22
3. Katz M: Family crisis training: Upgrading the police while building a bridge to the minority community. Journal of Police Science and Administration, Vol. 1 No. 2, 1973, p. 32
4. Warner CG et al: San Diego County Protocol for the Treatment of Rape and Sexual Assault Victims. City of San Diego, Fall 1978, pp. 69-74
5. Warner CG: Comforting and caring for the rape victim. In Using Crisis Intervention Wisely. Horsham, PA; Nursing 79, Books Intermed Communications, Inc., 1979, p. 122
6. Warner CG: Comforting and caring for the rape victim. In Using Crisis Intervention Wisely. Horsham, PA; Nursing 79, Books Intermed Communications, Inc., 1979, p. 123
7. Hyde D: Helping the victims of child abuse. In Using Crisis Intervention Wisely. Horsham, PA; Nursing 79, Books Intermed Communications, Inc., 1979, p. 113
8. Auten J: The domestic disturbance: A policeman's dilemma. The Police Chief, October 1972, p. 17
9. Croushore T: Recognizing and protecting the suicidal patient. In Using Crisis Intervention Wisely. Horsham, PA; Nursing 79, Books Intermed Communications, Inc., 1979, p. 93

10 DYNAMICS OF AN INTERVIEW

Carmen Germaine Warner, RN, PHN

Interviewing is a process. It represents much more than recording a victim's history. Instead, it constitutes the essential ingredients in a successful clinician-patient (victim) relationship. Appropriate, careful, and successful interviewing provides the foundation for understanding which leads to optimum results. The skill of interviewing is a technique which should be mastered and utilized by all law enforcement, health, and counseling personnel throughout the assessment and intervention process.

THE INTERVIEW: ITS SCIENTIFIC APPROACH

The interview, as defined by Kahn and Caunell, is a specialized pattern of verbal interaction initiated for a specific purpose and focused on some specific content area, with the consequent elimination of irrelevant material.[1] In essence, the interview process for first responders must incorporate this philosophy. In order for either the initial or the follow-up interview to produce optimum results, the interviewer must facilitate communication while at the same time keeping in mind the need to guide or even limit it. In cases when the victim or the family is confronted with the trauma of rape, the remorse of child abuse, or the vacillating feelings associated with spouse abuse, it can be inappropriate to ask a large number of specific, sensitive questions. This may cut off communication or limit it permanently.

In establishing a comfortable interview foundation, the first responder must incorporate a specific blueprint for planning. This plan is addressed in Table 10.1.

Table 10.1. Points of Consideration in Interview Planning.

Establishing and maintaining good communication skills.
Developing an attitude of openness.
Incorporating an element of curiosity.
Developing the desire to learn as much as possible about the victim and
    family.
Perfecting the capacity to transcend any cultural or social barriers.

Acquiring a thorough knowledge of rape, child molestation, child abuse, spouse abuse, sexual abuse, and suicide.

The bottom line in any first responder interview is sensitive data collecting. This ultimately leads to a mutual decision which is the best for all associated parties. Clinical decision making is rarely an isolated event in cases of social and domestic violence. It is a continuous process which extends from the initial assault or abuse and into the follow-up period of intervention. Each interview continues to build a data information bank and is appropriate for the specific phase the victim is experiencing.

If the initial and subsequent interviews are conducted with support and gentleness, a victim's trust and confidence will develop and grow throughout the entire process.

First Responder's Attitude and Behavior

The interviewer, based on his or her own attitude regarding social and domestic violence, can have an influence on the victim's openness to change. Often a victim may be encouraged to consider and evaluate what is best for their particular situation through the supportive, caring nature of the first responder. A victim can explore the possibility of a changed environment, personal relationships, individual ideas regarding the assault or abuse situation, and one's own concept of self.

The interviewer can assist the victim to identify first the types of changes that would be appropriate to the situation, and secondly how these changes can best be accomplished.

Methods of implementing change. The process of change involves the conscious cooperation of victim and interviewer. The harmony of this relationship begins in the initial interview and continues throughout the intervention process. Factors which contribute to the successful design of this harmony require that the first responder:

- Accept the victim as a person with real feelings, fears, and confusion.
- Maintain thorough awareness of the problem of abuse and assault.
- Participate actively in the interviewing process.
- Maintain respect for the victim's self-image.
- Demonstrate empathy toward the victim.
- Provide support throughout the crisis reality phase.

- Display genuine liking for people.
- Encourage and guide the exploration of alternatives.
- Initiate extreme patience.
- Practice active listening skills.

The first responder, when listening to the victim, should understand some of the points outlined in Table 10.2.

Table 10.2. Goals in Listening.

How the victim thinks and feels about his or her self.
How one feels about significant others and people in general.
How the victim perceives family and significant others as viewing the rape or abuse.
How the victim responds to the first responder and the material under discussion.
What are the victim's aspirations, ambitions, and goals?
What defense mechanisms the victim is using.
What coping mechanisms the victim possesses.
What are the victim's philosophy and values?

---

*Ideas developed from materials in Reference 2.

CHARACTERISTICS OF THE INFORMATION

The first responder will gleen information in two separate ways: (1) by listening to what the victim says, and (2) by observing the victim's behavior.[3] It is essential to observe the way the victim walks, talks, holds him or herself, breathes, sits, and behaves toward the interviewer. This is helpful in making the appropriate decisions regarding intervention. From the victim's response and observation of behavior, four types of information as noted in Table 10.3 can be gathered.

Assessing all aspects of the information attained is critical as a data base for the decision-making process. First responders should not attempt to predict victim or family behavior based on knowledge of social class or ethnicity.

Interviewing Skills

First responders will be directed in the interview by guidelines set forth as institutional procedure. Specific forms require that the victim answer optional questions. Even though this procedure is required, certain elements are important to develop an honest re-

Table 10.3. Classes of Information.[4]*

Class of Information	Information Gained	Method Used to Gather Information
Biological	Organic aspect of the abuse or assault.	Verbal and nonverbal communication and data from the physical assessment.
Psychological	Victim's mood, response to interviewer, attitude, perceptions, thinking processes, and intelligence—in essence, *mental status*.	Verbal expression called *content* and behavior called *process*.
Social	Victim's residence,** occupation of self or parent, personal tastes, cultural orientation and manner of spending leisure time, social mobility.	Direct questioning, review of existing health or medical records.
Cultural	The way of life, language, attitudes, skills, value systems, and shared ethical judgments.[8]***	Observation with attention to the victim's speech and manner, assessment of specific social and historical data.

*Certain pieces of information for the design of this table were gathered from Enelow and Swisher.

**Socio-economic status is a determinant of the physical and environmental factors that might play a role in the production as well as the intervention with abuse and assault victims.[5] Social mobility can also impact reactions to abuse and assault. There is some evidence that social movement may create difficulties of such magnitude as equated to a life crisis.[6] Parker and Kleiner present evidence that in Negroes (blacks), both upward and downward social mobility correlate with significantly higher rates of mental illness than social stability does.[7]

***Cultural factors will influence what a victim regards or reports as abusive or traumatic, as well as the way it is reported.[9]

lationship, while at the same time conducting an effective interview. These include:

- Trust and confidence: this develops in the victim when the first responder displays a supportive, caring attitude and respects the victim's autonomy.
- Participation and autonomy: incorporating mutual participation, where the victim feels some responsibility for a successful outcome and for his or her own behavior.
- Continuity and flexibility: specific interviewing procedures may require uniformity in its basic structure, yet the first responder must be flexible enough to adapt to the sensitivity of each particular situation.
- Victim expectations: the victim anticipates a certain amount of comfort, support, and physical and emotional intervention. The ultimate outcome may not always be as the victim desires or sees it to be, but it is important for them to believe the first responder is assisting in every way possible.
- Nonverbal communication: first responders should be aware of the role nonverbal communication plays throughout an interview. Forms of silent communication such as facial expressions, posture, tone of voice, and gestures are indicators of feelings or concerns which may not yet be expressed verbally. The first responder alert to these signs can investigate their origin and intensity when appropriate throughout the interview.

SPECIAL CONSIDERATIONS OF INTERVIEWING

Sexual Assault Investigations[10]*

The emotional state of the victim should be of primary concern to the first responder. The victim's emotional suffering may be minimized by conducting the interview tactfully, supportively, and with the victim's well-being in mind.

Responsibilities of the First Responder

- Respond immediately to the victim.
- Give attention to the victim's medical needs.

---

*Material in this section was taken from the *Protocol for Rape and Sexual Assault* (1978) by Carmen Germaine Warner, M. Joan Koerper, Doris Spaulding et al.

- Establish rapid radio broadcast and search.
- Preserve the crime scene and the most *crucial source of evidence*—the victim.
- Accomplish all of the above in the most organized, efficient manner possible.

At this point, departmental policies and resources vary regarding the availability of sex crime investigators. The following is addressed to those who are responsible for the investigative process whether they be police officers, deputies, or investigators.

The Initial Interview

The initial interview conducted by police authorities should be more than an investigative tool. It should:
- Serve to acquaint the victim with the complicated legal, medical, and investigative process.
- Be supportive in nature.
- Be used to assessing the emotional status of complainants.
- Serve to establish trust between the officer or investigator and complainant which will result in complete and accurate information being obtained from the complainant.

The appropriate place of interview is one which provides comfort for the victim, privacy, and minimal distraction. Unless the victim requests otherwise, the indepth interview should not be conducted at the crime scene with family or friends present or in the Emergency Department.

Rape investigation should be the responsibility of highly-trained officers, male or female. The sensitivity and ability of an officer is determined by his or her attitudes toward the crime and victim, not sex. If a female police officer or investigator is requested by the victim, the request accompanied by the above explanation should be met. If a female police officer or investigator is not available, the victim should have the option of having another woman present.

The support which a victim can receive by the presence of concerned parties from local crisis centers should *not* be ignored. Police departments benefit when such organizations have good relations with police officers and encourage victims to report. These organizations can also be invaluable in giving the department a greater picture of what is going on in their jurisdiction without violating the confidence of the complainant (reporting the location, time, date, and occurrence of a specific crime) through third-party reports which otherwise would go unreported. All departments should encourage cooperation between those in the community and those serving the community.

Community rape crisis centers can provide supportive counseling for the victim and her "significant others." These community agencies or family and friends, depending on the circumstances, can be especially valuable when the victim is being transported to the hospital, police station, or the prosecutor's office. Although the family or friends should not be in on the detailed interview by the investigator, they should take part in the investigation.

It is important that the family or friends be given information regarding the crime of rape and its aftermaths. If this phase is omitted, it is likely that the emotional adjustment of the victim will be lengthy and more difficult due to erroneously preconceived notions regarding the crime itself. The "significant others" can be the most important link to the complete recovery of the victim, and the investigator can be instrumental in this process.

Although rape is thought of as a crime which only happens to women, forced anal and/or oral intercourse can happen to women and men alike. In 1976, 24 percent of all reported rapes in San Francisco were male victims. It is safe to assume more men will be reporting these crimes in the future. In such cases, the victim should be treated with the same considerations, respect, and sensitivity as his counterpart. The procedure outlined here will remain the same in handling male victims. All evidence collection procedures are applicable except for the presence of sperm in the vagina and pregnancy prophylactics.

The use of a tape recorder in the interviewing process can sometimes be beneficial to the victim as it provides an uninterrupted exchange between the officer or investigator and the victim. Presently, however, the recording itself can be subpoenaed as evidence to impeach the victim's credibility. It is strongly suggested that written records rather than tapes be used for the interviewing and investigation process.

Complainant's Interview

- Record time, date, and place of interview.
- Introduce yourself.

- Begin by telling the victim the purpose of the interview, that it may be unpleasant but it is necessary for him or her to be frank and to give a detailed account of the incident. Nothing he or she says will shock you. This approach serves two purposes: (1) to let the victim know the purpose of the questioning; and (2) to establish rapport.

In all crimes it is necessary to first establish what crime has been committed. The officer or detective, if they are the first to interview the victim, should first obtain a brief verbal statement about the act itself—this is to establish whether rape, assault with intent to rape, sodomy, or other act, is being dealt with. After the crime has been established, proceed to ask the victim to explain what happened in its entirety. The investigator or officer should interrupt only to clarify and/or redirect the conversation back to the needed details. Record all statements in legible form.

In the course of an interview, the following information must be obtained:

- Who, what, where, when, and how?
- When was the defendant first observed—where observed?
- What he did—what he said; what complainant said, did?
- Who else may have observed the situation (establish possible witnesses), heard complainant's yell, glass breaking, saw running, or other action?
- Does complainant know defendant—has she ever seen him before?
- Did he ejaculate? Explain that this is necessary for evidence collection purposes. Do not imply anything sexual about the ejaculation.
- Where did he ejaculate? Semen will not be found in the orifice of the anus or vagina if the perpetrator ejaculated on the victim's hair, clothes, or elsewhere.
- Record victim's action subsequent to the assault, such as clothing change, douching, toothbrushing, defecating, and vomiting.
- Record all directional movements, such as he ran east down the alley beween such and so. Drawings can be very useful to clarify this information.
- What was left at the scene?
- Inform complainant that many times victims are sodomized (anally penetrated) and are embarrassed to tell. Did this happen to him or her?
- Can complainant identify defendant?

- Will complainant prosecute?
- Did complainant have consensual sexual relations within the last 24 hours? This information is necessary only to ascertain whether there would be contamination of the semen. It is not attempting to pry into the victim's sex life.

Details of Assailant(s)

Description of perpetrator(s):
- Age, height, weight, race
- Complexion
- Eye color
- Eye defects (bulging, different colors, crossed, or other deformity)
- Hair color
- Hair type (bushy, kinky, curly/wavy, or other style)
- Teeth (gaps, irregular, protruding, or other noticeable features)
- Speech (during crime—lisp, accent, stutter, or other trait)
- Beard (goatee/beard, heavy/bushy eyebrows, or other style)
- Facial oddities (birth marks, moles, freckles, thick lips, thin lips, receding chin)
- Facial scars (location, size)
- Nose (broken/crooked, broad/flat, large/long)
- Build (thin, very thin, medium, muscular, stocky)
- Body scars (location, size)
- Amputations (arms, ears, fingers, foot, hand, leg)
- Deformities (bowlegged, cauliflower ears, crippled arms/fingers/legs, limps)
- Tattoos (locations of and description)
- Ears (protruding, large, small, close to head)
- Face (thin, round, long, broad, Caucasian features, Negroid features)
- Was defendant circumcised?
- M.O. (Modus Operandi)
- Detailed description of weapon
- Detailed description of vehicle
- Description of items stolen and their value (jewelry, guns, television, radio, or other items)
- Identify possible items touched by the defendant to aid in the investigation.
- Collect evidence from the complainant.

- Re-evaluate the need for use of tracking dogs and/or evidence technicians.
- The items in Table 10.4 regarding the appearance and behavior of the victim should be noted on the officer or investigator report.

When you complete the interview, take a minute to reread it. It is also advised that it be read back to the complainant as well to make sure all statements are correct. At this point, the victim may clarify some point previously misinterpreted. This procedure puts the complainant at ease because he or she knows exactly what the officer has recorded about the incident.

Table 10.4. Officer or Investigator Report.

Bruises or marks
Disarrayed clothing
Facial discoloration
Smeared make-up (when applicable)
Disheveled hair
Confused or dazed behavior
Bewilderment or disorientation
Crying, shaking
Attitudes of fear
Incoherent or jumbled speech
Any or all of these points can be used to corroborate the victim's testimony

---

Venue (Crime Scene) Check

- Note lighting conditions.
- Document scene and evidence location—diagram and narrative.
    1. Yourself.
    2. Utilize evidence technician—when available.
    3. Utilize city or county planning department (will have plans of parking, structures, buildings, and more data; also will be able to draw plans not available).
    4. Aerial photos when needed for severe attacks outdoors.
- Search scene yourself and the surrounding area for possible evidence.
    1. Collect undergarments, clothing, bedding, rugs, or other appropriate items bearing seminal fluid or blood stains.
    2. Collect torn clothing or bedding, broken objects or

weapons which would tend to prove forcible compulsion.

3. Collect washcloths or towels which suspect may have used to cleanse attacker's genital areas. These may contain semen stains.

4. Collect objects, bottles, glasses, or cigarette butts which were touched by suspect. (These objects may contain latent prints.)

5. Search scene for foreign items such as buttons, hair, pieces of torn clothing.

6. If crime occurred in an automobile, gather sweepings from floors, search floor mats, seat covers, or blankets for stains. Check door handles for hair of victim or suspect if victim was forced to lie on seat or floor.

7. If entry was forced into victim's residence, note jimmy marks and other appropriate burglary evidence.

- Carefully collect, mark, and preserve all evidence.
- Identify location where evidence is found. When preparing your notes, be sure to give exact location where each piece of evidence was found. Examples:

1. One white Olga bra, left strap torn, found on the ground 20 feet west of the Organ Pavilion, Balboa Park. Taken by P.O. West #222 initialed JGW 1/22/77 2:10 a.m.

2. One white washcloth found on the bathroom floor 5 feet from door at base of toilet. Taken by P.O. West #222 initialed JGW 1/22/77 8:50 p.m.

- Photograph crime scene, particularly where physical evidence of a struggle is present (furniture overturned, broken lamp, or other features).
- Request specialized resources necessary:

1. Evidence technicians
2. Latent print expert
3. Scientific lab personnel
4. Tracking dogs available through Sheriff's Department Search and Rescue Unit
5. Helicopter

- Locate, identify, and interview all witnesses.

1. If an investigator, check information from officer(s), first at scene—individual activities of same.
2. Interview detained witnesses at scene.
3. Canvas area at scene for additional witnesses.

- Transport complainant to hospital (include parents if victim is under 18).

Investigators should be made available to the crime scene as soon as possible. It is good practice to return to the crime scene with the victim. However, this can be terrifying to the victim if the procedure is not explained. Sometimes it is imperative that the victim retrace his or her steps—he or she is the only one who knows them. However, at other times the victim may not be essential. At this point, ask if he or she wishes to come or stay in the car. Never walk off and leave a victim in the police car without an explanation.

Hospital Procedure

Whether you are escorting the victim to the hospital or are responding to a radio run at the hospital, the same procedure should be followed when you reach your destination.
- Check in with admitting.
- Establish rapport with the examining physician and nurse and victim's family or friends.
- Secure complainant's medical chart number and record it on your report.
- Secure examining physician's name and print that name on your report.
- Ascertain that all signs of trauma or injury, as well as the emotional state of the victim, are recorded on the hospital examination report.
- Obtain a copy of the hospital examination report.

Sensitivity and continuity throughout these initial procedures will prove extremely beneficial in establishing a secure foundation of trust for the victim and family members.

Interviewing Considerations in Child Abuse Cases

Recognizing that communication with children is largely nonverbal, first responders can learn a great deal by saying nothing. If at all possible, the child should be observed initially in a waiting area where they are unaware they are being watched. Such things as the child's general appearance, relationship with parents, and selected position in the room should be noted.

Toys during an interview. Considerable information can be obtained by observing a child at play. Initial and changing interests reflect a child's play patterns. The choice of toy would be a valuable observation as it reflects a mode of expression. According to Lourie and Rieger, several categories of behavior have been symbolically associated with different toys[11] as noted in Table 10.5.

Table 10.5. Toys in an Interview.

Toy	Behavior
Dolls, puppets, play houses, animals	Relationship interests
Cars and airplanes	Motor control
Soldiers, guns, inflatable clowns, punching bags	Aggression
Toy telephones and typewriters	Communication
Blocks, puzzles, clay	Construction and destruction
Dolls, clay, painting, drawing	Creativity
Clay and drawing	Constructive interests

The first responder might find that personal feelings of anger, hostility, and frustration develop when working with child abuse victims. It would be detrimental to the child and his or her safety if objectivity and sensitivity were not displayed at all times.

The first responder must consider the following points during any child abuse interview.

- Questions must be presented thoughtfully and carefully.
- Use open ended questions so the parent and the child have the opportunity of presenting his or her version of the situation.
- Attempt to identify the forces that bind the adults and child together, as well as those that make life difficult.
- Always display a nonthreatening, nonjudgmental attitude.
- Refrain from giving advice, guidance, or counseling.
- Do not act on the basis of superficial information or premature conclusions.
- Identification should not be made primarily with the child.
- Offer parents the opportunity to vent personal feelings of anger and frustration.

If the first responder is unable to conduct follow-up interviews, he or she should act as a liaison with the party who will. This will assist in maintaining continuity and reduce the chance of destroying the trust that has developed.

Considerations during an interview involving incest. A family frequently is placed in a state of imbalance when a case of incest or sexual abuse is reported. The first responder conducting the interview should be very knowledgeable about the problem and all the possible pressures which are placed on the parents, other siblings, and the victim.

A solid foundation of empathy, sensitivity, and trust must be initiated immediately and continue throughout the interview. The questioning process is slow and should incorporate many questions about school, friends, and hobbies in order to build a solid relationship.

As the interview progresses, some of the following questions should be considered.[12]

- What are the siblings like?
- What activities do the siblings do for fun?
- What are the siblings' relationships with their friends?
- What are the siblings' relationships with mother or father?
- What is the quality of the relationships between victim and siblings?

Slowly work into the area of parents and some general information about them.

- What is the child's perception of the marriage?
- What do mother or father do for fun?
- What does the child like or dislike about parents?
- What do mother or father do when angry? How does that make the child feel?
- How do mother or father discipline?
- How do mother or father show affection?
- Does either parent compliment the child on achievements?
- Are there any traumatic events in the child's past?
- Have there been any significant losses or separations?
- Did the child ever move away from close friends and/or relatives?
- Was the child ever attached to any pets that got lost or died?
- When did these losses occur? How old was the child and how did the child deal with these losses?
- What brings the child joy or happiness?
- When did his/her body start to mature?
- Did he/she know what was happening to his/her body?
- Did any family member talk to her about menstruation or her breasts developing?
- Did he/she take sex education classes in school? What did he/she learn?
- Is he/she sexually active now?

- Does he/she have a girlfriend/boyfriend in school?
- Does he/she date?
- Do males make sexual advances toward her? How does she deal with that?

Depending on the first responder's findings and recommendations, siblings and parents may be asked to participate in the interview process. Should ongoing intervention be advised, the delicate process of referral must be initiated.

SUMMARY

Victims of assault and abuse, along with their families and significant others, face traumatic injuries involving physical, psychological, and social ramifications. The first responders represent the initial contact with the outside world. They can either open the door to an intervention process of cooperation and team effort, or initiate feelings of resistance which ultimately will block and destroy all attempts to alleviate the problem.

It is essential that the first responder possess a thorough understanding of assault and abuse, maintaining an open mind and supportive attitude throughout the intervention process.

REFERENCES

1. Kahn RL, Caunell CF: The Dynamics of Interviewing. New York, John Wiley and Sons, Inc., 1957
2. Benjamin A: The Helping Interview, 2nd ed. Atlanta, GA; Houghton Mifflin Co., 1974, p. 46
3. Enelow AJ, Swisher SN: Interviewing and Patient Care, 2nd ed. New York, Oxford University Press, 1979, p. 14
4. Enelow AJ, Swisher SN: Interviewing and Patient Care, 2nd ed. New York, Oxford University Press, 1979, pp. 14-23
5. Graham S: Social factors in relation to chronic illness. In Freeman HE, Levine S, Reeder LF (eds): Handbook of Medical Sociology. Englewood Cliffs, NJ; Prentice-Hall, Inc., 1963, pp. 65-98
6. Susser MW, Watson W: Sociology in Medicine. London, Oxford University Press, 1971
7. Parker S, Kleiner RJ: Mental Illness in the Urban Negro Community. New York, The Free Press, 1966
8. Susser MW, Watson W: Sociology in Medicine. London, Oxford University Press, 1971
9. Enelow AJ, Swisher SN: Interviewing and Patient Care, 2nd ed. New York, Oxford University Press, 1979, p. 21

10. Warner CG et al: San Diego County protocol for the treatment of rape and sexual assault victims. pp. 57-62
11. Lourie RS, Rieger RE: Psychiatric and psychological examination of children. *In* Arieti S (ed): American Handbook of Psychiatry, 2nd ed. New York, Basic Books, 1974-1975, Vol. 2, p. 1
12. Gottlieb B: Incest: Therapeutic intervention in a unique form of sexual abuse. *In* Warner CG (ed): Rape and Sexual Assault: Assessment and Intervention. Germantown, MD; Aspen Systems Corporation, 1980

SUGGESTED READING

Arbuckle D: Counseling: Philosophy, Theory and Practice, 2nd ed. Boston, Allyn and Bacon, 1970
Ekman P: Body position, facial expression and verbal behavior during interviews. Journal of Abnormal and Social Psychology, 68, 1964, pp. 295-301
Ekman P et al: The Face and Emotion. Elmsford, NY; Pergamon Press, 1971
Fiedler FE: The concept of an ideal therapeutic relationship. Journal of Consulting Psychology, 14, 1950, pp. 239-245
Fiedler FE: A comparison of therapeutic relationships in psychoanalytic, nondirective and Adlerian therapy. Journal of Consulting Psychology, 14, 1950, pp. 436-445
Heller K et al: The effects of interviewer style in a standardized interview. Journal of Consulting Psychology, 30, 1966, pp. 501-508
Maslow A: Motivation and Personality, 2nd ed. New York, Harper and Row, 1970
McGowan JF, Schmidt LD: Counseling: Readings in Theory and Practice. New York; Holt, Rinehart and Winston, 1962
Reik T: Listening with the Third Ear. New York; Farrar, Straus, and Giroux, 1972

11 SPECIAL CONSIDERATIONS OF INTERVIEWING

Ronald James Cooper

Initial interviews for first responders will vary considerably based on the type of abuse or assault case under investigation. Victims of child abuse or child molestation will require a different form of interview than the spouse who has just been beaten or the geriatric rape victim. A first responder may face a situation of possible abuse as well as calls dealing with victims who have been severely abused, beaten, or raped. Whatever the case, special consideration must be taken to relate to the victim in a sensitive, personalized manner.

Police, paramedics, social workers, community crisis workers, and sometimes physicians and nurses respond to urgent calls. Police departments, paramedic stations, and hospital Emergency Departments function on a twenty-four hour basis in order to deal with various emergencies. These facilities, along with quick response by Protective Services*, insure special coverage for the victim anytime.

Protective Services will usually have a social worker available to respond to cases of rape and abuse. It is not uncommon for these social workers to seek assistance when responding to the private surroundings of an abuse or rape call. Therefore, the worker will call the local law enforcement agency and request that a police officer respond to the same call and to provide additional support to the worker.

During a call, when information reveals that an aggravated abuse of rape has occurred and medical attention is needed, the police will contact the hospital Emergency Department or designated facility and an ambulance will be dispatched to the scene.

Upon arrival at a home where a child or adult is suspected of being abused or raped, the respondents must be familiarized with the exact degree of authority they have been granted and how to properly utilize it.

---

*A division of the Department of Social Services, Denver, Colorado

Interviewing Techniques for First Responders

Paramedics responding to a residence must be able to assess the physical evidence of abuse or rape that the victim displays. Because paramedics are constantly on call for all emergencies, the analysis of each situation must be dealt with quickly. The type of interview conducted by paramedics focuses on obtaining specific facts regarding injuries. That is, how the injury was received, what is the nature and extent of injuries, proper on-site intervention, and transportation of the victim to an Emergency Department or clinic for additional medical care.

This may appear elementary; however, many emergencies have been assessed and decisions made prior to obtaining all available information with unfortunate results. A specific example occurred in a case of child abuse where two small children were scalded in a bathtub. Paramedics responded immediately to the scene. One child was floating in the tub, but the other was being held by the mother. The victim in the water was given immediate medical attention and rushed to the hospital. The police officer obtaining information from a neighbor at the time returned to the apartment and observed the second child was still there. Another ambulance had to be dispatched and the victim taken to the hospital after much delay.

In cases of severe child neglect where a child ingests a poisonous substance, the paramedic should obtain all the necessary information regarding the type of substance swallowed, how much was taken, and when it occurred. If a child swallows a dangerous medication it is wise to take the container with the victim to the hospital. The information listed on the container can be useful in determining proper intervention.

In situations involving sexual assault, the paramedic should be very careful in assessing the injury. Rape victims may be reluctant to reveal the extent of their injuries or may not be aware of the degree of trauma sustained. Severe lacerations may be present in the vaginal or rectal areas and not manifest any external symptoms. Internal injuries due to blunt trauma may also be present. It is imperative that knowledge be gained regarding the use of any weapon or instrument.

In essence, the type of interview used by paramedics at the scene will vary with the type of call. If the call is not a life-threatening emergency, information can be obtained in a less hectic atmosphere, yet thoroughness in fact gathering remains essential. In cases of sexual abuse, paramedics can assist in arranging for appropriate support services. Certain situations where the family resists admission of the victim to the hospital require that the paramedic obtain the legal assistance of the police. In many instances, paramedics will use the information already gathered by the police, thus limiting the interview. A medical and social history will usually be obtained at the hospital.

Interviewing Techniques for the Social Worker

Social workers responding to the scene of child abuse or spouse abuse will obtain related facts from the family. It will be the social worker's ultimate goal to make a decision regarding placement of the child, or, in the case of spouse assault, presenting her with existing alternatives.

The social worker and police officer begin their interviews in very much the same manner. All facts related to the abuse assault must be obtained. However, as the investigation continues, the social worker's and police officer's functions will separate. The social worker will deal with a civil court hearing, while the police will be involved with criminal filing.

Once the initial facts regarding the abuse or assault are obtained, the social worker will investigate the social history of the family. Due to the nature of a civil court hearing, the social worker must direct the interview toward attainment of appropriate information. The social worker will also interview the family to obtain information regarding abusive tendencies by other members, or, in the case of rape, feelings of blame, denial, or hostility. Hearsay evidence, along with abusive profiles and the past social history, can be used in civil court.

A procedure used by the Denver Police Department and the Denver Department of Social Services in specific cases of child abuse orders the parent(s), babysitter, or person of custodial care to appear at the Denver Crisis Center for a more complete interview. This occurs after a decision has been made for temporary child placement. If a social worker makes the initial response to a school, hospital, or other public place, the interview should be limited. After the initial interview, a decision is made regarding removal of the child. Occasionally, the social worker and the police have different opinions and procedures, causing a conflict among agencies. That is why a short but complete interview is necessary. This provides a basis for a sound decision regarding placement. The child's safety is at stake and must be kept in mind at all times.

In all cases of abuse or assault, a problem may arise where the social worker and police become personally involved with the situation. This will affect their decisions and ultimately their interviews; thus, the interview must be objective at all times. If not, the interview and the entire process will be destroyed.

The social worker will be responding to child abuse, spouse abuse, and sexual assault calls that will range from a casual call to one that might be very traumatic. The degree of severity of each call will dictate the type of interview to be conducted. It is suggested that a brief, thorough, factual interview be conducted on the initial visit. A follow-up interview should be performed within a day or two at a location that is mutually favorable. Interviews conducted in a home usually grant the family a feeling of superiority. The social worker must always maintain complete control of the interview. By the time of the second interview, the social worker will have gathered data from the victim, family, nurses, physicians, and police. This information will be extremely helpful in completing the interview.

Techniques in a Police Interview

The initial police interview is similar to that of the social worker's. However, after the initial facts are obtained by the uniformed officer at the scene, the information is transferred to an investigating detective.

The initial interview, which deals with the basic facts of the abuse or assault, should be written so that a permanent record can be obtained. The interview should include time, location, victim's name, the perpetrator's name, and the extent of injuries. It should be noted whether or not the victim was able to make a statement.

Throughout the interview, police are bound by stringent rules and procedures set down by municipal, state, and federal courts. In complying with these rules, the officer must first be responsible for the safety of the victim. Specific action to be taken by the officer is predicated on information obtained from the initial interview. If the information reveals that abuse or rape did occur, the victim will need to be taken to a hospital Emergency Department or some other type of medical facility.

After safety is provided for the victim, police must seek additional information. If witnesses are available, they must also be interviewed. These procedures vary among police departments. If the department is large, the uniformed officer's interview can be completed and sent to the investigative division. In smaller departments, the uniformed officer will have to conduct both interviews.

All 50 states now have specific reporting laws for child abuse.[1] Incorporated into these laws are definitions of child abuse. During the initial interview of such cases, it will be necessary for the police officer to direct his or her other interview toward the question of whether an abuse has actually occurred.

As previously stated, in some municipalities an "order in" system is used for a follow-up interview. The follow-up interview will be a more thorough interview, and the team concept is sometimes used. This is where the investigating police officer and the assigned social worker will conduct the interview together.

Both parties must be well versed in the investigation of child or spouse abuse for this type of interview to be effective. Some of the difficulties with this type of interview are that the basic facts of the abuse are important to both parties, but social histories and abusive profiles cannot be used by the police in a criminal court filing. It must be remembered that the police mission ends after the suspect is prosecuted in court. Of course, not all investigations of abuse cases are filed in criminal court, nor should they be. In situations of rape, it is different as filing is usually encouraged.

The Suspect Interview

The interview of the suspect in cases of child abuse is usually a parent or person of custodial control. In cases of spouse abuse, the partner is suspect. In either situation, the suspect will be advised of their rights prior to any interview involving the facts of the case. This procedure sometimes becomes cumbersome for the social worker because the suspect will possibly react by not talking. Therefore, both the social worker and the police officer must decide whether a joint interview would be advisable. In the more aggravated abuse cases, separate interviews would be advisable if possible. In situations of rape, the suspect is frequently interviewed in cooperation with an evidence collection process at the hospital. Specific procedures for this interview vary from city to city.

After advising the suspect of their Miranda warnings, the police officer will initiate the interview with general questions including location and time. Very specific questions involving type of weapon, if applicable, and reasons for the abuse will follow. Each investigator develops their own special skills to find out the answers to what, where, why, when, who, and how. Once a skill has been developed, interview consistency should be applied.

If the abuse or assault victim is a very small child who cannot relate the circumstances, the investigating officer will have to focus the interview on other sources of information. These will include such sources as the physical evidence the victim displays or material obtained from the crime scene. Information will also be obtained from attending physicians and nurses. Sometimes, information gathered from witnesses and neighbors in abuse cases may indicate a pattern of life style used by the family being interviewed.

If serious injuries or death has occurred, the interview should be conducted in the presence of a legal stenographer. This will assure that the interview will become an accurate, permanent record. If possible, a deputy district attorney should be present to witness and assist in the interview. It is also advisable to have the social worker present. This way, information previously obtained can be interjected into the formal interview. It would also be advisable to have the suspect's attorney or public defender present to insure the validity of the interview.

The formal interview should be planned well in advance. Police departments and social services agencies keep historical records which provide essential information for future investigations. It must be kept in mind that each law enforcement agency has its own rules and regulations regarding interviews. Resources also may differ, but the critical thing to remember is the welfare of the victim.

Interrogations

An interview can change and become an interrogation (see Table 11.1*). There are times when the investigating officer will not know who committed the abuse or the rape assault. An interview will reveal facts that can change the entire process. If the person being interviewed becomes a suspect, the person must be advised of his or her constitutional rights. Interviewing is the process by which an officer seeks, obtains, and evaluates information given to him or her by persons who have personal knowledge of the events or circumstances of a crime, accident, or other matter of police interest.[3]

---

*Note: The above comparison is used in *The Patrol Operation*, 2nd Edition, Chapter XII (1970), p. 144.

Table 11.1. A Comparison of Interviews and Interrogations.

Interview	Interrogation
Why (Purpose)	
To gather and to test validity of information to determine the particulars of the matters under investigation.	To gather and to test validity of information to determine whether the subject was responsible for or involved in the matter under investigation.
Who (Subjects)	
Victims and witnesses who are willing to provide police with any information they possess about the matter under investigation.	Persons suspected of crimes as well as others who may have information but are reluctant to offer it.
When (Timing)	
Interviews should take place as soon as possible after the event has occurred so statements of witnesses are not affected by memory loss, influence of talking to others, and other factors. Immediate gathering of information enables the investigator to prepare for interrogation of suspects.	Interrogations should take place ideally when the investigator has gathered enough information to know how truthful the subject is. They are more fruitful after witnesses and victims have been interviewed and phsyical evidence has been located and evaluated.
Where (Location)	
At a place convenient and familiar to the subject—or in a neutral setting. The subject's home, place of business, or any place where privacy is assured is preferred.	The police station is best since it enables the officer to control completely the security of the subject, as well as other factors that might tend to be distracting.
How (Method)	
Low pressure, informal atmosphere is preferred to allow the subject to tell in narrative style what he or she has to offer. Specific questions should be used to gather more detail and to jog the witness's memory.	Basically the same method as with interviews, but the atmosphere is more formal and the officer works toward a more specific purpose.

In many instances, runaway children are apprehended by the police and through careful interviewing, it is revealed that the child has been a victim of sexual abuse. This is true for males as well as females, although it is more common with females.

An investigating officer should not regard all runaway children as offenders of law. Females in their early teens are sometimes the victim of a sexual abuse by their father, stepfather, or boyfriend of the mother. If the girl has been sexually abused, she usually has a feeling of guilt. The victim then decides she cannot stay in her environment any longer and decides to run away.

Many teenage prostitutes were victims of sexual abuse when they were younger, which may have influenced the way their life developed. If the child is addressed in a tactful manner, information can be received regarding the real reason why the child ran away. It may be unhealthy to return a child to the same disruptive environment. The Juvenile Division of the Denver Police Department recognized this problem, and every runaway child that is processed is interviewed by a crisis social worker in an attempt to prevent reintroduction into a negative environment.

Summary

The types of interviews will vary depending on the personnel and agency involved. The goals and objectives of paramedics, social workers, and police officers must be based on protecting all victims; this includes male, female, child, and adult victims. Even though agency functions are different and interviews may differ, the individual conducting the interview must remain nonjudgmental and supportive yet thorough in the data gathering process.

REFERENCES

1. DeFrancis V, Lucht CL: "Child Abuse Legislation in the 1970s." From a conference booklet titled Sexual Abuse and Neglect. International Association of Chiefs of Police, 1978
2. The Patrol Operation, 2nd ed, Chapter XII. Gaithersburg, MD; International Association of Chiefs of Police, 1970, p. 144
3. The Patrol Operation, 2nd ed, Chapter XII, Gaithersburg, MD; International Association of Chiefs of Police, 1970

12 DOMESTIC VIOLENCE: RESPONDING TO VICTIM'S NEEDS

Ashley Walker-Hooper, BA

PROBLEMS RESULTING FROM POOR AND INAPPROPRIATE INTERVENTION WITH VICTIMS OF DOMESTIC VIOLENCE

It is difficult for many service providers to comprehend the dynamics of the battering couple. Because of the difficulty in understanding why women stay and why men batter, the intervener often imposes his or her own value system upon the victims. The results may be (1) hostility directed toward the intervener; (2) increased feelings of helplessness by women; (3) acceptance of blame or guilt by the woman; (4) feelings of futility and prejudice by the intervener; (5) victims not seeking assistance to avoid the criticism and judgment of "helpers"; and (6) implied justification or acceptance of the abuser's behavior.

Victim's need immediate, objective assistance that is not influenced by personal feelings or inclinations. Because the problems of domestic violence are so complex and the cultural stereotypes of men's and women's roles are so ingrained, it is necessary to initiate policy changes in systems to effect the care given to battered women. It is not appropriate to allow personal discretion to be the order of the day, especially in law enforcement, medicine, and social services. It should not matter that police officers are tired of going to John and Susan's house every Friday night. It should not matter that Susan has been in the Emergency Department four times or that she always goes back. An understanding of the personal involvement of the victims and their continuous need for assistance over a prolonged period should lead systems to reevaluate their response.

Over the last 15 years, systems have slowly developed protocols for dealing with victims of child abuse, neglect, molestation, and rape. It took a great deal of community education before the public was sensitized to their plight. If battered women can be defined as helpless victims because of early socialization, history of family violence, poor self-image, lack of resources, and emotional and economic dependence, then they too will receive comprehensive, sensitive care and assistance. As with rape victims, battered women have often been seen as the responsible persons, those who cause and provoke the violence. With this prevailing attitude, there is little hope for consistent, positive intervention.

Law Enforcement

Nonintervention and nonarrest policies in police departments reinforce the hopelessness of victims and reinforces their sense of isolation and vulnerability. When women are discouraged from making citizen arrests and their protective orders are not enforced, they are subtly told that there is no hope and that they must stay and take the abuse. The paternalistic attitudes of law enforcement agencies often help to keep "women in their place." The assailant gets the implied message that it is all right to beat his wife and that no one cares. The police are the only agents in the culture who have the power to intervene, stop the violence, and protect the victims. When this does not happen, there is no one with the sanction to do so, no one whom the abuser will respect and fear as a force greater than himself.

Medical Personnel

By treating only the physical complaints of victims and not making referrals to other agencies, medical personnel keep patients isolated and often dependent upon drugs. Making patients aware of the existence of "help" services may make the difference for many women and save them from years of abuse.

Crisis Workers

By not being offered expression and acknowledgment of their feelings and a clear focus and framework for their immediate crisis, many women are left more confused and anxious. When crisis counselors mirror the mood of callers, it reinforces their anxiety. The counselor should be a calming agent who synthesizes the problem, helps to give callers focus, and provides a sense of control and self-competency.

Therapists and Counselors

When therapists encourage and reinforce traditional cultural values about family life and the role of women, clients feel they are failures. When counselors seek to "rescue," they reinforce women's dependence and discourage the achieving of control over their own lives. When counselors do not understand and challenge the myths of battering and do not make women aware of their options and choices, they become a part of the oppression of the victims.

TECHNIQUES FOR RESPONDING TO VICTIMS

The following section on counseling of battered women will be helpful to all professionals. Sections on the understanding of clients' anxieties and apprehensions and their emotional reactions are important for both short and long-term intervention. All information that helps explain the stress, confusion, ambivalence, and fear of victims will increase the victims' chances for sensitive assistance.

Table 12.1 shows the lack of and inappropriate responses of systems to battered women. Table 12.2 shows a more comprehensive, enlightened approach. Most battered women have interacted with the systems listed in Table 12.1. The responses, or lack of responses, have helped keep women physically trapped by telling them that there was nothing that they could do, or psychologically trapped them by reinforcing the concept of family togetherness thereby making them feel they are to blame. In order for battered women to have chances at new lives, these systems must begin to respond in a more supportive and flexible manner. They must not add to women's victimization.

It is not easy for systems to readjust their policies and retrain their personnel to become sensitive to the plight of battered women. Table 12.2 lists a few of the changes which must occur if battered women and their children are to attempt a life style without physical violence or threats of violence. Re-education about the dynamics of battering is mandatory if personnel are to respond to the physical and psychological nature of domestic violence as the intolerable, dangerous crime that it is. Help for battered women should no longer depend upon personal inclinations of one sensitive police officer or one understanding physician. Only policy decisions can assure fair, impartial administration of justice, health care, or social services. Battered women are victims and deserve protection and assistance in a consistent manner.

Table 12.1.   Lack of and Inappropriate Responses of Systems to Battered Women.

LAW ENFORCEMENT—POLICE
—orientation toward non-enforcement and non-intervention
—feels it is dangerous work with few rewards
—prosecutors and courts are too lenient
—feels woman won't press charges
—feels man's home is his castle
—arrest is a waste of time

FAMILY SYSTEMS, NEIGHBORS, FRIENDS
—unaware of resources
—threatened by batterer
—thinks husband has right
—feels she always goes back
—thinks she is a nuisance
—feels she is his only hope
—feels it is a personal family problem
—thinks she is lying because they have never seen him behave in that manner

MEDICAL PERSONNEL
—treats only physical symptoms
—do not make appropriate referrals
—make few chart notations
—fear court appearances and loss of 'expensive' time
—cost of treatment prohibitive for many women
—medication

LEGAL ASSISTANCE—ATTORNEYS
—inadequate drafting of T.R.O.'s
—costly—do not want cases because women don't follow through and lack funds
—do not adequately explain restraining orders
—low status
—do not make appropriate referrals
—are not aware of current domestic laws

THE BATTERED WOMAN
Low Self-Esteem, Guilt, Self-Blame, Embarrassment, Isolation, Anger, Fear of Insanity and Loneliness, Doubt, Learned-Helplessness, Economic Dependency, Pain, No Resources, Emotional Dependency

SOCIAL SERVICES
—traditional family counseling perpetuates violent relationships
—sees woman as drain on welfare coffers
—treats drug & alcohol dependency separate from battering
—sees woman as housing concern
—does not support single-parents as whole persons
—treats woman for "her" problem(s)

EMPLOYERS
—battered women as poor workers with sporadic attendance
—get harrassed by irate husbands
—do not support battered women by calling police when husband appears
—sees woman as source of problem

LAW ENFORCEMENT—
PROSECUTORS, COURT(S)
—waste of time, women do not follow through
—legal process deliberately slow, to weed out women and discourages women and preserves violent families
—make few or no referrals
—conciliation efforts minimize violence
—patriarchial system lenient with batterers

EDUCATION
—school system does not interact with parents
—underachievement by children
—mother misses classes or drops out
—school ignores abuse/neglect of children. Do not report as mandated

Ashley Walker-Hooper, San Diego, CA, November 1979

Table 12.2. Suggested Response Changes in Dealing with Battered Women.

LAW ENFORCEMENT: POLICE WITH EACH INCIDENT	FAMILY SYSTEMS, NEIGHBORS, FRIENDS	MEDICAL PERSONNEL	LEGAL ASSISTANCE—ATTORNEYS
—restore peace	—understand why woman stays or returns	—make chart notations when domestic violence is suspected	—become aware of dynamics of wife-abuse
—protect victim	—never accept rationalizations for violence.	—offer women more options than tranquilizers	—stay abreast of current legislation, police and court procedures that affect your clients
—take appropriate legal action	—never condone violence	—make in-house or other social service referrals	—believe her story
—enforce protection orders	—become aware of resources	—inquire as to safety of woman and children	—advise women of their rights—you will probably be the first
—make referrals	—offer help as "revolving door" as often as needed	—involve police and crisis hotlines as indicated	—make referrals to counseling, hotlines and other support systems
—transport for medical assistance			
—protect victim as she prepares to leave, transport, if possible			
—understand why women stay or return			
—treat abuser as any other suspect			

THE BATTERED WOMAN
A feeling of Self-Worth, Emotional Interdependence and Independence, Calm, Self-Assured, Unafraid, Responsible Decision-Maker, Economically Self-Sufficient, Friendly, in control of her life and her children.

SOCIAL SERVICES
—assess your own values
  and therapeutic
  modalities before working
  with battered women
—offer woman options and
  information/referrals
—keep client reality-based
—be aware of dynamics of
  battering and escalation
  of violence
—work on client's feeling
  about self
—remember all marriages
  cannot be saved

EMPLOYERS
—if woman has been good
  employee, support her.
—employment and
  economic self-sufficiency
  are necessary to break
  cycle of violence
—call police when harassed
  by batterer, do not send
  woman out as sacrificial
  lamb
—become aware of problem
  and allow woman time for
  counseling

LAW ENFORCEMENT—
PROSECUTORS, COURT
—make referrals that offer
  woman a support system
  whether you prosecute or
  not
—speed up cases when they
  are intentionally 'set
  aside' to prevent
  harassment and fear
—handle custody and
  visitation expeditiously

EDUCATION
—be aware of child
  abuse/neglect and
  mandatory reporting
—be aware of child's lack of
  concentration and
  achievement
—when possible, make and
  sustain home visits
—support mother's interaction
  in school programs

Ashley Walker-Hooper, San Diego, CA., November 1979

Counseling

Many advocates for battered women have hesitated in making referrals to mental health professionals and agencies. In a substantial number of cases, experience has shown this to be detrimental to the victims. They are not supported in their efforts to stop the violence or to leave the relationship. Most psychotherapy emphasizes keeping the family intact. They are branded as "sick," "crazy," or "hysterical." Their low self-esteem and sense of failure are confirmed by an expert usually, but not always, male.

The violence is rarely the issue of primary concern. Behavior and symptomology (constant stress, immobilizing fear, repressed anger, inability to trust, and suspiciousness) are the focus of the therapy. Victims are labeled and treated without a thorough investigation of sources of the symptoms. The way women have learned to cope with violence is seen as evidence of personality disorders and not, as Dr. Lenor Walker states in "Battered Women,"

> " . . . situationally imposed emotional problems caused by their victimization. They do not choose to be battered because of some personality defect; they develop behavior disturbances because they live in violence.¹"

As women increase their contact with other women, they find they are not "sick." They express similar feelings, ideas, and experiences, and find what they lack is a sense of self and identity that can stand alone outside of home, husband, and children. As stated by Phyllis Chesler in "Women and Madness:"

> "Both psychotherapy and middle-class marriage isolate women from each other; both emphasize individual rather than collective solutions to women's unhappiness; both are based on a woman's helplessness and dependence on a stronger male authority figure. . . . Both psychotherapy and marriage enable women to express and diffuse their anger by experiencing it as emotional illness, by translating it into hysterical symptoms: frigidity, chronic depression, phobias. . . . Each woman, as patient, thinks these are unique and her own fault; she is 'neurotic.' She wants from a psychotherapist what she wants—and often cannot get—from a husband: attention, understanding, merciful relief, a personal situation—in the arms of the right husband, on the couch of the right therapist.²

Who Should Counsel?

A recurring issue is: "Who should counsel battered women?" There seems to be uniform consensus among feminist and other "enlightened therapists that women should not enter a therapeutic relationship with a Freudian psychoanalyst. The inherent attitudes toward women are not conducive to positive self-concept and control over their own lives.

Lenore Walker states:

> "I strongly recommend that at this time only women psychotherapists treat battered women. Battered women are similar to rape victims in that they respond more easily to a female therapist who is trained to understand the effects of such victimization. These women need to learn to trust other women as competent, strong professionals. The role model that such a woman therapist provides for a battered woman facilitates therapy. Then, too, women can share intimate problems with the other woman in a way that also facilitates the therapeutic process.[3]"

She does not negate the possibility that a male therapist can accomplish the same goals. She states that it takes longer and complicates the process because victims will relate to the male in her old, seductive, and manipulative ways.

The Feminist Referral Committee of Philadelphia feels that no matter how sensitive or sympathetic the male counselor, battered women will most likely view him as a male authority figure. The chances of this happening with a female therapist are less and can be handled with greater ease. The Committee feels that women's socialization will cause her to seek approval, guidance, and their sense of self-worth from the male counselor instead of from their intrinsic personal strength. If men are to be effective with battered women, they must come to grips with their position of power and its oppressive actions and attitudes toward women. Therefore, a therapist must involve himself in a personal struggle. It would be difficult not to involve the victims through his feelings of guilt and defensiveness. The Committee feels that if a male therapist works with battered women, he should augment the therapeutic process by requiring their attendance in a woman's support group.

Charlotte Holt Clinebell, in her manual *Counseling for Liberation*, states:

> "Probably gender of the therapist is not crucial to good counseling. Many women counselors have 'made it' in a male-dominated system and have been so co-opted by the system that they see their role as that of helping their clients adjust to the respective 'femininity' and 'masculinity' demands of society. Certainly, a woman cannot hear the cry of another woman if her own consciousness is not raised. Ideally, a woman counselor with a raised consciousness, one who is struggling with her own journey toward liberation, would be a better counselor

for women than a man would be and vice versa. But a liberated male
counselor is better than an unliberated female counselor (for women
and for men).[4]"

She lists important characteristics of a good counselor, one
who is involved in the constant struggle for liberation.

- Values being female equally with being male. A woman
  counselee cannot learn to value herself from a counselor who
  devalues women.
- Believes in complete equality between women and men at
  all levels and in all areas of public and private life, on the job
  and in the home.
- Is aware of the fact that deeply imbedded cultural
  stereotypes are likely to have their influence on him or her at
  an unconscious level, even though intellectually he or she
  rejects such stereotypes.
- Is nondefensive, unpretentious, and nonjudgmental.
- Holds the basic philosophy that it is his or her job to help the
  client find out who he or she is and wants to be. This may
  mean raising the issue of other options and choices for persons who are not raising that issue for themselves.
- Is constantly aware of his or her limitations in working with a
  person of the opposite sex.
- Is in the process of becoming (and encouraging counselee
  and client to become) a more fully androgynous person.[5]

Defining the Options

Whether the most effective counselor is male or female will continue to be debated. It is crucial, however, to acknowledge the fact
that traditional therapeutic methods do not work for battered
women. The emphasis on keeping the family together only serves
to keep women in an abusive, demeaning, and potentially *deadly*
relationship. If agency or personal philosophy do not allow frank
discussion with the victims about the absolute need for intervention to stop the violence, then the agency becomes, in essence, part
of the cultural oppression of the victims. The choice of staying or
going must always be the victim's. However, the counselor must be
aware of the options and must make the victims aware that the
options are limited and fairly unattractive. (1) They can stay, constantly changing their behavior, steadily increasing their survival
skills, and hoping that their partner will change. (2) They can
leave, facing the loneliness, reduced economic stature, harass-

ment, and often a single-parent life style. (3) They can stay, increase their survival skills, without hoping that their partner will change.

Some basic strategies for working with female victims, their children, and systems have been developed by Frances Woods and Miriam Habib. They are necessary to any counseling foundation for working with battered women.

STRATEGIES FOR WORKING WITH ASSAULTED WOMEN, THEIR FAMILIES, AND THE SYSTEMS AROUND THEM[6]

INTERVENTION WITH WOMEN. In working with victims of wife assault, the following are important.

- Affirmation of the woman is of primary importance. Her strengths, the efforts she has and will take to end her being assaulted are very important.
- A group approach—working with more than one woman at a time is useful for several reasons. It cuts down on the isolation that most women who have been assaulted feel; it provides concrete information that is accurate and sensitive to the women's needs. Other women who have experienced the problem are the best experts on it.
- Recognize that *women don't identify themselves as abused* because to do so would make them susceptible to society's blaming, e.g., there is something wrong with me if I put up with it, it's my fault, I must be stupid, etc.
- Sensitive listening is of utmost importance. We are just learning what this crime is all about. The usual experience of battered women is that no one listens to them or takes them seriously.
- Stress the fact that the woman is not all alone; stress the fact that you can help the woman.
- Where possible, give *concrete information* and aid. For instance, have a lawyer available to give legal advice or, better, representation. Be available for going to court with the woman, taking her to welfare, etc.
- Help the woman develop *alternatives*—where she can go to spend the night, what job training is available, etc.
- Recognize and deal with the extreme mental and physical exhaustion.
- Recognize and deal with guilt and shame.

- Recognize and deal with the fear of being murdered or seriously hurt.
- Some women will want to try marriage counseling again or for the first time. Some women will recognize that their mates need help. In our experience, these approaches are successful only if both partners are sincerely interested. This means the male is willing to deal with the issue of his violence and is willing to work on his own problems, with some motive besides keeping the wife in the marriage.
- Women tend to rationalize and feel sorry for the man since he is 'mentally ill,' drinks, etc. Help her take care of herself first.
- Recent evidence about assaulted women point up that most women can end the abuse only by leaving the marriage. Discuss this in a straightforward manner which recognizes that it may take the woman some time to reach a decision. Let her know that you support her no matter where she is in her decision-making process.
- Recognize the usual pattern of going in and out of the relationship until a final decision is made. This includes the woman's decision to try marriage counseling for the first time or again.
- Recognize and deal with all the societal pressures and role expectations on the woman for keeping her family together at all costs, e.g., "It's my duty to stay with him, the kids need a father," etc. Particularly important are the financial reasons for which a woman stays with her husband.
- Help women work out the particular responses which are most helpful to her, e.g., should she fight back, go to court, etc. Remember this is individualized.
- Work on developing all independence skills—education, jobs, assertiveness, love of self, self-worth.
- A social-political perspective to this assault on the woman will help her combat her tendency to accept society's myth that she blame herself for being beaten.

WORKING WITH CHILDREN. In working with the families of assaulted women, the following are important.

- Recognize and deal with the child's fear of being in a home where violence may erupt. Such children feel very vulnerable, although this may be hidden by a tough facade.
- Many children learn from their parents that violence is a way to solve problems—fighting, hitting, brute aggression. These children often have not learned the skills of talking

about their feelings so they act them out aggressively. Help
the mother, teacher, etc., to help these children talk about
their feelings rather than act them out. It is especially useful
with some mothers to teach them to model this behavior for
kids.

- Some children react to violence in the home by withdrawing.
- Many children have a low tolerance for frustration. They are
  easily upset and thrown off balance.
- Children have a difficult time separating out their own identity since they are so caught up in their intense conflict. This
  may result in difficulty with peers.
- A common dilemma for the child is to be in the middle of the
  struggle between the parents.
- Some children become involved in protecting their mothers
  from physical harm. This may result in their feeling angry at
  their fathers and, consequently, feeling guilty about this. It
  may also result in the children feeling very resentful toward
  their mothers (disliking them for being weak), etc.
- Getting the father to be responsible to them is a big problem
  for children of both sexes.
- Boys desperately want their fathers' attention. They may relate to the father only on a play level. They make no demands
  for understanding or parental responsibility. They sometimes actively side with the father against the mother. Some
  sons identify with their fathers to the point that they fear
  marriage because they don't want to become like their
  fathers. Others take on the same stance as their fathers—
  become 'bullies.' A high percentage of men who beat their
  wives saw their fathers beat their mothers.
- Girls also want their fathers' attention. Because they have
  often been severely punished for being angry or showing
  anger to their fathers, they tend to identify with the aggressor, feel sorry for their fathers and become angry at their
  mothers. Girls often grow up insecure about their ability to
  get men to love them and be caring toward them. Some girls
  attempt to seek affirmation from men in sexual modes. Many
  girls learn to fear and distrust men and have difficulty forming equal partnerships in marriage. Such daughters may
  marry violent men because they learned to expect beatings
  as normal and inevitable.
- It is important to help children and mothers assist the children in dealing with the realities of the father's behavior.
- Many mothers, not wishing to turn their children against

their fathers, protect the father and make excuses for him. Mothers must be helped to deal more realistically so they can help their children.

- Help the mother to discuss honestly the new financial situation with the children. Many mothers, not wanting to worry their children, hide the facts from them. Consequently, the children do not understand and cannot react appropriately.

- Mothers under severe stress don't have the energy to nurture their children, so they are deprived and neglected. It is important to give active support to such mothers—for instance, day care for younger children, involve supportive school counselors with older children, etc.

- When, as is often the case, the child acts out in school, a mother's tendency is to get angry with the child and to punish him or her. It is important to help the mother see how this isolates the child and to help her see how she can support the child in his or her difficulty.

- In most families, violence is never spoken of openly. Help the children and mother to talk about it so they can share their fear, hurt, and anger.

INTERVENTION WITH SYSTEMS

- Recognize wife assault as a broad social problem which requires institutional changes.

- Attempt to sensitize and form cooperative approaches with other agencies—courts, police, hospitals, etc.

- Recognize and deal with the resistance there is to seeing wife assault as more than a family issue. Resistance will come in the form of trying to blame women and to keep the family together at all costs. Male authority of systems may be threatened when the issue of battered women is raised.

- A shelter for women needs to be set up. A stop gap measure is a shelter network of private homes.

Dispelling Myths

Dr. Elaine Hilberman and Kit Munson, M.S.W., in their report "Sixty Battered Women," discuss the "complex mythology" about wife beating that *must* be challenged and eliminated early in the counseling-therapeutic relationship.

> " . . . (a) the violence is perceived as a norm; this is most likely when the victim comes from a violent home of origin; (b) the violence is rationalized; he is not responsible because he is sick, mentally ill, alcoholic, unemployed or under stress; (c) the violence is justified; she deserves it because she is bad, provocative or challenging; (d) the violence is controllable; if only she is good, quiet, compliant, he will not abuse her.
>
> The victim utilizes this group of beliefs to 'explain' the brutality. This reinforces her tenuous denial and protects her husband and her marriage at the expense of her self-esteem and autonomy, if not her life. It allows her to remain totally enslaved while believing that she is in control.
>
> The second group of myths prevents dissolution of the marriage even when she perceives the violence is inappropriate: (a) she loves him; (b) she can't survive without him; (c) she stays 'for the sake of the children'; (d) he will change. There is usually ample data to confront these beliefs with a multitude of broken promises and betrayals, blatant evidence of disturbed or abused children, and the reality that she is surviving in spite of a husband who provides neither emotional nor financial support for his family."[7]

The authors see this as a time when the victims start to favor some active position and formulate embryonic plans for work, education-training, and termination of the relationship. They stress, as will be stressed throughout this article, the necessity of not pushing women beyond what they perceive as "safe" boundaries in acknowledgment of their anger and taking action to confront the husband. It is crucial for counselors to accept a woman's assessment of "her own controls, the extent of the danger to herself and her children, and her husband's potential for violence as accurate."[8]

Reducing Client Apprehension and Anxiety

Seeking assistance from a counselor or therapist is an anxiety-provoking situation for most people. For the battered woman, there are reality-based fears which must be dealt with before a session materializes. These concerns should be assuaged during the initial telephone contact. These first few minutes reduce the number of issues of concern to women before the session and increase the probability of follow through. Building the trust level of women must begin with the *first* interaction, whether in person or by telephone.

The following issues should be handled when the initial intake is scheduled: (1) confidentiality; (2) openness and free choice in goal setting; (3) freedom to give or withhold experiences; (4) personal interest and professional nature of the counselor; (5) problems with being labeled socially as "battered" and psychologically with some mental disorder; and (6) child care. The victims' comfort level increases with their feelings that the counselor understands their concerns and their situation.

Identification and Understanding of Client's Emotional Reactions

The following discussion of emotional reactions and suggestions for counselor understanding and interaction is available in "Counselor Training Manual #1 by Resnick.

A. *Loss of Control/Helplessness*
    Feeling at the mercy of someone's mood fluctuations and outbreaks of temper is a very frightening and frustrating way to live one's life, and can easily lead to a feeling of having no control over one's life. . . .
    Efforts at seeking help have often proved to be deadends for many of these women—again leading to feelings of helplessness.
    Tremendous fear may result and/or a sort of emotional paralysis, so that the victim feels passive and experiences all that happens around her as being done *to* her. It is important to help the victim get back in control of the situation, and this can be done in many ways. Helping her to identify her feelings is one way to calm down her chaotic state of mind. Getting her to seek medical, legal, and social services attention that she needs helps her to take action on her own behalf.
    Again, it is of crucial importance that the counselor *help* her to make decisions; if she is told what to do, it will only increase her sense of helplessness and lack of control. Further, she may lean too heavily on the counselor for decisions in the future, if decisions are made for her at this time.
B. *Fear*
    It is important to reassure the client of the confidentiality of

---

*This statement is not part of Resnick's manual; however, in many states it is applicable.

her help-seeking contacts (except for filing a criminal complaint against the assailant) and mandatory child abuse reporting.* She should be helped to make a realistic assessment of her imminent danger. If she is not living with the assailant, suggestions can be made about changing locks on the doors, locking the windows, and other security measures. If she is living with the assailant and is in imminent danger, suggestions should be made for temporary, alternative housing. Legal measures, such as divorce, prosecution, or restraining orders, may be the route to take, but the client should never feel pressured into this route. Legal processes should be thoroughly explained.

C. *Anger*

All victims will be experiencing anger at some level about their situation. Some victims will be able to express their anger directly on or at the assailant, but others will not. It is very important to help the victim express anger and to focus it in the proper direction—this is at the assailant. If this is not done, the victim may well internalize the anger, getting angry at herself instead of the assailant, thus leading to feelings of guilt and self-blame. At other times, the victim may ventilate the anger toward police, medical, and social service personnel, or at the counselor.

D. *Guilt*

As mentioned above, guilt often has its roots in misdirected anger—anger turned inward. Guilt also arises from some all too commonly held beliefs that if a woman gets beaten, she deserves it; therefore, it goes that she must be a bad woman, wife, or mother. Another belief is that women are by nature masochistic and thus expect and enjoy physical abuse. It is important to explore these beliefs and misconceptions with the victim to let her know that the counselor does not believe these things are true.

E. *Embarrassment*

A woman may well feel embarrassed to admit that she is a battered woman. She may well be ashamed of her scars, may feel foolish to have made a domestic commitment to a physically abusive man, as well as being ashamed of herself to have put up with the repeated beatings. Considering the embarrassment a victim of domestic violence might feel, she may never have discussed her problems and feelings with anyone. In such cases, she will really welcome the opportunity to ventilate in a supportive atmosphere.

As counselors we must remember that each person has complex needs that motivate them to make decisions. Most of us have, at some point in our lives, misjudged another person's character or believed in the sincerity of someone's assurances that they would change for the better. The victim must be reminded that there is no reason to be ashamed of making mistakes as long as we learn by them.

F.   *Doubts about Sanity*

Some women have fears of insanity, particularly if they have strong feelings of lack of control. Living in constant fear of physical assault can have many emotional ramifications which may lead a victim to isolate herself socially. Once she is socially isolated, she has no one to confirm her sanity. Her only input is from the assailant and from herself.[9]

Support Groups

One of the major counseling modalities with battered women is the peer support group. Women working in cooperative, nurturing relationships with other women has resulted in substantial treatment gains. Embarrassment, fear, and guilt have lead to self-imposed isolation by battered women. Jealousy, physical attacks, and imprisonment by the husband caused forced isolation. The group experience: (1) decreases the sense of isolation and the feeling that they are the only ones with the problem; (2) offers ideas, support, and reassurance for women who have the same or similar experiences; (3) offers one of the few "safe" places for battered women to express their feelings, frustrations, and anger without fear of physical reprisal, psychological labels, or disbelief.

In order to assure success with this format, the facilitator is important. This person, preferably two persons, must have some knowledge of group dynamics. They must also be sensitive to group issues and serve as a source not only of resource information for victims, but also of exposure and eradication of social, economic, and cultural myths that keep women hostage. Two facilitators will: (1) reduce burnout caused by the crisis and demanding nature of the groups; (2) offer two sources of information and opinion; (3) allow the group size to increase; (4) give participants two persons to call on in emergencies; and (5) provide a useful training tool for less experienced counselors by pairing them with experienced ones. The group goals must be set by the group with the facilitator(s) acting as a guide to keep the sessions on track. The facilitator(s) also can synthesize a multitude of stories and experiences that appear different, identify, and label the common issue, and enhance the problem solving by focusing on the overall issue in a context that is understood by the participants.

The following is excerpted from a paper "Nontraditional Counseling Modalities" by Adrienne Berlin-Miller and Ona Rita Yufe of Battered Women's Services of San Diego, California. It gives insight into the family dynamics and explains two modalities (peer support group and couple counseling) that are experiencing some degree of success with victims.

NONTRADITIONAL COUNSELING MODALITIES

Melissa J. sits alone in her darkened living room. The front door is locked, the drapes are drawn, and the television is droning on. She wonders what to do now—her husband will be home from work in a few hours. Dinner is not cooked, the kids are screaming in the backyard, and the wash is done but the clothes have not been transferred into the dryer. The phone rings—she sits and listens until the ringing stops.

"It's all my fault," she thinks. "What can I do to change all this—I must be doing something wrong." The last argument, before Dan left for work this morning, ended with Melissa thrown against the wall and kicked.

"But it wasn't so bad this time," she thinks. "At least he stopped before I blacked out. It's getting worse, though—he's hitting me more now than he ever used to. During the eight years we've been married, it was never this often."

The phone rings again, and, as she aimlessly stares at the TV, she remembers the message that flashed on the screen with the hotline number for Battered Women's Services.

"Where did I hide it?" She searches her memory, knowing that precious number is scribbled somewhere on a scrap of paper. "My old purse," she thinks. "It's in my old brown purse."

Dan J. storms into his office, screams at his secretary to "hold all calls," slams the door shut and kicks the desk.

"Damn it," he fumes. "Three solid months of work on this project and now they tell me to scrap it." He pounds his fist on the work table, picks up his paperweight, and throws it across the room. The intercom buzzes.

"I thought I said no interruptions," he yells. The secretary's voice meekly announces, "You asked me to remind you about your lunch date with your new client." The last thing he needs now is to kowtow to a new client. He pours himself a double, slumps into his armchair and mutters, "Damn company—who needs it?"

He fears that he is trapped. He needs the job, despite the bitter frustrations, building anger, and gnawing resentment. He is the breadwinner, and he alone must provide for his family. His friend Bill recently bought his wife a new sports car. The neighbors are putting in a swimming pool.

"Oh, Christ, I wonder how badly I hurt her this time?" he thinks. "What's wrong with me—why do I do this? There's nobody to talk to and nobody would understand anyway. What can I do?"

Melissa and Dan are looking for help. Like dozens of others in their situation, they may find that help in peer support groups which are designed to address specific issues of domestic violence. Embarrassment, fear, and guilt may have led the victims to a self-imposed isolation. In contrast, peer support groups offer a cooperative and nurturing environment where the participants are encouraged to share their accounts and their feelings without fear of reprisal. The group experience:

- Encourages open communication and sharing and builds verbal skills.
- Allows honest emotional expression.
- Supports ambiguity and dissension.
- Brings together victims with similar experiences and needs.
- Provides a safe arena for peer confrontation.
- Stresses self-determination.
- Offers new information, ideas, and problem-solving techniques.
- Decreases isolation and feelings of helplessness.
- Teaches methods of stress reduction.

Support Group Format

A brief description of the dynamics of a peer support group begins with the role of the facilitator. This person needs to be aware of, and sensitive to, group process, have strong communication skills, be empathetic and nonjudgmental. The facilitator also should be knowledgeable in the area of domestic violence as an issue encompassing social, economic, and cultural stereotypes and myths. The key to a group's success depends upon the facilitator acting as a guide only, and not as a commander or a participant.

Groups are for participants only. No observers should be allowed. Family members or friends who may accompany the victims are welcome to join the group as participants.

Groups work best when they are informal, self-directed, and nonstructured in terms of specific topics for discussion. Participants have the choice of speaking or listening, but the facilitator has the responsibility of assessing the needs of the silent group members.

Open with a group introduction and sharing of each other's names. Circle seating is most conducive to a feeling of belonging. A brief welcome and procedural outline by the facilitator follows, including a description of the sponsoring agency, information taking for statistical purposes, assurances of confidentiality, setting of time limits and, if indicated, a leading statement or question designed to engage the group in active participation.

It is fundamental to the group's operation that only one participant speak at a time, and that the others direct their attention to the speaker. During this process, the facilitator needs to be aware of nonverbal reactions by the listeners, and prepare to ask them later if they care to comment.

A two-hour weekly time allotment is most effective with the average group of five to ten members. Because of the nature of the crisis, group size should not be limited. Membership is open to anyone at any time, and regular participation is not required. Because the number of participants varies from week to week, division into smaller groups is not indicated. Group functioning depends on a mix of newcomers and oldtimers. Nighttime or daytime groups are equally as effective.

The serving of coffee, soft drinks, or other snacks should be a group decision, and can be implemented by group members.

Whenever possible, child care should be offered to participants in women's groups. Small children are distracting when allowed to stay with their mothers during the sessions.

Support groups are not designed to deal with heavy drug, alcohol, or psychological problems. Appropriate assessment and referral are indicated in these situations.

There are several advantages to having more than one group facilitator. Co-facilitating enhances group function in that it offers another source of ideas and information, allows one facilitator to engage in the group process while the other concentrates on content, provides a second role model for victims, and reduces the risk of burnout.

It is vital that group facilitators protect their anonymity by using their first names and releasing only the hotline telephone number.

Couple Counseling

In an attempt to keep the relationship intact but end the violence, many couples become involved in couple counseling. The goal of the traditional therapeutic model ("marriage counseling") is to keep the couple together, whereas the goal of couple counseling in domestic violence is to extinguish the battering. Historically, women have been the consumers of mental health services largely because men have been conditioned to believe that the need for therapy is a sign of weakness. Mending a violent relationship is possible if both partners are not only attending the counseling sessions, but are willing to share responsibility.

"Thank you," says Melissa as she hangs up the telephone after having spoken with a hotline counselor.

"Now, how do I tell Dan?" she wonders. The phone rings and she jumps. It rings again—and again. She stares at it while it rings a fourth time, and finally reaches over and picks it up.

"Hello. . . . "

"Melissa—is that you? You sound so far away."

"Yes, it's me."

"How are you feeling? I'm so sorry. What can I say? Are you okay? The phone rang so long—I was worried that . . . " his voice trails off.

"Dan, we really need to talk. We need help. I found out about a place today. We can go there for help, if you're willing. Can we talk about it tonight when you get home?"

Dan sighs deeply. "You're right—we do need help. Yes, let's talk about it tonight."

The two basic problems encountered in a violent relationship and addressed in couple counseling are communication and behavioral response. Both areas are affected by socialization, sex-role stereotyping, and perpetuation of traditional ascribed roles such as, "breadwinner" and "housewife." The man's need to be in control and have the woman obey, coupled with the woman's need to be gentle and nurturing, and have the man strong and dominant, are manifested behaviorally by the man's coldness and the woman's hysteria.

By tuning in to both verbal and nonverbal responses, the counselor can filter out the couple's destructive masking devices and avoid the gaming by helping to reveal the basic existing conditions in the relationship.

The role of the counselor is to:

- Have clients identify themselves as batterer and batteree.
- Assist in diffusing anger.
- Share information to demystify stereotypes and dispel myths.
- Insist that clients own their feelings and take responsibility for their behaviors.
- Present new techniques for coping with stress and frustration.
- Rehearse new communication skills, particularly reflective listening and "I" sentences.
- Establish a trust relationship with the clients.
- Obtain individual psychosocial histories and couple profile.
- Provide a positive role model.

Achieving a relationship free of violence is the primary goal. Repairing the relationship without directing attention to individual growth, development, and personal needs is likely to lead to further battering. Individual strengths are based on self-awareness, self-esteem, self-fulfillment, self-acceptance, and self-disclosure. Unless these elements are fully explored by the couple in counseling, each person will be hampered in future attempts to develop and maintain violence-free relationships.[10]

Assertiveness Training

Assertiveness training is a method used by many counselors and clinicians with battered women. There are, however, some issues which should be addressed before the introduction of this technique.

Assertiveness is a behavior change method which makes a distinction between aggression and assertion. It implies an expression of feelings and an assertion of rights without violating another person's rights or negating their feelings. It encourages the exercise of one's own power and increases self-concept. Elaine Hilberman, MD, in her preliminary report "Sixty Battered Women," talks of progressing very slowly. It is frustrating and anxiety provoking for the counselor because of the " . . . knowledge that a client's self-assertion could prove fatal."[11] The inherent danger of her assertiveness being met with aggression is very high. Murray A. Straus, in his paper "A Sociological Perspective on the Prevention and Treatment of Wife-Beating," discusses the assertive steps which battered women must take if they wish a cessation of the violence. Battered women must seek assistance and involvement not only from friends and family, but also professional agencies. They must be prepared to leave. They must redefine the marriage license so that it does not include the unstated right to hit. They must find some means of economic support. Straus suggests getting a job even at the expense of other things because it further ". . . validates the threat to leave if violence occurs." Women must not wait until violence is upon them. They must take steps to alter the pattern. It is a positive proaction and not a futile reaction. ". . . The critical first steps of 'getting help,' canceling the hitting license and making it clear that one is prepared to leave" are all highly assertive, but nonaggressive acts. Assertiveness is vital if there is to be any hope of correcting the problem over which the violence occurs."[12]

In an undetermined number of instances, this assertiveness meets with no results or negative results. Upon entering any counseling relationship with a battered woman, it is mandatory to map strategies, long-term goals, and possible effects. Women meet with negative responses when the way they relate to situations is altered, without any effort or chance to alter the behavior and consciousness of the abusers. Nonsupportive or threatening responses by the partner cause women to either revert to old behavior patterns or become unable to tolerate the old situations. If the latter is the case, it is the counselor's responsibility to make sure that the victims are not acting in a vacuum and are prepared for the possible consequences.

Divorce Counseling

For many therapists and counselors, the thought of consciously assisting couples in the breakup of the family unit is appalling. An acceptance that the battering relationship is, at the very least, physically and psychologically damaging to women and children and, at the maximum, detrimental to the very existence of some women must be faced. Clinebell states that it is necessary to accept the fact that marriage is not the only place where one can meet their needs, and that both the married and single states have very distinct advantages.[13] A look at the factors which got couples into the marriage and factors that are forcing them out is necessary.

> "Divorce counseling is not the same as marriage counseling. Divorce counseling is based on the assumption that it may be better for some couples to separate, rather than on the traditional attitude of the church that a marriage must be saved if possible and that divorce is always a tragedy. A divorce may be the most humanizing option if a particular couple got married for all the wrong reasons in the first place, or if one or both persons would be better off single. Divorce counseling is a kind of counseling and consciousness raising that affirms singleness as an option for human wholeness."[14]

Some issues and questions about relationships and the pros and cons are discussed by Eugene Walder, Ph.D., in his book *How to Get Out of an Unhappy Marriage or an Unhappy Relationship*. These and similar issues should be discussed openly with battering couples to give some perspective to the relationship and to strip away the myths and rationalizations that keep the couple together. The couple may not choose to separate, but at least counseling will be done in a more reality-based setting. Facing the objective facts that the relationship is not fulfilling needs and is causing physical harm is a first step. The issues and questions in the following section help couples begin to pinpoint problems and issues that were not clearly understood.

> • *Are you tired, fatigued, tense? Suppressing your feelings can drain your energy. Pay attention to your body. It may be trying to tell you something about your marriage. But you will need a clean bill of health from your doctor before you can begin to diagnose physical symptoms as expressions of your unhappiness.*
> • *Do you get headaches when you are around your spouse? Have you considered that your marriage may be a big headache to you?*
> • *Do you get "the shakes" when you are with your spouse? You may be shaking with bottled-up rage.*
> • *Do you feel apprehensive about returning home? What scene are you picturing in your mind? Certainly not the loving spouse greeting you with a drink.*
> • *Do you feel irritable a lot of the time? If you do, you are angry about something. Try to identify the source of your anger. Monitor your*

feelings when you are with your spouse. Does what your spouse say irritate you? Do you experience a welling-up of anger? Do you suppress your feelings because of guilt, or fear of disapproval, or fear of loss of love?

• Do you get a sinking feeling in the pit of your stomach when you hear your spouse's footsteps? If you do, your marriage may be going under.

• Do you feel lonely and empty even when you are with your spouse? Isn't this a sign that your marriage isn't fulfilling your needs?

• Do you constantly pick on your spouse about little things?"[15]

Are You Willing to Risk Living Alone?

Downs

- Coming home and having no one to talk to.
- Being afraid of intruders.
- Staring at the four walls.
- Sleeping alone.
- Being sexually frustrated.
- Going on vacation alone.
- Becoming ill and having no one to take care of you.
- Feeling unwanted and unloved.
- Waking up from a bad dream and having no one to comfort you.
- Dying alone.

Ups

- Coming home when you want to. How many times have you come home to your spouse when you didn't want to? Your home is your castle. Has it been under constant siege in your marriage?
- Being content. If you're not at war with your spouse, you can be at peace with yourself.
- Experiencing new sexual adventures. You'll be free to be *yourself.*
- Pursuing the activities you've never had the time for—or the energy. Does your spouse waste your fuel by idling your engine?
- Spending an evening by yourself. You'll be with someone you enjoy being with.

- Regulating your own life. You'll be self-regulating.
- Seeing whom you want. You won't be entertaining his friends or her friends. You'll be entertaining *your* friends.
- Being responsible for yourself. You've been voting since you were eighteen. When was the last time you gave yourself a vote of confidence?
- Meeting new people. Your friendly attitude will be inviting to others. Yours will be an "open" house.[16]

Are You Willing to Have Custody of the Children? (Wives Mostly—Husbands if Applicable)

Downs

- Being a homemaker *and* breadwinner.
- Working around the clock with no relief.
- Being the disciplinarian.
- Running yourself ragged.
- Supporting babysitters.
- Having desirable men (or women) run scared.
- Feeling overwhelmed by it all.
- Having to make decisions about the children by yourself.
- Being both mother and father to your children.

Ups

- Getting a big promotion. You'll be running the family business. You'll make it a going enterprise.
- Becoming yourself. Finding your own identity, and your children will get to know *you*.
- Being more than *just* a housewife. You'll give up coffee klatches for coffee breaks.
- Providing a healthy atmosphere for your children. All noise and pollution will be eliminated.
- Declaring yourself Head of the Household. You won't be a dependent anymore. You'll be independent.
- Being living proof to your children that life doesn't have to have a knock-out punch. You'll be steadier on your feet than ever. You'll never have been so up.
- Becoming yourself for yourself. You won't have to seek your spouse's approval or avoid your spouse's disapproval. You

can just be you. You'll approve of yourself.

- Being fully with your children when you're with them because you'll be a whole person.
- Sharing the wealth with your children. Your newly discovered personal resources will be a bonanza.[17]

Are You Willing to Risk Supporting Yourself? (Wives Mostly—Husbands where Applicable)

Downs

- Going out to work every day.
- Hating your job.
- Not making enough to make ends meet.
- Being laid off or fired.
- Paying bills.
- Balancing a checkbook.
- Having no marketable skills.
- Having a boss.
- Balancing a budget.
- Living on one salary.

Ups

- Getting paid for your labor.
- Being your sole support. You won't have to lean on anyone else.
- Getting a raise in salary. Your labor will be appreciated.
- Brushing up on old skills. You'll be making yourself attractive to your employers.
- Learning a new job. You'll be using your head.
- Establishing an identity through who you are instead of whom you're married to.
- Enjoying what you do. You'll have found a meaningful form of self-expression.
- Becoming an interesting person. You'll carry yourself with pride.
- Getting a promotion. You'll be 'growing' up in the world.[18]

Are You Willing to Risk Relocating?

Downs

- Selling the house.
- Pulling up roots.
- Adjusting to a new community.
- Leaving old familiar friends.
- Giving up the comforts of home.
- Making a new circle of friends.
- Apartment or house hunting.
- Saying goodbye to the good memories you shared together.
- Leaving behind your shattered dreams.

Ups

- Starting out afresh. You'll leave all your dirty laundry behind you.
- Making new friends who accept you for yourself, by yourself.
- Joining what you want to join. You won't do anything because it's the thing to do unless it's *your* thing.
- Leaving the past behind you. You'll say goodbye to the old, unpleasant memories. By living fully in the present, you'll have a storehouse of new, pleasant memories for the future.
- Giving your children a fresh start. They'll be able to breathe again because the home environment has been cleaned up.
- Finding out who your friends are. There's no distance between close friends, no matter how far away you are.
- Decorating your house or apartment. Everything will be in good taste because it will be the way *you* like it.
- Moving out because you're on the move. You can really go somewhere.[19]

Are You Willing to Risk Facing the Unknown?

Downs

- Going from the frying pan into the fire.
- Being worse off than before.
- Getting cold feet and calling the whole thing off.
- Not finding anyone else.
- Hurting your spouse.
- Being a two-time loser.

- Being overwhelmed by all the pressure.
- Hurting your children.
- Not having emotional security.
- Not knowing if you can change your life and yourself.

Ups

- Taking a chance on a better life. Can it be much worse than it has been? What do you have to lose?
- Realizing your potential. You'll never know what you're capable of until you give yourself the chance to find out.
- Having your sexual fantasies come true. Is sex with your spouse an unpleasant reality? You may find that sex can be 'unreal' with the right partner.
- Planning for the future. Think of all the things you've wanted to do. You can do more than plan. You can do.
- Saving your children's future. Watch their emotional resources grow. By the time they're old enough to leave home, they'll be able to support themselves.
- Doing your spouse a favor. Your going-away present will be a very special gift—the opportunity to make a better life with someone else.
- Discovering your natural resources. Were you unable to locate the 'mine' because you hadn't dug below the 'ours?'
- Becoming a different person. You really can't become a different person. You can become only yourself. You'll be amazed at how much you've changed.
- Being all charged up about life. You can free your energies for the things that really matter to you. You can become a self-generating power plant. You can make your life hum.[20]

SUMMARY

In this section the author has dealt with a variety of issues and problems which demand resolution and acknowledgement when dealing with family violence situations.

It is crucial that all interveners know and play their proper role in this tragic situation. One of the chief problems faced by first responders is that they misunderstand their roles in the resolution of the crisis state. This inevitably leads to frustration, disillusionment, and a sense of failure.

REFERENCES

1. Walker LE: The Battered Woman. New York, Harper and Row, 1979, p. 202
2. Chesler P: Women and Madness. New York, Avon Books, 1972
3. Walker LE: The Battered Woman. New York, Harper and Row, 1979, p. 203
4. Clinebell CH: Counseling for Liberation. Philadelphia, Fortress Press, 1976, p. 21
5. Clinebell CH: Counseling for Liberation. Philadelphia, Fortress Press, 1976, p. 22
6. Woods F, Habib M: Strategies for working with assaulted women, their families and the systems around them. Metuchen, NJ; unpublished, 1976
7. Hilberman E, Munson K: Sixty battered women. Unpublished paper prepared for a special session of the American Psychiatric Association Meetings on Battered Women: Culture as Destiny, Toronto, 1977
8. Hilberman E, Munson K: Sixty battered women. Unpublished paper prepared for a special session of the American Psychiatric Association Meetings on Battered Women: Culture as Destiny, Toronto, 1977
9. Resnick M: Counselor Training Manual No. 1. Ann Arbor MI; Domestic Violence Project, November 1976
10. Berlin-Miller A, Yufe OR: Nontraditional counseling modalities. San Diego, CA; Battered Women's Services, unpublished
11. Hilberman E, Muson K: Sixty battered women. Unpublished paper prepared for a special session of the American Psychiatric Association Meetings on Battered Women: Culture as Destiny, Toronto, 1977
12. Straus MA: A sociological perspective on the prevention and treatment of wife beating. In Roy M (ed): Battered Women. New York, Van Nostrand-Reinhold, 1977
13. Clinebell CH: Counseling for Liberation. Philadelphia, Fortress Press, 1976, p. 29
14. Clinebell CH: Counseling for Liberation. Philadelphia, Fortress Press, 1976, p. 29
15. Walder E: How to Get Out of an Unhappy Marriage or an Unhappy Relationship. New York, G. P. Putnam's Sons, 1978
16. Walder E: How to Get Out of an Unhappy Marriage or an Unhappy Relationship. New York, G. P. Putnam's Sons, 1978
17. Walder E: How to Get Out of an Unhappy Marriage or an Unhappy Relationship. New York, G. P. Putnam's Sons, 1978
18. Walder E: How to Get Out of an Unhappy Marriage or an Unhappy Relationship. New York, G. P. Putnam's Sons, 1978
19. Walder E: How to Get Out of an Unhappy Marriage or an Unhappy Relationship. New York, G. P. Putnam's Sons, 1978
20. Walder E: How to Get Out of an Unhappy Marriage or an Unhappy Relationship. New York, G. P. Putnam's Sons, 1978

13 SPECIFIC RESPONSE TO CHILD ABUSE VICTIMS

Linda Walker, BA, MSW

In the early 1960s, Drs. Kempe and Helfer of the University of Colorado Medical Center identified what they called the Battered Child Syndrome, after recognizing that a certain number of children were admitted to the hospital for treatment of injuries that were determined to be the responsibility of their parents.[1] Since that time, as there has been a growing awareness of the rights of children, many others across the country (and in other countries, as well), from the more traditional institutions such as medicine, law enforcement, and public welfare, to the newer community-based agencies in the private sector, have broadened understanding of the family that may hurt its children.[2] All states now have laws that mandate the reporting of child abuse; many are developing service systems that provide treatment for these dysfunctional families as well.

Traditionally, first responders to child abuse cases have been medical personnel, who identified and treated injuries, and law enforcement representatives, who basically dealt with holding the offenders legally accountable and providing protection for the abused children. The end result was often perceived as family separation and legal prosecution. As time has gone by, other professionals have also become involved, and in an increasing number of instances may also be first responders. With the emphasis largely changing from a strictly medical/legal perspective to include a treatment orientation, first responders are frequently viewed as the beginning step of a process[2] which ultimately results in a potential for positive change and family reunification. Because of this major change in focus, the one most important predictive impact of the first responder upon the abusive family is that the tone is set by them for future relationships with professionals in other fields.

Currently, first responders to child abuse victims may be persons who are of many different backgrounds.[1,3] First responders may be:

- Police
- Hospital or other medical personnel (paramedics, MICN's)

- Social service personnel (for example, protective services)
- Mental health staff
- Teachers or other school staff
- Clergy
- Neighbors, family members

In a sense, there may actually be several "first" responders. Since there may be many different people involved in responding to a single child abuse case, and some of their functions are quite separate, the victim and family may perceive of individuals from different professional orientations as each being a first responder from their own groups. Because numerous different individuals may be in contact with family members, the first person within his or her own professional system may be viewed as the first responder from that system. For example:

Professional System	*Individual Within Professional System*
Schools	Teacher
	Principal
	Nurse
	Counselor
	Office staff
	Custodian
Medical/Hospital	Nurse
	Receptionist
	Physician
	Lab technician
	X-ray technician
	Orderly
Criminal Justice	Patrolman
	Detective/investigator
	District attorney
	Defense attorney
	Judge
	Probation officer
Social Service	Welfare department social worker—intake
	Welfare department social worker—on-going
	Receiving home staff
	Foster parents
Mental Health	Therapist—intake
	Therapist—on-going

As an example, follow this sample case through a series of contacts:

A child is observed by her teacher (first responder #1) to have questionable injuries. After discussing the source of the injuries with the child, the teacher then calls in the school nurse and principal. Subsequently, the school personnel call the police, and a patrolman (first responder #2) arrives, interviews the child, takes her to a hospital for a medical examination (first responder #3), and then to the county receiving home. There she is interviewed by a social worker (first responder #4). Following these contacts, she may eventually be seen by other representatives of the legal system (detectives, lawyers, district attorney, judges), service providers (physicians, mental health professionals, social service staff), and foster parents. (In counties having team response systems, or where social service staff provide the primary response to child abuse cases, some of these steps may be eliminated or combined.)

Response may be due to identification directly by the victim, or because some other person, adult or child, is acting on behalf of the victim asking for intervention.[3]

Professional Responsibility

When the responder is acting in a professional capacity, it is the expectation of those requesting assistance (including the victim) that the responder is knowledgable about his or her responsibility, and will act accordingly. Consequently, it is the responsibility of the responder to personally acknowledge any lack of pertinent information, procedurally or otherwise, and seek out assistance whenever necessary and appropriate.[1] It is also particularly critical in the case of child abuse and related problems for the individual to resolve for him or herself his or her own feelings regarding these cases so as not to impact the victim and family members with his or her own biases and/or emotional involvement.[2] Careful evaluation of the responder's own values regarding the issues involved in child abuse cases (such as excessive discipline) is also necessary.

In responding to a child abuse case, it is impossible to ignore the relationship of the family (in particular the parent, or other primary caretaker) to the total picture.[3] Even in cases of injury at the hands of the parents, a child will often retain close emotional ties to the family unit, and frequently specifically the abusive parent.

Threats toward the family may be very upsetting to the child, as they are interpreted as threats to himself, as well. Because of the commonly found role reversal in abusive families, children frequently believe that they are responsible for the well-being of the family unit, and grieve deeply when they feel they are responsible for the family disintegration. Additionally, since children identify personally with their parents, being told that there is something wrong with their parents often means that there is something also wrong with them. Therefore, their own self-image becomes questionable, along with the image of their parents.

Inappropriate Response

Inappropriate responses can take many forms. For instance, it is inappropriate, and a potential set-up for continued abuse of the victim, for a response to be "He (the victim) must have deserved it," the parent "has a right to do anything he wants to his child," or "I do worse to my child," when a child is presented with injuries resulting from excessive discipline. Additional damaging responses may include moralizing, making derogatory comments about the condition of the victim in his or her presence (for example, "He looks terrible," "Look at these bruises!"), and making derogatory comments about the child's parents (such as, "They can't possibly love him," "They must be crazy").

Inappropriate response to the victim of child abuse by the first responder, as described above, may result in the following:

- Poor communication with both the victim and his or her family.
- Hostility on the part of the victim and/or his or her family.
- Lack of cooperation.
- Repression of evidence or information, withdrawal, and/or cover-up.
- Breakdown of trust between the victim and his or her parent.
- Lack of trust by victim for responder, and other professionals later involved.
- Resistance to supportive future involvement by other professionals for both victim and family members.

Special Nature of the Problem Area

It is critical for those working with abusive families to develop some understanding of this particular problem area.[2] Specifically, it is helpful to recognize that many parents who abuse their children physically, sexually, or emotionally, come from abusive histories of their own. Acting in a violent or sexual way toward their children may force parents to review their own childhood, often reliving negative experiences. The resultant confusion, hostility, anger, and guilt seriously impairs their ability to respond cooperatively when openly confronted by the current abusive behavior. Because abusive families tend to act out the abusive behavior at times of stress, and are generally isolated from supportive community or familial relationships,[1] there is a tendency for family members to put pressure on the victim to not cooperate with outsiders, or to apply force in the form of additional abusive incidents or threats in order to accomplish the same thing. In this case, a non-threatening, non-confrontive approach[2] will maximize cooperation while minimizing interference with the victim by family members.

Needs of Victims

Victims of any form of child abuse have specific needs to be met by first responders from any professional orientation. These needs are not different from the needs of victims of other crimes, with one exception. Since all victims of child abuse are children, attention must be paid to focusing the approach in an age-specific manner. In general, it is important to take note of the age of the victim and maturity level. And, since children are tremendously affected by adults, it is important to identify which adults are present, how they relate to the victim, and what impact their reaction to the situation has upon the child's behavior. Other needs of victims of child abuse include:

- *Compassion/Support*—A clear sense of support from the first responder, with recognition of not only the physical discomfort, but the emotional discomfort, as well.
- *Honesty*—Adults tend to think of children as being unable to understand processes and issues that seem complicated. What is often not recognized is that children not only understand more than we give them credit for, but that if adults do not give them straight answers to questions, children often make up their own inaccurate answers. While it is important to phrase explanations in language appropriate for the age and maturity level of the victim, it is equally important to be as complete as possible in clarifying processes at each step. Children will cooperate most fully, and be much less fearful, if they are as familiar as possible with the process through which they are going.

- *Trust/Rapport*—An effort must be made by the responder to lay the groundwork for trust and rapport to be built with the victim. This often takes time initially, but pays off in the long-run by establishing a cooperative nature within the child. Particularly critical is not rushing into a confrontive interview, spending time getting to know the child first.
- *Sensitivity*—Perhaps the most important need of the victim is to interact with someone who is sensitive to his or her needs. While training may ultimately be the responsibility of those who assign staff to work these cases, individuals in these assignments can also independently become knowledgable about intervention in child abuse cases and, in general, increase their own awareness and sensitivity through participation in workshops and reading on their own.

Interviewing the Child Victim

Because of the special needs of children, care must be given to adjusting interviewing techniques appropriately to allow for maximum input from the child while minimizing the negative impact caused by fear, the implication of threat, or the pressure of having to continually verbally recreate abusive incidents. First responders must seriously reconsider their own skills in preparing for interviews with child victims.

The following excellent outline for interviewing child victims of sexual assault was prepared with support from grant #77-DF-10-0016 awarded to the Sexual Assault Center* by the Law Enforcement Assistance Administration, U.S. Department of Justice. Developed specifically for use with criminal justice system personnel, it is clearly applicable to other professional groups, as well, for use in interviewing victims of *all* forms of child abuse.

INTERVIEWING CHILD VICTIMS[4]: GUIDELINES FOR CRIMINAL JUSTICE SYSTEM PERSONNEL

BACKGROUND INFORMATION

The following issues affect the child's ability to give a history of sexual assault and influence the cooperativeness of victim and family.

---

*Sexual Assault Center, Harborview Medical Center, 325 Ninth Avenue, Room IC-60 Seattle, WA 98104, (206) 223-3047

I. Child's Developmental Level

A child's cognitive, emotional and social growth occurs in sequential phases of increasingly complex levels of development. Progression occurs with mastery of one stage leading to concentration on the next.

Cognitive—Preconceptual, concrete, intuitive thinking in the young child gradually develops toward comprehension of abstract concept. Time and space begin as personalized notions and gradually are identified as logical and ordered concepts.

Emotional—The young child perceives her/himself egocentrically with little ability to identify her/himself in a context. S/he is dependent on the family to meet all needs and invests adults with total authority. The child often reflects the emotional responses of the parents. S/he gradually shifts to greater reliance on peer relationships and emotional commitments to people outside the family.

Behavioral—The young child is spontaneous, outgoing, and explosive with few internal controls and only a tentative awareness of external limits. S/he has a short attention span. A child most often expresses feelings through behavior rather than verbally. As the child grows, s/he develops internal controls and establishes a sense of identity and independence. Peers and other adults have increasing influence on behavior.

II. Sexual Assault

Characteristics of the assault affect the child's emotional perception of the event and to a great extent determine the response. The closeness of the child's relationship to the offender, the duration of the offense, the amount of secrecy surrounding the assault, and the degree of violence are the factors which have the greatest impact on the child's reaction. The child may very well have ambivalent feelings toward the offender or be dependent on him for other needs.

III. Response to Child

The child is fearful of the consequences of reporting a sexual assault. The response of the family support system and official agencies will directly affect the resolution of the psychological trauma and her/his cooperativeness as a witness. The child fears s/he will be disbelieved or blamed for the assault and almost always is hesitant about reporting.

INTERVIEWING CHILD VICTIMS

I. Preparing for Interview

Prior to interviewing the child, obtain relevant information from parents/guardian, and if applicable, Child Protective Services caseworker, physician, and/or Sexual Assault Center/Rape Relief counselor.

A. Explain your role and procedures to above personnel, and enlist their cooperation.

B. Determine child's general development status:
  - Age
  - Grade
  - Siblings
  - Family composition
  - Capabilities
  - Ability to write, read, count, ride a bike, tell time, remember events
  - Any unusual problems: physical, intellectual, behavioral
  - Knowledge of anatomy and sexual behavior
  - Family terminology for genital areas

C. Review circumstances of assault (as reported already by child to other person):
  - What, where, when, by whom, and to whom reported
  - Exact words of child
  - Other persons told by child
  - How many have interviewed child
  - Child's reaction to assault
  - How child feels about it and what, if any, behavioral signs of distress (nightmares, withdrawal, regression, acting out) have occurred

D. Determine what reactions and changes child has been exposed to following revelation of the assault(s):
  - Believing
  - Supportive
  - Blaming

- Angry
- Ambivalent
- Parents getting a divorce
- Move to a new home

II. Beginning the Interview

A. *Setting*—The more comfortable for the child, the more information s/he is likely to share.
  1. *Flexibility*—A child likes to move around the room, explore and touch, sit on the floor or adult's lap.
  2. *Activity*—Playing or coloring occupy child's physical needs and allows her/him to talk with less guardedness.
  3. *Privacy*—Interruptions distract an already short attention span, divert focus of interview, and make self-conscious or apprehensive child withdraw.
  4. *Support*—If the child wishes a parent or other person present, it should be allowed. A frightened or insecure child will not give a complete statement.
B. *Establishing a Relationship*
  1. *Introduction*—Name, brief and simple explanation of role, and purpose: "I am the lawyer (or legal person) on your side; my job is to talk to children about these things because we want them to stop happening."
  2. *General Exchange*—Ask about name (last name), age, grade, school and teacher's name, siblings, family composition, pets, friends, activities, favorite games/TV shows. (It often helps to share personal information when appropriate, e.g., children, pets.)
  3. *Assess Level of Sophistication and Ability to Understand Concepts*—Does child read, write, count, tell time; know colors or shapes; know the day or date; know birthdate; remember past events (breakfast, yesterday, last year); understand before and after; know about money; assume responsibilities (goes around neighborhood alone, stays at home alone, makes dinner, etc.).

III. Obtaining History of Sexual Assault

A. *Preliminaries*
  1. Use language appropriate to child's level; be sure child

understands words. (Watch for signs of confusion, blankness, or embarrassment; be careful with words like incident, occur, penetration, prior, ejaculation, etc.).

2. Do not ask WHY questions ("Why did you go to the house?" "Why didn't you tell?") They tend to sound accusatory.

3. Never threaten or try to force a reluctant child to talk. Pressure causes a child to clam up and may further traumatize her/him.

4. Be aware that the child who has been instructed or threatened not to tell by the offender (ESPECIALLY if a parent) will be very reluctant and full of anxiety (you will usually notice a change in the child's affect while talking about the assault.)
   The fears often need to be allayed.
   • "It's not bad to tell what happened."
   • "You won't get in trouble."
   • "You can help your dad by telling what happened."
   • "It wasn't your fault."
   • "You're not to blame."

5. Interviewer's affective response should be consonant with child's perception of assault (e.g., don't emphasize jail for the offender if the child has expressed positive feelings toward him.)

6. Ask direct, simple questions as open-ended as allowed by child's level of comprehension and ability to talk about the assault.

B. *Statement*
   1. WHAT
      • "Can you tell me what happened?"
      • "I need to know what the man did."
      • "Did he ever touch you? Where?"
      • "Where did he put his finger?"
      • "Have you ever seen him with his clothes off?"
      • "Did you ever see his penis (thing, pee pee, weiner) get big?"
      • "Did anything ever come out of it?"
      Once basic information is elicited, ask specifically about other types of sexual contact.
      • "Did he ever put it into your mouth?"
      • "Did he ever make you touch him on his penis?"

2. WHO

Child's response here will probably not be elaborate. Most children know the offender and can name him, although in some cases the child may not understand relationship to self or family. Ascertain from other sources what is the exact nature/extent of the relationship.

3. WHEN

The response to this question will depend on child's ability, how recently assault happened, lapse between last incident and report, number of assaults (children will tend to confuse or mix separate incidents). If the child is under six, information re: time is unlikely to be reliable. An older child can often narrow down dates and times using recognizable events or associating assault with other incidents.

- "Was it before your birthday, the weekend, Valentine's Day?"
- "Was it nighttime or daytime?"
- "Did it happen after dinner, 'Happy Days', your brother's bedtime?"

4. WHERE

The assault usually occurs in the child's and/or offender's home. Information about which room, where other family members were, where child was before assault may be learned.

5. COERCION

What kind of force, threat, enticement, pressure was used to insure cooperation and secrecy?

- "Did he tell you not to tell?" "What did he say?"
- "Did he say something bad would happen or you would get in trouble if you told?"
- "Did the man say it was a secret?"

C. *Assessing credibility and competency*

1. Does child describe acts or experience to which s/he would not have normally been exposed? (Average child is not familiar with erection or ejaculation until adolescence at the earliest.)

2. Does child describe circumstances and characteristics typical of sexual assault situation? ("He told me that it was our secret"; "He said I couldn't go out if I didn't do it"; "He told me it was sex education.")

3. How and under what circumstances did child tell? What were exact words?
4. How many times had child given the history and how consistent is it regarding the basic facts of the assault (note times, dates, circumstances, sequence of events, etc.)?
5. How much spontaneous information can child provide? How much prompting is required?
6. Can child define difference between truth and a lie? (This question is not actually very useful with young children because they learn this by rote but may not understand the concepts.)

IV. Closing the Interview

A. Praise/thank child for information/cooperation.
B. Provide information.
   1. Child—Do not extract promises from child regarding testifying. Most children cannot project themselves into an unknown situation and predict how they will behave. Questions about testifying in court or undue emphasis on trial will have little meaning and often frightens the child (causing nightmares and apprehension).
   2. Parent—Provide simple, straightforward information about what will happen next in the criminal justice system and approximately when, the likelihood of trial, etc.
C. Enlist cooperation—Let them know who to contact for status reports or in an emergency; express appreciation and understanding for the effort they are making by reporting and following through on process.
D. Answer questions; solicit responses.

SUMMARY

In responding to any child abuse case it is important to carefully evaluate each situation individually. Where there are many general similarities between cases, the individuals composing family units must be considered separately in order to fully understand the uniqueness of each case. An understanding of the impact of each family member upon the other is critical in predicting responsivity, family functioning, and potential risk factor.

An effort should be made to have professionals working in this field be those with special training, expertise, and sensitivity to issues involved in the entire family. Further, an evaluative process needs to be made at the time of initial response that allows for avoidance of family separation whenever possible.

Finally, emphasis is placed upon the fact that it is often the first responder's approach to family members that directly influences how responsive family members will be to those professionals they will have contact with in the future. Since we know that most children wind up with their natural parents at some point, even when they have been removed initially, it is imperative that the groundwork be laid at the time of the initial contact to allow family members to view service providers in general as being potentially helpful.

REFERENCES

1. Helfer RE, Kempe and Henry C: Child Abuse and Neglect: The Family and the Community. Cambridge, MA; Ballinger Publications, 1976
2. Summitt R: Sexual child abuse, the psychotherapist and the team concept. In Dealing with Sexual Child Abuse, Vol. 2. Chicago, National Committee for Prevention of Child Abuse, 1979
3. Justice B, Justice R: The Abusing Family. New York, Human Sciences, 1976
4. Sexual Assault Center: Interviewing Child Victims: Guidelines for Criminal Justice System Personnel. Material prepared with support from grant #77-DF-10-0016 awarded to the Sexual Assault Center, Harborview Medical Center, 325 Ninth Avenue, Room IC-66, Seattle, WA, 98104; by the Law Enforcement Assistance Administration, US Department of Justice.

14 IMPORTANCE OF COMMUNICATING WITH VICTIMS OF RAPE

Doris Spaulding, RN, BSN

The crime of rape now has been recognized as a crime of violence rather than one of sexual gratification. It is this violence that leaves the victim with a sense of hopelessness and powerlessness to regain self-control over actions and decisions. This violence, however, need not be physical in nature. Body language or the tone of voice can be just as frightening as actual physical violence and/or injury. The act of rape constitutes an injury.

The American Psychiatric Association's nomenclature includes "post-traumatic stress reaction." Rape is specifically included.

Even if the offender is apprehended and removed from society, the victim's ordeal continues. The trauma that results can be alleviated by the numerous agencies now available. Rape crisis centers and rape hot lines have been established in many cities throughout the United States. Since calls are made at any hour of the day or night, those who are victims are able to avail themselves of the services offered throughout a 24-hour period, seven days a week. The service alluded to is not long-term therapy but immediate contact by telephone. The caller may have been a victim of rape weeks, months, or years earlier, but recognizes the need for moral support. Even though a victim has resumed a normal routine, there may be times when a reminder of the attack causes a disruption in life. Symptoms vary widely, but may include shaking, clammy-feeling hands, increased heart rate, hyperventilation, and others. The ordeal of the attack is being relived and this is extremely frightening. A number of events can trigger this response:

- Seeing someone who resembles the rapist.
- Hearing about another person's ordeal.
- Attending a lecture which focuses on crimes against women and children.
- An "anniversary reaction"—the day of the week on which the crime occurred or one year following the attack.

If this occurs, moral support is needed immediately. In the event that support is lacking from family and/or friends, the immediate telephone contact available through a crisis center can allay fears that a tragedy is imminent. The caller may voice the fear that "I must be losing my mind." The calm, reassuring voice of a knowledgeable, trained crisis line advocate can mean the difference between a period of extreme anxiety versus relative calm. This frequently is very obvious from either a change in tone of voice of the caller, or through a statement such as "I feel so much better now—thank you for listening." Frequently, the resolution of the trauma depends upon the manner and competence of the first responder, irregardless of whether a responder is from an agency or from another source, such as a family member.

The attitude of family and friends can cause guilt and a sense of worthlessness if thoughtless or hostile remarks are made. Loved ones are in a difficult position. They not only need to assist the victim, but must also deal with their own particular trauma. Loved ones may not know how they should treat the victim and may ask "Should I protect her to the point of babying her?"

Not knowing exactly what the victim requires, loved ones often become impatient with symptoms of rape trauma, not realizing how necessary patience is in this situation. It is hard to remain in the background, allowing the victim to make decisions. This may be even more difficult for someone who has not dealt with this particular crime before and who may be tempted to think or say, "If that had been me, I'd have kicked him. I wouldn't have let him rape me." One must remember that each individual reacts to given circumstances in her own way. It is impossible to state positively how one will or will not act, especially in a crisis. Rape is a life crisis situation. It would be detrimental to give the impression that the victim is being judged.

While the temptation to seek for the rapist is a natural one, this should be left to law enforcement personnel. At this time, the victim needs the presence of those she loves, but only if an atmosphere of security can be maintained. A friend or family member who is visibly upset should try to be composed in order to provide the victim the type of strong support needed. An emotional reaction by loved ones is not only a natural reaction, but moral support is needed for the loved ones of the victim as well. A feeling of worthlessness and rejection may be perceived if support is sought but not given. This situation can occur if a victim, having been humiliated and degraded, seeks comfort and receives none.

A victim may feel the need to be with someone or to talk to someone, hoping that whoever is chosen will take time to listen. If the victim seeking support is turned away by statements such as

"You should be glad he didn't beat you up," or "Forget it, it's over now," the sense of dejection is overwhelming. A very shocking situation occurs when a friend, neighbor, or stranger turns the victim away by any number of reactions and statements.

Responses such as "I don't want to get involved" or "Stop crying. I have my own worries," leave the victim feeling worthless or deserted. This can prolong the resolution of rape trauma to a significant degree. The victim may feel that no one cares, that there is no help available. This is one reason rape crisis lines are so vital. Reassurance from a nonjudgmental advocate can help re-establish confidence in a victim.

It must be remembered that the reaction following an *attempted* rape can be just as devastating as a completed rape. Therefore, moral support is as necessary as in the victim who has been raped by vaginal penetration.

At the time of the ordeal of rape, survival is uppermost in the victim's mind. A statement such as "I was so afraid he'd kill me, I said I'd do what he told me to if he would just leave afterwards," is common. After the rapist leaves, the victim must then decide the first step to be taken.

The crisis created by the rape now makes decisions mandatory, even if that decision is to do nothing. If the victim chooses to do nothing immediately, that decision is not necessarily final. In a short time, the need for security may determine what step to take first. Having others around her may give that sense of security and thus make her feel she is safe from further intrusion.

Safety

Safety is the prime concern. Since law enforcement personnel represent protection, the victim's first instinct may be to call the police. Prosecution is of no concern at this point, although for some victims it soon becomes an issue, realizing that without the willingness to prosecute the rapist, he is free to repeat his heinous crime. Fear is the driving force—fear that the rapist will return, and that the safety of the victim will again be jeopardized. Other reassurances will soon be required. Feelings of guilt may emerge. The victim may ask, "Was I somehow to blame for what happened?" A common expression of guilt may be "If I hadn't taken the dog for a walk at 10:30 at night, this wouldn't have happened." The victim needs to hear that she was not at fault. She had the right to go for a walk, but the rapist had no right to attack her.

Our present culture still views rape with skepticism. This is shown in attitudes and comments such as "She deserved what she got; look how she was dressed." This creates a sense of guilt on the part of the victim despite the fact that the crime was committed *against* the victim. Attitudes of professionals and loved ones assume great importance.

Treated as an Individual

The needs of victims vary from one person to another. In addition to safety, the victim needs to be treated as an individual, not as "the rape case." An atmosphere of haste or unconcern is not helpful to the victim who needs moral support. The assault has left the victim feeling dirty, degraded, and used. To restore self-esteem to the victim, those coming in contact with her must sincerely care about people and their feelings.

Initial Response

A hypothetical situation can demonstrate the specific, immediate needs of victims of rape. A woman awakens suddenly and sees only a shadowy figure. The body initiates a chain of reactions due to this intrusion: tenseness, increased output of adrenalin, a pounding sensation in the ears, pounding heart beat, and/or actual immobilization (in some instances).

The immediate need is safety and self-preservation. A victim thinks, "This is my home; no one has the right to invade it." The powerful instinct to survive cannot be underestimated. Many victims have submitted to sodomy, oral copulation, and/or rape because of the threat by a rapist, "If you don't do what I tell you to, I'll bury you."

Protection by Law Enforcement

After the rapist leaves, whoever the victim calls or sees can be instrumental in the resolution of the trauma of rape. If police are called, they have the responsibility of physically protecting the victim. The police officer need not be a woman. Manner and competence are much more important than the sex of the officer. The victim has the right to be treated with dignity and respect. The rapist treated the victim like an object, and the victim now feels worthless. Her self-esteem is at a very low ebb and is in need of moral support so that she knows she is still a worthwhile person.

Listening

Another responsibility of the police is to listen to what the victim says. For many years, a woman who said she had been raped was not believed. Many assumed she was "crying rape" to avenge a former boyfriend.

There are many in today's society who believe that unless a woman struggles and *shows results* of that struggle that rape did not occur. If rape is equated with sex and pleasure rather than force and violence, difficulties arise. The violence need not mean broken bones, cuts, or bruises. Many victims have been terrorized by an attitude or tone of voice. It is not essential that a weapon be seen or used in order to instill fear.

Dislike/Distrust

One natural reaction would be not only distrust of all men, but also dislike. All men are not rapists. An early, comfortable experience with a male is, in many instances, beneficial to the victim. An unpleasant experience occurs occasionally when a police officer makes remarks that demonstrate a lack of knowledge for the feelings of a rape victim. This not only shows lack of respect for the individual, but can prolong resolution of the trauma.

Since many victims feel a sense of guilt, comments regarding the reason the rape occurred are not in order. The officer who listens patiently as the victim relates the details necessary for a complete report, establishes a rapport that can restore confidence both in the victim and in significant others.

Role of the Advocate

If a victim calls a crisis line, the calm voice of the advocate can be very reassuring. The fact that a knowledgeable, caring person is only a telephone call away is of great comfort to one who is frightened. The advocate can continue to talk by telephone to the victim until the police arrive. While some information may be exchanged, the prime purpose is reassurance:

- That she did the right thing; it is better to have survived rather than fight to the death to preserve honor.
- That she was not asking for rape; a hitchhiker is asking for a ride, not rape.
- That advocates will be available for moral support throughout all procedures.
- That the decision is hers to make whether to report, or whether to prosecute.

INTERVENTION BY MEDICAL PERSONNEL

Paramedics are in a unique position to help victims of rape. At times, victims do not tell anyone of the rape but, for physical reasons, may go to a private physician or a hospital. The initial attitude that the victim *perceives* can affect in a positive or negative manner. It is not the position of medical personnel to judge. Their responsibility is to attend to the physical needs of the victim and to give moral support. Information regarding referral should be given so that the victim will have that information on hand to use when she so decides.

At times, the first responder may be a friend or relative whom the victim has called. Often, those closest to the victim are so emotionally involved that they cannot give the moral support that is needed. They may feel useless in this situation and may ask, "What can I do or say to show my concern?" or "How do I treat her?" If they call a crisis center, suggestions can be made as to the victim's needs, not only immediately but in the days to follow. Moral support may consist of nothing more than being willing to listen whenever the victim wants to talk. Retelling details is distasteful and difficult. Feelings and how to deal with emotions concern her more. Loved ones can be aware of certain changes in the victim, as listed below.

- Does she only feel secure when she is with people?
- Do crowds bother her?
- Do sudden sounds frighten her?
- Is she reluctant to have any physical contact?
- Is she uneasy in the presence of men?

It would not be appropriate to ask for details of the attack. Understandably, the victim would like to put the event behind her, as if it had not happened. It would also be undesirable to intimate that the victim was in any way to blame for what happened or that she should have done something once the rapist started his intimidation. Comments such as "Why didn't you scream?" or "Why didn't you kick him?" should not be made. Now that the assault has taken place, the victim may be asking, "Why didn't I do something?" This is a natural reaction. Now the victim feels relatively safe, but the attack is uppermost in her thoughts.

ROLE OF THE FIRST RESPONDER

Resolution of rape trauma and/or the willingness to prosecute may depend upon the response of those who surround the victim. If that response elicits negative feelings, the victim may decide not to proceed further, not to prosecute, or even report the crime. She may never see that particular person again, but the lack of established rapport reinforces negative feelings. Thus, the importance of trained, concerned personnel who respond to the rape victim's call should be given consideration.

Fortunately, even though the attitude of a police officer, paramedic, physician, or nurse is far from acceptable in some instances, many victims proceed with reporting and prosecution. However, future adjustment is to be considered as well as immediate reaction.

The possibility of VD and/or pregnancy is cause for concern. Some victims ask for this information immediately and seem more concerned about this aspect than emotional reactions.

Any information by medical personnel should be given in writing. Oral instructions are soon forgotten. It must be remembered that victims are usually preoccupied with other matters such as safety, and often do not hear all that is said. The abundance of information and/or advice seems overwhelming. These instructions are actually bouncing off the victim, and the need for repetition is common. Conversation is difficult because of preoccupation with the attack.

Responding to Children

Difficulty in responding to a child victim is due not only to emotional reaction, but also to the inability to explain to many children why this crime occurred. A mother is frequently the first to know a crime was committed. Irritation around the genitalia may be discovered at bath time and, upon questioning, the child may then tell what happened. If this occurs, the parent (or relative or babysitter) must be careful not to display shock, although that may be the first inclination and understandably so. It is essential that a calm atmosphere surround the child. No hint of blame should be placed on the child as the victim did not do anything bad or dirty.

Although it will be difficult, parents of child victims must remain calm in the presence of the child. A parent's reaction will be quickly perceived by the child and, if the child feels rejected, the adjustment will be prolonged. If the parents seem angry, the child may assume that it is they who have caused this anger because "Mommy and Daddy told me not to get in a car with people I didn't know, and that's what I did and now they're mad because I disobeyed them." Children perceive emotions and reactions in a different manner from adults and in a very difficult situation, such as molestation, the child may arrive at conclusions that are incorrect.

Maintaining a calm atmosphere is not an easy task; therefore, parents require a great deal of moral support. When first responders reassure the parent, both the parent and child will benefit since the parent's reactions will affect the child.

PERSONAL REACTIONS

Reactions to this crime vary as the victim comes in contact with different people. The reaction to a loved one may be very different from that of a law enforcement officer or paramedic. Family and friends may tend to blame the victim for putting herself in a "questionable" position. Remarks such as "I told you not to dress like that" or "I knew you'd get into trouble if you went out with that crowd" are made as a result of frustration and inability to help in this situation.

SUMMARY

In the crime of rape, control is taken from the victim. In order to restore control, it is essential that no one pressure the victim to make decisions. A degrading, humiliating crime has been committed against the will of the victim. Moral support during the adjustment that now takes place is necessary. It will not be an easy task to restore confidence in herself or in others. While the victim cannot foresee the various phases of rape trauma that are natural reactions to such a crisis, those who have had experience with this crime can see the problems. Gradually care and treatment are improving, thereby improving the quality of support needed by the victim. This is a highly specialized field and requires specially-trained personnel. There is an art to listening, and victims' self-esteem can be enhanced by one who listens well. The team approach to this crime produces excellent moral support which is vital to a satisfactory resolution of rape trauma.

RECOMMENDED READINGS

Burgess A, Groth J, Holstrom L, Sgior S: Sexual Assault of Children and Adolescents. Lexington, MA; Lexington Books, D.C. Heath and Co., 1978

Burgess A, Holstrom L: Rape trauma syndrome. American Journal of Psychiatry, September 1974

Hunt G: Continuing Education. Treatment of Rape Victims, March 1978

Information Pamphlet No. 12: Rape: The Crime and Its Prevention. Office of the Attorney General Crime Prevention Unit, October 1978

Interviewing the Child Sex Crime Victim. International Association of Chiefs of Police, 1975

15 CONSIDERATIONS AND INTERVENTION WITH FAMILIES OF SEXUAL ABUSE

Carmen Germaine Warner, RN, PHN

First responders are seeing an increasing amount of people who are victims of abusive behavior. With the uncovering of a large number of adult rape and sexual assault victims has come the awareness that numerous children are victims of this same trauma. A compounding issue is that sexual abuse includes not only cases of child molestation but incest also. As professionals have gained a greater working knowledge of the problem, they have begun to develop intervention networks geared toward the child, the siblings, and the parents as well. It becomes essential to deal with the entire family as the entire system is affected in sexual abuse cases.

RECOGNIZING THE PROBLEM

First responders may occasionally see children whose chief complaint is openly identified as sexual abuse. However, in the majority of instances the abuse is only detected when the first responder experiences a strong degree of suspicion. According to Rosenfeld, there are four categories which lead to specific identification of the problem. They are: (1) genital difficulties, (2) common childhood problems, (3) alterations in behavior, and (4) acting out behavior.[1]

Sexual abuse, even with evidence of genital injuries, irritations or discharge, may be overlooked or dismissed as a possible cause. Only when there is evidence of venereal disease do professionals receive a clear-cut signal as to the problem. To clarify this point, Branch and Paxton record that the incidence of gonorrhea in children aged one to nine years is increasing and is proven to be caused by sexual contact.[2]

Consideration of common childhood problems and alterations in behavior are outlined in Chapter Seven. These changes should be understood and used as supportive data throughout the questioning and interview process in an attempt to facilitate proper problem identification. Along with behavioral difficulties is the need to understand normal child development. This serves as an excellent comparative base for assessing problems.

Behavioral changes of an acting-out nature are frequently noted in adolescents who have been abused sexually. Specific indicators of this problem include running away, drug and alcohol abuse, suicide attempts, sexual acting out, intense fears regarding sexual activity, and teenage pregnancy.

When sexual abuse is suspected, first responders should secure appropriate incident-related information and initiate appropriate referrals. Because of the sensitivity of the problem, the family is placed in an uncertain and frightening imbalance and must be directed to persons with extensive knowledge about sexual abuse.

Disclosure has created great stress in the family, and the need to close ranks becomes quickly apparent. The ensuing pressure is witnessed by verbal and nonverbal attempts to re-establish family harmony.[3]

First responders should utilize conversation such as, "I recognize this is difficult for you to talk about, but you are doing the right thing," or "You do not have to live with these fears."

These opening indications of understanding will make it easier for others to assume and continue the intervention process. Recognize that the transition period between first responders and medical or counseling professions is difficult. There are several major considerations regarding initial intervention which will make this transition easier. They include:

Self-esteem: Each family member has frequently experienced times of feeling ashamed, put-down, or exploited. It is critical that each family member be helped to regain a positive sense of self-worth and self-love.

Family role identification: Existing roles have been confused. The redefinition of an individual member's responsibilities is important in re-establishing open communication.

Sex education: Minimal or no previous understanding regarding physical maturation and body functions is a frequent accompanying situation. Honest, open communication about sexuality will alleviate some of the existing anxieties.

Basic skills in assertion: Although difficult for individuals with minimal self-esteem, it is helpful for family members to be guided in learning how to protect what they feel is theirs.

INITIAL INTERVENTION CONSIDERATIONS

The child may be overwhelmed with all the confusion of strangers, anxious family members, and personal feelings of guilt and fear. In an attempt to minimize the trauma, there are several considerations which should be followed by all first responders:

- Demonstrate an attitude of concern for the child's physical and emotional well-being.
- Do not question anything the child may tell you, recognizing that a doubting attitude will result in withdrawal.
- Initiate contact with appropriate medical personnel.
- Provide support and assurance that the child is okay and will be safe.
- Answer any questions the child might have openly and honestly, but do not pressure the child to communicate if he or she chooses not to.
- Never appear surprised, disgusted, or angry.
- Respect the privacy of the child by not permitting multiple interviews or questions.

ONGOING MANAGEMENT AND INTERVENTION

As first responders proceed into the interview process, it is of ultimate importance to remain calm, thoughtful, and gentle, although constantly maintaining a professional attitude. The appropriate level of language must be spoken at all times so the child will not be confused with unfamiliar terminology. Questioning the parents regarding the child's vocabulary is in order.

The ultimate goal, according to Leaman, is to resolve all feelings about the abusive event so that family functioning may return to normal as quickly as possible.[4]

In an attempt to achieve this level of functioning, the following steps should be initiated.

- Interview family members and the child separately. The child is easily influenced in his or her answer when parents are present.
- Indicate openly your awareness of the nature of the abuse both in molestation and incestuous cases. This will reduce the potential for denial.
- Identify the need for medical attention and explain the specifics of the necessary procedures.
- Assist parents in understanding that their reactions will strongly influence those of the child.
- Stress the importance of returning the home life to normal as quickly as possible.

- Encourage parents to communicate their feelings on the abuse.
- Assist in identifying various social, medical, public health, and legal services for both child and family members.
- Document accurately all the results of your initial interview.

Detailed initial interviews and treatment evaluations focusing on the specifics of the incident itself, the child's living patterns, the parents' personal history, and intrafamily relationships are not the role of the first responder. This usually occurs throughout the next intervention steps. Significant importance does rest in the first responder's role of careful evaluation of such things as: (1) parent/child interaction, (2) the emotional status and defenses of the parents, (3) the overall quality of family relationships, and (4) the quality of the family members' self-evaluation. These data will be helpful *if* passed on to those continuing the evaluation and intervention process.

CONSIDERATIONS OF SIBLINGS AND PARENTS

Interaction with Siblings

The effect of sexual abuse on siblings, although uninvolved in the encounter, may easily be overlooked. It is crucial that they be included in the evaluation process to the degree that it will benefit them. It is likely that siblings ten years old and older have at least a subconscious knowledge of the abusive incident or relationship. Parents may deny this awareness, but this is primarily in an attempt to establish a family rule of silence.

In reiteration of the ultimate goal to restore family functioning, the chronological age and the developmental level of each sibling should be assessed in determining the degree of involvement necessary. The type of questions frequently asked a sibling relate to such topics as:

- Their ages.
- Sleeping accommodations for all children.
- Existence of role reversals between siblings and parents, or siblings and victim.
- Means of demonstrating family affection.
- Interaction among siblings.
- Sibling and victim's interaction with relatives outside the immediate family, should molestation be suspected.

- Assessment of sibling and victim's level of interaction with little-known friends of the family or strangers.

Interaction with Parents

Specific interviews with parents or relatives are of two basic types. One is to assess the situation and determine the validity of the allegation. The second is for evaluating the type of intervention deemed necessary.

Assessment of the Situation

Whether the case is child molestation or family sexual abuse, it is important for the father or the alleged perpetrator, if known to the family, to be in the presence of a social worker during the interview. This is a very difficult and trying time. Whatever mechanisms are available for enhancing self-esteem and assisting the accused to be amenable to treatment are strongly encouraged.

The accused should never be made to feel that they are not accepted, even if their behavior is in question. One essential aspect that must be kept under the control of the interviewer is allowing no room for denial. The accused should be clearly aware of the allegations and should be informed of his legal rights.

The interview with the mother is established on the foundation of providing adequate protection for the child. From the start, the mother must provide support and attempt to ease any feelings of guilt within the child. Blaming the child for the incident, whether it occurred inside or outside the family, can create an enormous barrier against family resolution.

Assessment for Intervention

The intervention interview is geared primarily toward assessing the type of referral treatment deemed necessary. According to Gottlieb, some of the items to be addressed include:[5]

- Evaluate each parent's personal history.
  1. What was the relationship with their own parents?
  2. What type of affection did they receive as children from their parents?

3. What methods of discipline did they experience as a child?

- Identify what each parent did for fun and what their work was.
- Outline the parents' personal feelings with their own siblings.
- Note any losses, separation, or traumatic events in their lives.
- Identify past sexual experiences.
  1. When they learned about sex.
  2. From whom.
  3. What type of sexual experiences did they have?
- Outline the feelings each parent had toward the same *and* the opposite sex.
  1. Do they have close friends of the same or opposite sex?
  2. What activities do they share with members of the same or opposite sex?
- Clarify how each parent deals with frustration, anger, joy, and sadness.
- Identify the marital history.
  1. How they met.
  2. When they married.
  3. Likes and dislikes about the spouse at time of marriage.
  4. Likes and dislikes about the spouse now.
  5. What communication skills are used in the family?
  6. What feelings exist about their sexual relations.
- Question the friends each parent had or has.
  1. Did each parent have few or many friends while growing up?
  2. Were friendships close?
  3. What was the quality of the friendship?
- How does each parent feel about him or herself?
  1. Do they like or dislike themselves?
  2. What would they change about themselves?
  3. What is their level of self-esteem?
- Clarify each parent's view of the child victim.
  1. Do they perceive the child as basically good or bad?
  2. Can they identify the child's likes and dislikes?
  3. How does each parent view their spouse's relationship with the child?
- Analyze the parents' view of parenting.
  1. What are their roles and responsibilities?
  2. Do they feel this child is difficult to parent?

These two assessment components of the initial interview can gather valuable information at a time when data are not greatly affected by fears, guilt, hostility, or withdrawal. The greater the period of time which elapses between the abuse action and actual intervention, the less chance there is of developing a sense of trust and a working communication base.

SUMMARY

Specific intervention techniques will vary based on departmental protocols and policies. Despite these variances, a common thread of nonjudgmental, open, supportive attitudes is a necessary first step for all first responders regardless of personal beliefs. Unless this support is provided, one is at risk of jeopardizing the family's reception toward initial and ongoing intervention.

REFERENCES

1. Rosenfeld AA: The clinical management of incest and sexual abuse of children. JAMA 242:16, October 19, 1979; p. 1761
2. Branch G, Paxton R: A study of gonococceal infections among infants and children. Public Health Representative, No. 80, 1965, pp. 347-352
3. Gottlieb B: Incest: Therapeutic intervention in a unique form of sexual abuse. *In* Warner CG (ed): Rape and Sexual Assault: Management and Intervention. Germantown, MD; Aspen Systems Corporation, 1980, Chapter 9
4. Leaman K: The sexually abused child. Nursing 77, May 1977, p. 70
5. Gottlieb B: Incest: Therapeutic intervention in a unique form of sexual abuse. *In* Warner CG (ed): Rape and Sexual Assault: Management and Intervention. Germantown, MD; Aspen Systems Corporation, 1980

16 SUICIDE INTERVENTION FOR FIRST RESPONDERS

Drew Leavens, MA

A tragedy occurred recently in San Diego. It was one similar to many that happen yearly in the United States. A young mother of two was despondent because she had been evicted from her apartment. She was on welfare and knew from experience that rentals for single parents on welfare were difficult to obtain. She did have some resources available to her; mainly, a gift of 500 dollars from her parents. With this money she arranged to charter a helicopter. While on the flight, she asked the pilot to increase his altitude from 500 to 2000 feet. When he leveled the craft at the higher altitude, the pilot turned and watched helplessly as his passenger climbed out and jumped from the helicopter. Later, during the investigation, several notes were found by her telephone which listed and compared the prices of various air charter services. Unfortunately, nobody recognized this, or other clues, which may have prevented her suicide until it was too late.

Suicide is a major health concern in the United States today. For adults, it is the tenth leading cause of death.[1] However, among adolescents, suicide is second only to accidents as the highest cause of death.[1] It is believed that for every suicide there are about ten unsuccessful suicide attempts.[2] Based on that ratio, it is estimated that between one-quarter and one-half million Americans will experience a suicidal crisis this year.[2] About 30,000 people will take their own lives during this time (see Table 16.1).[3]

Table 16.1. Suicide in the United States.[3]

YEAR	NUMBER OF SUICIDES	SUICIDE RATE*
1977	28,681	13.3
1970	23,480	11.6
1960	19,041	10.6

*Suicide rates represent the ratio between the number of people who commit per every 100,000 population.

This figure is considered conservative because statistics underestimate the extent of the problem. One reason for this is that suicide is still considered to be a societal taboo. Some survivors feel guilt or embarrassment when suicide is listed as the cause of death. This stigma, coupled with the possible loss of insurance monies, often causes survivors to put considerable pressure on coroners to establish another cause of death. One coroner in a southern state disclosed that he would not list suicide as a cause of death unless a suicide note was found. Due to reasons such as these, the number of cases reported will inevitably be lower than the actual number of suicides committed.

In a potential or actual suicide situation there are many possible first responders. The focus here, however, will be on those normally called upon to save lives, such as policemen, firemen, paramedics, nurses, and crisis workers. There are also many informal first responders like the beautician, bartender, the teacher, and others who often learn of another's despondent feelings through casual communication. These informal contacts can be very important and especially beneficial if the despondent person is able to confide in someone and discharge some feelings. If, after contact with this type of first responder, the individual in crisis can be helped into the community health care system it is possible that many serious crises could be averted.

CHARACTERISTICS OF A SUICIDAL CRISIS

People who are feeling suicidal are usually in crisis. A crisis state, according to Gerald Caplan, is a "disorganization of homeostasis . . . which cannot be solved quickly by the individual's normal range of problem solving mechanisms."[4] In other words, the individual becomes overloaded and unable to process current stressful stimuli by previously learned coping methods. Crises are also time-limited. Something must change to resolve the stress of a crisis state. It is this desire to change on the part of the individual that causes him or her to seek help. Additionally, once a therapeutic contact is made, the person in crisis is usually more motivated to do what is necessary to work through the crisis and re-establish equilibrium in his or her life.

Communication with significant others is often difficult when one is in crisis. A suicidal crisis can be instigated by stresses or other crises in a person's life. What may have been started by a lost job can turn into an internal dialogue questioning ones own self-worth. Prolonged, the person's thoughts may turn to suicide. The individual often feels guilty and embarrassed by such feelings but still attempts to communicate them with others. If this communication is not well received, the suicidal person may feel a growing sense of isolation and despair. The individual may then make a suicide gesture in an attempt to communicate his or her feelings and as a call for help. Through all of this, the original feelings of inadequacy over the lost job are hidden, and the suicidal crisis has taken on an identity of its own. Communication is an important factor in all phases of a suicidal crises and its intervention.

Another characteristic of a suicidal crisis is the concept of ambivalence. Ambivalence is the conflict between the suicidal person's will to live and his or her urge to die. The individual might be feeling intolerable pain and see death as the only way out. Yet there may still be hope that his or her situation will improve. Ambivalence can be readily seen in examples of (1) a man who calls a crisis center saying he wants to talk to a counselor before he kills himself, and (2) a woman who calls a hospital after she has taken a lethal dose of sleeping pills.

It would be rare for a first responder to intervene in a suicidal situation with an individual who is not ambivalent. A person who is no longer in a suicidal crisis, or has completed an act of suicide, is not ambivalent. The first responder, however, will work with potential victims who are in crisis and are ambivalent about future actions. In performing suicide intervention, it is essential to recognize and work with the potential victim's ambivalence about dying. It is this undecidedness on the part of the client which makes a suicide intervention possible. Since people have a greater will to live than to die, the worker can ally him or herself to that will and offer hope for the future.

PRECIPITATING FACTORS

Why do people try to kill themselves? Do they really want to die? Although there are exceptions, for the most part the answer is no. Persons who have been revived from unsuccessful suicide attempts appear to feel relief at having failed. If this is so, then why are these attempts made in the first place?

People attempt suicide for many reasons. One of the most common is in an attempt to relieve intolerable pain and suffering. Such pain can originate from real or imagined sources and vary in how it is perceived from one person to the next. Among stimuli causing the greatest pain are losses of any kind and debilitating physical or emotional problems. One woman with a history of emotional problems called a crisis center and reported wanting to "open her veins to let the pain out."

Some suicide attempts are manipulative in nature rather than a sincere desire to die. Such attempts often stem from relationship problems with significant others. One partner, fearing a possible separation or divorce may attempt suicide in a manipulative effort aimed at controlling the other. This can be seen especially in situations where one party is extremely angry at the other but knows that the anger will only further alienate the love partner. At this point, the angry party takes the "acceptable" action of turning the anger inward and making a suicide gesture. Again, the object of such actions is to express feelings and to manipulate the other. Individuals have been known to call crisis centers and say, "Would you call my wife and tell her I'm going to kill myself if she doesn't come back to me?"

Suicide might also be intended as a "cry for help." The individual is unable to communicate certain feelings until those feelings build to a breaking point. A suicide attempt may then be made to communicate those feelings. This type of suicidal gesture is rarely an actual wish to die as much as an attempt toward communicating feelings that appear too intense to verbalize. These suicide gestures may come in the form of superficial wounds to the wrist, ingestion of small amounts of drugs, or can occasionally be more serious. Upon recovery, it is essential that the problems be dealt with and resolved in order to avoid recurrence.

Individual Responses to Crises

People experience a broad range of emotional crises throughout their lives. They must cope with the deaths of loved ones, personal failures, rejections, poor health, loss of jobs or status, and a myriad of other similar situations. Many people have thought about committing suicide at a critical point in their life. Some may have put these thoughts into action by making some type of suicidal gesture. For most, the crisis that brought on these thoughts or actions was integrated and everyday life was resumed. For others, such problems go unresolved and resurface with each new crisis that is experienced. In her book, *Addicted to Suicide*, Mary Savage elucidates this point—"I lived there for four years, and I remember those years as the happiest of my life. I tried suicide only once . . . "[5]

While people possess many similarities in their responses to a particular crisis event, the way in which they integrate that experience into their life is very individualized. Cultural, ethnic, religious, family, and social interactions all influence and shape attitudes and belief systems that will be tested later. These past experiences, both joyful and traumatic, will dictate how a person will act or cope with future crisis provoking events.

Optimally, every crisis event should be coped with, resolved, and integrated into one's life experience. To be free of the effects of either a present or past crisis situation, the individual, at some point in his or her life must face it, resolve it, and see it in perspective within his or her present life. If this does not occur, it is likely that a person will find a maladaptive way of coping with the crisis. An example of a maladaptive response is an older woman who contacted a crisis center after an air disaster in Southern California in 1978 in which an entire planeload of passengers lost their lives. Her husband had served as a fighter pilot in World War II and had been killed some 30 years prior to the 1978 disaster. When she called the crisis center, it was her husband's death she wanted to talk about as that was what she was despondent about, not the present airline disaster. For her, the 1978 crash made her finally come to grips with the realities of her husband's death. Although this woman had been able to cope with her husband's death, she was never able to accept or resolve it.

There is no typical suicide-prone person. Everyone is exposed to the various life crises mentioned previously to a varying degree. The person who would choose suicide is generally one who can not cope with a present crisis or a long term accumulation of upsetting life events. In fact, it has been said that suicide is one of the few things in life that is truly democratic. It takes its toll among the rich, poor, educated, laborer, Christian, Jew, atheist, every ethnic group, male, female, those of all ages, and persons with every type of physical characteristic. There are the Marilyn Monroes, and the Freddie Prinzes as well as the anonymous derelict in the alley who has only a John Doe on his death certificate. A common factor among all appears to be whether or not the individual has either an innate or acquired ability to cope. The individual who does not, will likely consider suicide as a response to crisis situations. In "Suicidal Survival," Mary Savage writes, "Suicide is a protest to the pain of living, and I believe that the process of living is more painful for some than others; their thresholds are lower."[6]

EARLY WARNING SIGNS

Suicide is rarely an impulsive act. More often it is a response to an accumulation of pressure, stress, and pain. Those around eventual victims, such as family, friends, nurses, and therapists usually receive indications of what the individual is feeling. Warning signals often go unnoticed or are brushed off. In a family situation, for example, a wife may feel threatened if her husband communicates feelings of depression or insecurity. She might deny his feelings with statements such as "Everything will be OK" or "You couldn't really feel that bad." This lack of acceptance or understanding will further the feelings of isolation, despair, and hopelessness which can lead to suicide. Interveners must be aware of these feelings and other warning signs in order to respond appropriately.

The following are early warning signs to look for: (1) Verbal Communicated Intent, (2) Nonverbal Communicated Intent, and (3) Sudden Changes in Behavior.

(1) *Verbal Communicated Intent*—The need to communicate one's plight is often quite strong in a suicidal crisis. Eighty percent of the persons who have committed suicide have clearly communicated their intentions to other people.[7] Some do this in a straight-forward way by saying, "I just want to die" or "I think I'll just kill myself." Most lay people and many professionals do not know how to respond to such statements. The response is often one of denial, "You don't really want to die" or "Things can't be that bad." Some will overreact and become upset to the point that they are of little use to their clients or friends.

Suicidal feelings are more frequently verbally communicated in a less direct manner. Statements are made which reflect a helpless, hopeless, and isolated state which the individual is experiencing. It is important to recognize the lack of hope and despair even though the suicidal person may not vocalize these feelings directly. One might hear, "I've always been a failure" or "I've tried everything and things don't get better, what's the use?" An example which clarifies this point further is about an Arizona man. Sitting in his home he told his son, "Son, I'm going home." The son replied, " But, Dad, you are at home." Two days later the father was found hanging from a rope in the basement of his house.[8] The father's statements were verbal clues that suggested he was considering suicide.

Another illustration of a suicidal person who communicated intent was actor, Freddie Prinz. Most survivors were aware of his depressed state of mind, his repeated talk of suicide, and the fact that he kept a loaded gun. To many it came as no surprise when he actually did kill himself.

(2) *Nonverbal Communicated Intent*—Some potential suicides give clues of their intentions through their actions. Nonverbal warning signs are more difficult to recognize than verbal messages because, taken out of context, they appear to be normal in nature. It is only when matched up against previous behavior that such actions appear odd. Some examples are taking out large insurance policies, filling out or changing wills, purchasing a gun or ammunition, giving away prized possessions, and closing bank accounts. These acts may be suspect especially if accompanied with other warning signs.

Another example of this more passive means of communication, and one which may be overlooked initially, is the suicide note. While such notes provide little comfort after the fact, they are occasionally found before the suicide attempt takes place. As with all suicide related communication, the note should be taken seriously and acted upon. About one-fourth of all suicide victims leave some type of note or message."[9]

(3) *Sudden Changes in Behavior*—Sudden changes in behavior should be viewed suspiciously if accompanied by other warning signs. A sudden increase in drug or alcohol consumption may be indicative of growing inner turmoil. A normally placid person might become quick tempered and easily irritable. As the result of a crisis, an outgoing individual might appear unduly and inappropriately depressed and withdraw from those around him or her. In each situation these might be understandable behavior changes. However, if such behavior persists beyond those limits it can serve as an early warning sign to a possible suicide. Therefore, it is important that an individual's past standard of behavior be examined when evaluating the meaning of these sudden behavioral changes.

Another interesting phenomenon has been observed by survivors of suicide victims. In certain cases, the potential victim, depressed and in turmoil for a period of time, decides in his or her own mind to go ahead and commit suicide. Once this decision is made, the ambivalence around the conflict between life and death dissipates. At this point many eventual victims show relief as if their problems have suddenly gone away. Those associated with the victim often remark at this sudden improvement and are grateful that the victim has seemingly resolved his or her difficulties. Then, with what seems to be no "warning," the victim commits suicide. In this type of situation it is the calm *after* the storm that one should be suspicious of.

Assessing Suicide Potential

When first responders are confronted with a possible suicidal client, they must assess the individual's suicide potential. Calling a person suicidal is somewhat a misnomer in that it implies that all persons so-named are in equal danger or risk to themselves. Actually, suicidal persons vary in lethal potentiality from minimal to highly serious, and each person requires individual evaluation.[4] The main goal of the assessment is to be able to decide what degree of risk one should ascribe to the potential victim. The first responder needs solid critieria for assessing the situation in order to prevent decisions from becoming arbitrary or emotional.

Some procedures for understanding and evaluating suicide potential have changed recently. Health care professionals used to evaluate suicide risk by putting great emphasis on the age and sex of the potential victim. If, for example, the client was a middle-aged man, one would immediately assume him to be high risk. Statistics have reinforced that assumption. Men commit suicide two to four times as often as women depending on the year and age group (see Table 16.2). Additionally, men over 50 have consistently had the highest suicide rates. Knowing the age and sex of high risk groups will be helpful but it is not always the most reliable indicator of suicide risk. Age and sex must be placed in context with other criteria. The following section explains these criteria.

Table 16.2. Male Versus Female Suicide.[3]

YEAR	MALE SUICIDES	MALE RATE*	FEMALE SUICIDES	FEMALE RATE*
1977	21,109	20.1	7,572	6.8
1970	16,629	16.8	6,851	6.6
1960	14,539	16.5	4,502	4.9

*Suicide rates represent the ratio between the number of people who commit per every 100,000 population.

Criteria which should be considered by the health care professional when assessing the potential suicide are as follows:

1. The Suicide Plan
2. Attitude of Hopelessness–Helplessness
3. History of emotional and/or physical problems
4. Age–Sex
5. Presence of stress
6. Availability of Support Systems

(1). **The Suicide Plan.** The plan is one of the most reliable determiners of lethality. According to the Los Angeles Suicide Prevention Center, there are three main components of a suicide plan which provide the basis for assessment. They are: (A) the lethality of the proposed method, (B) the availability of the means, and (C) the specificity of the details.[4]

A method is highly lethal when it has the potential to cause immediate death. A plan that involves a gun, jumping, getting into an automobile accident, or hanging, is of greater risk than a plan relying on pills or wrist slashing. Use of pills is an example of a less lethal method in that death is not immediate and allows for the possibility of being rescued before death.

Once the proposed method of suicide is discovered, the responder must know whether the individual has the means at hand to follow through. If the individual talks of shooting himself or herself, the responder should find out if he or she has a gun and/or ammunition. Those who have procured the means for their proposed method are at greater risk than those who have not.

Persons whose suicidal plans are well thought out and specific in nature will be of higher risk than those whose plans are sketchy. If the individual has taken care of specific details such as taking out an insurance policy, giving away prized possessions, buying a gun, and setting a time for killing himself or herself, then the degree of suicide risk would be rated high. A plan that seems spontaneous or impulsive in nature, would be categorized as less risk.

(2). **Attitude of Hopelessness–Helplessness.** This determiner is helpful, but a less tangible indicator of lethality than the suicide plan. People who feel hopeless and helpless about their situation will make statements such as, "I've tried everything and nothing worked," and, "What's the use; nobody cares anyway." A person may try to improve his or her life only to find that, with each failure, comes a reduction in self-esteem which can lead to feelings of hopelessness. Hope for the future is a necessary motivating force among people. When individuals are feeling hopeless, their desire to live wanes. Persons having chronic physical and/or emotional problems may be especially prone to feelings of hopelessness.

(3). *History of Emotional and/or Physical Problems.* A knowledge of certain areas of the client's past is essential in making an assessment. As already stated, persons with chronic emotional and/or physical problems are more likely to attempt and commit suicide. Mental illness, as diagnosed by a physician, was the second leading reason for suicide in San Diego County according to a six-year study by the coroner's office. Additionally, a history of previous suicide attempts increases the chances that an individual will commit suicide. "Twenty percent of those who attempt suicide will repeat the behavior and each subsequent attempt tends to be more lethal."[9] Poor physical health, on the other hand, was the primary reason for suicide according to the same study. A long term physical health problem can lead to poor self-image and the hopeless feelings found in many suicide deaths. Knowing that a client has previously attempted suicide or has a chronic physical or mental health condition must add to the risk factor.

(4). *Age–Sex.* Age can be a helpful adjunct in suicide assessment. First, statistics help identify trends and current high risk groups. Second, within certain age groups there are factors which contribute to the incidence of suicide within that group. A knowledge of these factors and statistics relating to age groups is important to the first responder when attempting to assess the lethality of the individual (see Tables 16.3 and 16.4).

As mentioned previously, middle aged men (40 to 60) have committed the highest number of suicides and consistently have had the highest suicide rates.[3] Recently there has been a dramatic rise in the number of suicides among young adults (20 to 24). Since 1960, the suicide rate in this age group has more than doubled, while the total number of suicides is nearly five times greater.[3] Although the suicide rates for the 20 to 24 year age group are now close to those of other age groups, the total number of suicides is much higher than other age groups due to the high number of young adults in the population.

There are certain factors which relate to the problems associated with each age group. One study has shown, for instance, that suicide among young children under the age of 11 centers around the actual or fantasized loss of a same sex parent and the wish of the youngster to join the parent in an after-life.[2] Evidence from the same study indicates that in children up to age 15, as many as one-half of eventual suicide victims may have been diagnosed as having a learning disability such as hyperactivity or dyslexia.[2]

Table 16.3. Numbers of Suicide by Five-Year Age Groups.[3]

YEAR	10-14	15-19	20-24	25-29	30-34	35-39	40-44	45-49	50-54	55-59	60-64	65-69	70-74	75-79
1977	188	1871	3694	3272	2555	2044	1911	2163	2254	2133	1818	1615	1316	914
1975	170	1594	3142	2784	2257	1875	2075	2345	2421	2171	1792	1562	1167	849
1970	130	1123	2005	1880	1636	1768	2129	2359	2279	2186	1798	1427	1158	772
1965	103	685	1191	1268	1453	1888	2176	2143	2411	2259	1783	1405	1120	866
1960	90	475	764	983	11301	1649	1767	2077	2173	1993	1697	1337	1187	834

Table 16.4. Suicide Rates By Five-Year Age Groups.[3]

YEAR	10-14	15-19	20-24	25-29	30-34	35-39	40-44	45-49	50-54	55-59	60-64	65-69	70-74	75-79
1977	1.0	8.9	18.6	18.6	16.6	16.6	17.1	18.8	19.0	19.3	19.4	19.1	21.4	22.5
1975	0.8	7.6	16.5	16.5	16.2	16.2	18.6	19.9	20.2	20.6	19.4	19.3	20.2	21.2
1970	0.6	5.9	12.2	13.9	14.3	15.9	17.8	19.5	20.5	21.9	20.9	20.4	21.3	20.1
1965	0.5	4.9	8.9	11.3	13.2	15.8	17.6	18.9	23.1	23.7	23.5	21.5	21.0	24.7
1960	0.5	3.6	7.1	9.0	10.9	13.2	15.2	19.1	22.6	23.6	23.8	21.4	25.0	27.3

The factors and personality characteristics associated with young adult suicides, 19 to 25, include loneliness, isolation, and the lack of meaningful relationships with peers and parents. Among the elderly there are two dominant contributing factors for suicide. These are chronic or debilitating health problems and vital losses such as a spouse or job.[10]

The sex of a person has been given less emphasis as an assessment tool although it remains a factor to be considered. Men complete suicide about three times as often as women although women attempt suicide three times as often as men.[2] This is possibly due to cultural conditioning in which men, in general, are less likely to disclose their feelings directly. It is this capping of feelings, however, which escalates their sense of isolation and alienation toward others. Men who are experiencing severe depression and anxiety may have suicidal thoughts underneath. This possibility should not be underestimated, especially when other warning signs are present.

Women tend to be more expressive with their feelings and the expression of their emotions is more readily accepted by others. Possibly because of this, many women will reach out to family, friends, or other support systems when in crisis. By these actions, they can often dilute the crisis before it reaches more serious proportions.

(5). *Presence of Stress.* When assessing a potential suicide it is necessary to know how much stress the person is experiencing and how it affects his or her current life situation. Stress may be related to certain life development stages such as puberty, moving away from home, getting started in a career, starting a family and later in life, retirement and menopause. Stress can also result from situational crises like natural disasters, death of loved ones, marital problems, and so on. Positive life events, such as having children, graduating, or moving to a new town also produce stress. In reacting to the stress, the individual may be feeling any of a multitude of symptoms. Resulting from these symptoms are a variety of related problems, such as loss of appetite, sleep disorders, social withdrawal, apathy, and despondency.[4] These symptoms of stress need to be taken into account by the responder when the initial contact is made. The responder should also find out why the individual is seeking help at that time. In doing so, he or she can get an idea of what is causing the stress that the person is reacting to.

(6). *Availability of Support Systems.* A support system is something an individual can fall back on in time of need. This may be personal in nature such as a spouse, family member, or friend. It could also be in the form of community oriented services, such as 24-hour telephone crisis lines, outreach teams, and mental health evaluation and outpatient services. Crises seem to occur most often after 5 P.M. and on weekends, and it is essential that communities have services available during those times. Many people in crisis do not have adequate support systems to help diffuse their crisis situation. In addition to evaluation of an individual's personal support system, it is the responsibility of the first responder to know what resources are available in a community at any given time. For example, a worker in a crisis intervention service contacted an ambulance to transport a suicidal client to the hospital. When the man arrived at the hospital he was informed that the psychiatric unit was full and he would have to wait until a psychiatrist could be summoned. This made an already difficult situation even more frustrating. If the crisis worker had contacted the hospital initially, then other alternatives could have been explored with the client.

Intervention with Potential Victims

How does one approach potential victims? What are the necessary questions to ask? How is the seriousness of the situation determined? The following four-step intervention guideline should provide a framework for interaction with potential victims. The four steps are:

1. Establishing a trusting relationship
2. Obtaining specific information
3. Making an assessment
4. Forming a plan of action

(1). *Establishing a Trusting Relationship.* This is probably the most important step in crisis intervention counseling with potential suicide victims. Unless the worker is able to gain rapport, other intervention techniques will likely be futile. Rapport is the establishment of a trusting, sympathetic relationship. Most first responders have the ability to gain rapport with clients because they care and are concerned about those with whom they work. Often a relaxed and confident approach will be enough to bridge the gap between the helper and client.

The technique for gaining rapport centers on the use of active, reflective, and empathic listening skills. Because the potential victim is often feeling isolated and withdrawn, being heard by the responder can be very therapeutic. Permitting a client to vent feelings will often diffuse the tension and anxiety from a crisis situation. It is important that the intervener transmit this willingness to really listen to the client.

While the client is talking, the responder should provide active verbal and nonverbal reinforcement. Verbal reinforcement should come in the form of single words and short phrases like, "uh-huhs," "yes," "I understand" and "I hear you." This type of response is especially important when working with a client over the telephone. When making an in-person contact, nonverbal clues are equally important. Actions such as nods, smiles, and eye contact can be very reassuring to the client. Also, certain types of body language such as being on the same physical level as the client or an occasional comforting physical touch can be helpful rapport builders. By the responder's actions, it is hoped that the client will begin to feel the trust necessary for further crisis work to take place.

While listening actively the first responder should be asking him or herself, "What is really being said here?" or "What are the feelings behind those words?" For instance, a statement like "Nothing ever works out for me" might be summed up and reflected back to the client as "It sounds like you are feeling hopeless." When the worker identifies the feelings among the client's words, these feelings should be fed back to the client for clarification. This feedback should take the form of an explicit observation such as "You sound upset, depressed, angry" or "You look sad." The object here is to try to help the client identify and clarify what he or she is feeling. If the worker is wrong in identifying the feeling, the client may correct him. For example, in response to the hopeless nature of statements made by a client, a worker inquires, "Are you thinking about suicide?" If the answer is "Yes," then lines of communication open up as the client begins to talk about this sensitive area.[7] The responder should not worry about planting the idea of suicide in a person's mind. If the person has not thought about it, it is probably not an action he or she would consider. If the client is not suicidal, he or she clarifies the situation and the rapport is not lost. The client is shown that the worker is willing to talk about even the most threatening of subjects.

When the worker identifies the client's feelings correctly, he or she should make an empathic statement about those feelings. Empathic listening means that one is able to understand and identify with the feelings of another. An empathic response might be, "I can understand how you might feel that way" or "I can see why you might feel jealous and hurt." Such responses help the client to feel that the worker is an ally and can be trusted. It is this trust and acceptance which is essential in establishing the desired rapport.

Additional factors in building this relationship would be for the worker to project an accepting and nonjudgmental attitude. The suicidal individual is probably feeling isolated, anxious, and guilty. The worker must let him or her know it is all right and acceptable to have those feelings under the circumstances. It is equally important that the worker have the ability to accept any anger, frustration, or other negative emotions the client may express. The client must be able to vent such emotions without the worker becoming upset and taking them personally.

As mentioned previously, individuals cope with stress or crisis in different ways based on their background. Because of this it is essential that stresses which lead to suicide be viewed from the client's eyes, not from those of the crisis worker. These feelings should be validated and accepted regardless of the worker's own values. For example, avoid value statements like, "You shouldn't be so angry (sad or lonely)," but rather empathize by saying, "I understand how that would make you angry (sad or lonely)."

(2). *Obtaining Specific Information.* As the intervener gains the trust of the potential victim he or she must also gather specific information. Due to the individualized nature of a crisis response it is the responder's task to piece together the total picture of what is happening and how the suicidal individual is affected by it. For example, a paramedic must know a considerable amount of information before making medical decisions. The same process must take place when making decisions based on an individual's behavior or announced suicidal intentions. In making the behavioral assessment, there are simply different questions and criteria involved in the decision making. The information an intervener needs to know in order to make credible decisions is previously listed in the section relating to assessment. The following are some typical questions which can eventually provide the information necessary for sound decision making (see Table 16.5).

If the client is resistant to answering these questions, it is possible that rapport has not yet been established. For the most part, however, the active disclosure of personal information on the part of a client should increase the rapport if handled well by the responder. Some questions will automatically lead to others until, bit by bit, the responder is given a clear picture of the situation at hand.

Table 16.5. Questions That Will Provide Information For Assessment Criteria.

Are you thinking about suicide?
How had you thought you would kill yourself?
Do you have a gun (or other means) available?
Have you ever made a suicide attempt before?
How long have you been feeling this way?
Have you been under stress recently?
How old are you?
Are you currently seeing a therapist or counselor?
How is your work going?
How are you feeling about your family and/or spouse right now?
How are you feeling physically?

---

(3). **Assessment.** Making an assessment of the client's situation is the next part of the intervention. The first responder must determine whether the potentially suicidal individual is of a high, moderate, or low risk. All the information gathered must be evaluated. Several questions must be answered before a workable course of action can be implemented. Is the suicide plan well thought out, lethal, and imminent in nature? Has the client previously tried to commit suicide? To what degrees do other assessment factors, such as poor emotional or physical health, stress, or depression convey an overall feeling of hopelessness on the part of the client? Has the client improved in the course of the intervention with the first responder? The answers to these questions formulate a worker's assessment and provide a basis for action.

The information may indicate a situation which is high risk in nature and which requires emergency measures by law enforcement or paramedics. It may, however, be less urgent, where on-the-spot counseling and referral to an appropriate mental health program will suffice. In either case, the decision making must be based on the evaluation of the information provided. If the information received is incorrect, then it is likely that the situation will be assessed incorrectly. If the assessment is not valid, it will likely be due to a lack of or incorrect information.

It is important for the responder to know that the assessment is accurate. While there is no foolproof way to be sure of this, mistakes in judgment will be minimized when the assessment is fed back to the client and, if possible, to co-workers. The client is entitled to hear what assessment has been made and how it affects him. In fact, with the exception of certain emergency cases, the assessment should be arrived at with the client's input. Co-workers, on the other hand, can help by providing objective second opinions when dealing with high risk or emotionally draining situations.

Finally, there are many difficult situations to assess, such as persons who have been drinking, persons with chronic emotional problems, and persons who use suicidal threats to manipulate. When confronted with these situations a worker should utilize as much assessment criteria as possible. Some suicide attempters are very manipulative, and, unless the responder is able to neutralize this, he or she may be set up for a frustrating intervention. An earlier example was given of a man who called a crisis line and said, "Call my wife and tell her I'm going to kill myself unless she comes back to me." The responder should attempt to work with this kind of caller according to the intervention steps presented and evaluate his suicide potential by the criteria provided. If the caller is assessed to be of low risk, the responder might attempt to counsel him around his angry feelings, his fear of losing his wife, and/or his manipulative behavior.

When making an assessment of the suicidal situation, it may be necessary to take additional factors into account. The first factor is in regards to the potential suicide plan. Currently the predominant method of suicide among men is by violent means, such as gunshot or hanging, while the majority of women die from drug overdose. Although the use of drugs was described as a less lethal method previously, it is obviously used effectively by those intent on committing suicide. A first responder should not initially place less emphasis on a certain method until other assessment information is available.

The first responder also needs to be aware of individual differences, exceptions to the rules, and especially his or her own feelings during the process of the intervention. These feelings can be an important sixth sense in the assessment process when confirming or sending out a warning signal as the assessment is being concluded. While the assessment criteria are the essential guidelines in the decision-making process, the intevener's "gut feelings" can be an important adjunct. For example, while interviewing in a situation involving an adolescent girl, the responder learns that she is upset over recent rejection by her boyfriend. She has plans to go through her mother's medicine cabinet and find some pills. On the surface this might ordinarily sound like a low risk situation. However, the responder may feel the girl to be a serious risk by intangible factors such as the sound of her voice or the look in her eyes. In this case the responder should proceed as though it is a high risk situation until it is proven otherwise.

(4). *Forming a plan of action.* Once a situation has been assessed, a plan of action needs to be formulated. The plan is based on the client's needs derived from the assessment and on the availability of personal as well as community support systems. The type of action the first responder takes depends to a large degree on the risk factor established in the assessment.

In a high risk situation, the responders plan of action is dictated by the emergency nature of the situation. A serious suicide threat or attempt may be imminent or may have already been made. The priority in a high risk intervention is to get the client to professional medical and/or psychological services for further evaluation. Most of the decision making should be made by the responder due to the likely confused or agitated state of mind of the client. Additionally, in this situation, the worker may need to be very directive in his/her suggestions to the client. For example, a policeman may have to say "I would like to talk with you, but you must first put the gun down." Personal support systems can be utilized in high risk cases but not as the only resource. For instance, a family member or spouse might accompany the client to an Emergency Department with the responder. However, a high risk individual should rarely be placed with the family in lieu of a psychiatric and/or physical examination. Occasionally, the responder will not be sure whether a client is high risk or not and should seek other opinions (such as those of co-workers). If any doubt remains, it would be safest to have the client evaluated by a professional.

With low to moderate risk cases there is greater leeway in deciding on a plan of action. The responder may be able to link both personal and community supports into the plan. Client input is important both in making the assessment and deciding upon a workable plan. For instance, a caller to a crisis center assessed to be of moderate risk might be asked, "Do you feel that you can make it through the night?" The client's response of "No" would indicate the need for transportation to an emergency facility. However, if the client responds, "I think so" or "I'll try," then the responder might try bringing in support systems, or making a contract with the client to call the center again throughout the night if suicidal thoughts return. The responder is able to spend more time performing supportive crisis counseling and problem solving in low/medium risk cases because emergency services are not a priority. Family members may be called in to be with a client if it appears they would be able to provide additional support. The worker should then suggest that the client make an appointment with a local mental health service or private practitioner as soon as it is convenient.

Follow Up Services

The ability to provide follow up services depends largely on the resources available in the community's mental health system. A first responder has the initial responsibility to see that clients receive timely supportive counseling services. Subsequent to that, responders should facilitate the linkage of clients to professional mental health and/or medical services when necessary. When working with medium and high risk suicide cases, it is essential that the worker transfer rather than simply refer the client to needed services. Transferring of clients means that the worker provides the linkage between services and does not relinquish responsibility for the client until he or she is under the care of a qualified professional. Due to the confusion surrounding a suicidal crisis, clients do not always know or follow through with what is in their best interest. Once transferred to these services the overall care and responsibility for the client rests in the hands of that service system.

Though a first responder need not follow up beyond this point he or she can still impact the client's care. Clients have been known to enter and leave hospitals, mental health units, and other service systems with little or no resolution to their problem. This movement in and out of service delivery systems has been termed a revolving door syndrome. Many drug overdose suicide attempters are treated medically and released without receiving necessary treatment to prevent future suicide attempts. A responder can minimize this "revolving door syndrome" by asserting him or herself within the service system to assure that the client receives treatment. Mary Savage reports the treatment she received as a result of suicide attempts using drugs. "I was promptly taken to the hospital where I received an injection of caffeine and was sent home. I was saying "Help!" about something, but nobody paid any attention. Suicides are a dime a dozen in New York."[5]

When a responder transports a client to a hospital for medical attention following a suicide attempt, it is essential to request a psychiatric evaluation for that client. This will insure that the client has access to help that will set the stage for problem solving, a viable treatment plan, and an easing of the crisis. When transporting a client to a mental health facility, the responder should impart an encouraging and hopeful outlook to the client while enroute. This will be especially helpful for a client who is fearful or anxious and using such services for the first time.

Occasionally, responders will be transporting individuals who often make suicide attempts. Frustrating as this may be to the worker, he or she should continually remind the mental health facility personnel of this repetition. Such action may prompt the facility professional to take action necessary either to alleviate the crisis situation or to seek treatment alternatives. Direct communication between the first responder and medical and mental health practitioners can help impact the system on the client's behalf and reduce the incidence of "revolving door clients."

SUMMARY: A WORKING PHILOSOPHY FOR FIRST RESPONDERS

Suicide has been called a preventable death. While all workers have individual values about death, a first responder must assume a role of preventing death whenever possible. In working toward this end, the responder should avoid taking responsibility for the actions of others. Certain individuals will be successful in their suicidal efforts regardless of any action taken in their behalf. Workers will inevitably feel some guilt when this happens. They will think they could have done more. It is important to learn from such experiences rather than to assign blame or assume guilt. There may have been clues that were missed or improper intervention techniques may have been used. Examining these factors should be helpful in future prevention efforts. It would be truly self-defeating for the first responder to assume responsibility for the destructive actions taken by others.

The work performed by the first responder in the area of suicide intervention is very stressful. Important decisions must be made often under chaotic conditions. Usually there is little reward or recognition for those who perform this work day after day. It can become difficult to tell just how good a job one is doing without such positive reinforcement. The first responder must attempt to stay objective and to give credit when he or she is performing effectively. With such self-reinforcement, the first responder is able to give back to themselves and replenish the energy which is constantly being expended on others. In so doing, the first responder can continue to provide essential services consistently and with the quality that is expected of them.

REFERENCES

1. Hoff LA: People in Crisis: Understanding and Helping. Reading, MA; Addison-Wesley Publishing Co., 1978, p. 104
2. Peck ML: Understanding and preventing youth suicide. From a paper published by the Institute for Studies of Destructive Behaviors and the Suicide Prevention Center, Los Angeles, CA; p.4
3. National Center for Health Statistics, Mortality Statistics Branch, Division of Vital Statistics, Vital Statistics of the United States, Volume II Mortality Trend B and C Tables 291, 291A, 292
4. Farberow N, Heilig SM, Litman RE: Techniques in Crisis Intervention: A Training Manual. Los Angeles, Suicide Prevention Center, Inc., 1968, pp. 1, 5, 6
5. Savage M: Addicted to Suicide: A Woman Struggling to Live. Santa Barbara, CA: Capra Press, 1975, p. 19
6. Savage M: Suicidal survival. In a newsletter published by E. R. Squibb for psychiatric nurses, Volume 6, No. 4, July-August 1979, p. 1
7. Courses by Newspaper, University Extension, University of California, San Diego. Written by Edwin Shneidman appearing in San Diego Union, April 15, 1979, p. A-22
8. Suicide: Danger Signals are Subtle. An interview with Mary Miller appearing in San Diego Union, July 26, 1979, pp. B-1, B-10
9. Everything You Always Wanted to Know About Suicide. A fact sheet compiled by Mary Miller, p. 1
10. Miller M: Suicide After Sixty: The Final Alternative. New York, Springer Publishing Co., 1979, p. 7

17 INNOVATIONS IN SYSTEMS PLANNING

Carmen Germaine Warner, RN, PHN

First responders are being summoned to answer calls of social and domestic violence at a rapidly increasing rate. This is due not only to the increased number of people who are willing to report and seek professional help, but also because of the increased availability of paramedics and law enforcement specialty units who focus solely on rape and family violence incidents.

Along with this expansion of service comes the need for specialized systems planning which can address the needs of program development, service implementation, and an efficiency of service delivery.

NECESSARY CONSIDERATIONS FOR SYSTEMS PLANNING

Professionals attempting to plan for service delivery of the future must begin by developing an approach to plan making. According to Zweig and Morris, there are three steps in the plan making process:

1. Adopt a problem-focused approach to plan making.
2. Take nothing for granted regarding the target social problem.
3. View the plan as rational.[1]

In adopting a problem-focused approach to plan making, planners should first explore the nature of the problem relating to uniform services for victims of social and domestic violence.

Due to existing commonalities among victims of violence, assess whether there is a duplication of effort stemming from the current practice of separate units for each act of violence. Have separate training modules been designed to deal with each issue? Has a coordinated service delivery and referral mechanism been established? Can personnel be utilized in relating to victims of each form of violence? Some of these questions will assist in solving the problems of this issue.

While taking nothing for granted, planners must collect pertinent data regarding the population at risk, availability of community resources and referral opportunities, cost analysis for establishing a social and domestic violence unit, and available funding sources for such a unit.

Finally, planners must view the proposed plan as timely, rational, and appropriate for dealing with the problems of social and domestic violence. In determining its rationality, program objectives must be identified and their means of attainment clarified. Alternatives must be outlined and analyzed, and evaluation components designed.

The projected plan for the design of such a social and domestic violence unit, while progressive in thought, must be recognized as the trend of the future. Its philosophical basis, purpose, and objectives must be planned so comprehensively that the unit's conceptual framework could evolve automatically.

INCORPORATION OF NEEDED TOOLS FOR THE PLAN MAKING PROCESS

Stern and Sannoll have identified five classes of design tools which may be useful in program planning.[2] They include:

1. Statement of the problem.
2. Theories of causation relevant to the problem.
3. Intervention alternatives and their possible consequences.
4. Information about target population.
5. Value consideration.

Statement of the Problem

The first tool consists of early program conceptualization answering the questions who, what, where, when, why, how, and under what conditions should a special social and domestic violence unit be designed? The problem statement resulting from these answered questions should afford an accurate descriptive overview of the plan. Questions to be asked include:

- What community concern stimulated the consideration of improved services for victims of violence?
- Which social values are at risk with the increased incidence of violence?
- What agencies or organizations would be in support of such a plan?

A statement of the proposed program's goals and objectives should accompany the plan. Goals—because they serve as a comparative base between now and what conditions will be like once the program is achieved—and objectives—which will be general at first—will be defined as development continues and will serve as a measuring stick for progress.

Theories of Causation

The second class of design tools focuses on the causal explanation of the problem. This offers meaning to the problem statement by providing a cause-and-effect interpretation. A clearly understood and accepted theory of causation pertaining to medical and law enforcement violence units would clarify the need for specific social and domestic violence program plans. A thorough research and justification for a program plan implicitly shapes the format and develops alternatives.

Intervention Alternatives

Having completed the first two design tools, the vision of a proposed violence unit is quite clear, and appropriate means of intervention follow. An analysis of various modes of intervention should clearly identify a recommended course of action and outline choices not advisable. Thus, this tool will identify the strengths and weaknesses, the positives and negatives, of a given cause of action.

Dimensions of intervention may proceed along one of two proposed lines: the victim system or the service system. In the victim system, intervention attempts to deal with the facilitators and the inhibitors in the system, focusing on the management of victims of violence. The service system aims to deal with the bureaucratic and interorganizational conditions within the law enforcement, medical, or community service structure which accommodates or blocks actions aimed at improvement or change.

Information About Target Population

Considerable data should be collected in the justification for the formation and funding of violence service units. One segment focuses on a working knowledge of the population at risk. This would include such things as:

- The culture and life style of the population base in the proposed service delivery area.
- Ethnic make-up.
- Religious differences.
- Income characteristics.
- Trends of migration and growth patterns.
- Households and their population density.
- Housing and neighborhood characteristics.

The other segment would address the analysis of existing resources. This would include:

- The rate of inflation.
- The state of the economy.
- Current legislation and its restriction on service-related funds.
- Industrial development and investment phenomena.
- Manpower utilization trends.
- Public expenditure patterns.
- Private consumption patterns.
- Land use patterns.

The third segment would relate to knowledge of existing social standards. Factors to consider under this segment would be:

- Minimal health and welfare standards formulated by the community.
- Forms of organization for enhancing or policing standards.

These three segments are valuable in that they redirect the design guide with pertinent data toward a working reality.

Value Consideration

This final design tool is recommended in an attempt to answer such questions as "Is this plan appropriate?" and, "Will it work?" In essence, it is an evaluative basis by which planners, reviewers, and the community at large will be asked to accept the plan. This tool will afford the opportunity to examine any aspect of the plan not previously discussed, and provides a transition area between plan making and plan implementing. This constitutes the last analytical category of the plan and the first cycle of information input into a strategy of implementation.

TESTING THE PLAN

Originating with the problem statements, and expanding outward through the subsequent classes of design tools, offers an opportunity for testing the recommendations, and establishing a firm base upon which to construct the actual plan. The final test of the problem statement is the degree to which it can be divided into three multiple explanations and interventions. Thus, the planner is prevented from assuming it will work and is compelled to explore all potential options (see Figure 17.1).

This broadening concept opens a variety of alternatives to the

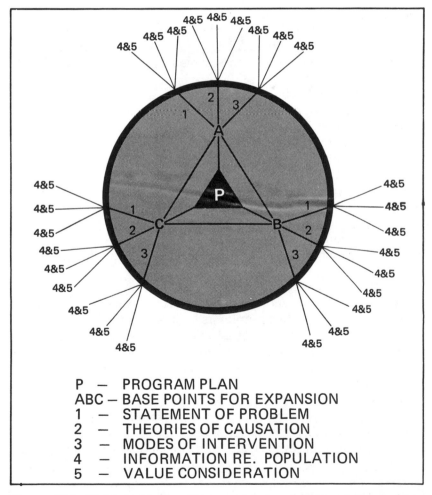

Figure 17.1. Multiple explanations and interventions of the problem statement.

planner. It is critical that the planner be able to select from these alternatives. The manner in which this is accomplished is through priority determination.

The design guide offers the planner various parameters for judgment and assists in testing one's professional assessment for existing gaps or needed supplementation.

IDEAS FOR THE DEVELOPMENT OF A SOCIAL AND DOMESTIC VIOLENCE UNIT[3]*

The Problem

There are a number of violence connected, interlinked crimes that are escalating at an alarming rate. These crimes manifest a number of distinctive interrelating elements (refer to Chapter One), two of which include:

- They all involve a type of assault.
- They emerge from a social framework.

Consequently, they will be called social assaults and include rape, all aspects of domestic violence, child abuse, neglect, and sexual abuse.

All these crimes derive their origin from within a social structure. In the case of domestic violence and child abuse, neglect, and sexual abuse the origin is from within the social structure of the family. In the case of rape and child molestation, the origin stems from within the structure of a social framework that has become law.

In addition to the social context within which all these crimes operate, they all have another very important similarity. In each case the victim of the crime manifests long-term suffering. Regardless of whether the victim is an adult or juvenile, male or female, social and domestic violence universally produce, in addition to the immediate trauma, long-term anxiety, confusion, fear, and shame.

Unlike most other crimes, this violence requires a highly specialized, interdisciplinary, sensitive, professional response. Law enforcement investigation and first responders must become intimately involved with medical expertise to develop the origin of the

---

*Ideas in part from a proposal submitted for consideration.

crimes. In addition, because of the unique social setting in which these crimes occur and because of the psychic trauma they involve, there is an imperative, commensurate need for social service involvement.

In the past, the response to these crimes has been fragmented or absent due to the complex interdisciplinary approach required and the lack of centralized resources. The shortcomings of this response, especially in relation to the resources provided to the victim, has received widespread critical public attention which has created a climate of increased community awareness and concern, and has generated a climate demanding improvement.

Terminal Objectives of the Proposed Unit

1. To improve the efficiency with which a violence team responds to the group of crimes defined as social and domestic violence, by responding with a highly professionalized, multidisciplinary team in a skillful and sensitive manner in which victims' needs are made a first priority during a more comprehensive and efficient investigation.

2. To improve the ability of the victim and their families to handle the emotional and psychological trauma suffered by the victims by professional support offered by trained investigators, medical, and social service personnel.

3. To develop the confidence of the victim and the community in law enforcement officials by skillful handling of cases to encourage reporting of crimes by future victims.

4. To ultimately lower the increasing rate of social and domestic violence by increasing the number of reported crimes due to public confidence in the police department, which will lead to a greater number of arrests due to increased reporting and an increase in suspect information yielded by trusting victims. A greater number of these suspects will be convicted due to the more complete bipartite investigation by the team leading to a decline in the rate of crimes.

Recommended Approach

To meet these demands, a violence team is proposed. The team will be a victim-oriented, interdisciplinary group under one centralized command composed of highly-trained law enforcement investigators, a law enforcement physician investigator, and highly skilled social service personnel.

Composition

1. Investigation: The team will be commanded by a lieutenant. Investigations will be composed of four sergeants and 24 investigators, who all will be intensively trained in interview techniques, crisis intervention, communication skills, evidence collection and preservation, and parapsychological facets of victim assistance. The investigators will be available on a twenty-four-hour basis and will respond to the patrol division to handle the defined crimes.

2. Medical investigation: The role of the physician investigator is unique to law enforcement. The position will be filled by a sworn, licensed physician. All social and domestic violence cases involve medical expertise. During the preliminary investigation of these crimes, both victim and suspects are examined by physicians, thereby developing a body of medical evidence. The medical investigator will review this data—the physician's physical findings, the X-rays, and the laboratory work—to establish and insure the completeness of investigation. The medical investigator will then compile a medical origin of the crime. The report will then be fused with the investigator's report to yield a complete historical and medical composite. Upon issuance by the prosecutor, both the regular investigator and the medical investigator would testify to the appropriate findings, avoiding the time-consuming need to seek out outside medical expertise.

The medical investigator will also act as a liaison between the team and the medical professionals in the community who see the victims and suspects during the preliminary investigation. Together they will develop uniform methods of handling the medical investigations of the violence cases and will develop improved methodologies of operation.

3. Social service: The team also will have three social service professionals trained in the complexities of social and domestic violence. By working directly with the team, these workers will be able to immediately become involved in the appropriate cases and begin necessary maneuvers at the onset of the investigation. The intimacy of this association with the team will in-

sure that the proper social support is offered to the victim.

4. Location: In the past, victims of violence were often further traumatized by being transported to busy, callous police facilities for interviews and processing. The team will be located in an area completely isolated from the main police facility whose setting will be redesigned to be nontraumatic to the victim.

5. Inservice education: Since the patrol division will be making the initial contact with the victims, the team will undertake an extensive in-service education program on handling victims of violence for the patrol division. This will include education in crisis intervention, sensitivity, interviewing, reporting, and evidenciary methods.

6. Community awareness: Since community awareness and cooperation are of prime importance in social and domestic violence, an extensive program to enhance a thorough understanding of the team's goals and objectives will be developed. Extensive lecture series will be arranged by members of the team, and both the telecommunication industry and the press will be fully utilized.

Concluding Statements

Team members will attack the crimes of rape, domestic violence, child abuse, neglect, and sexual abuse with a tripartite interdisciplinary team composed of law enforcement investigators, a medical investigator, and social service support operating under a centralized direction.

The unique structure of the team will offer an efficiency of operation not appreciated before now. Centralization of the investigations unit will allow the development of highly specialized techniques unique to social and domestic violence. The presence of a law enforcement trained medical investigator within the team will add a level of professional expertise never before appreciated within law enforcement. The presence of skilled social service personnel within the team will insure victim-oriented priorities.

The net result will be greater community confidence in the police department which will lead to the reporting of more crimes, leading to more arrests. Improvement in the handling of investigations will lead to more convictions and finally to a decline in the rate of social and domestic violence.

SUMMARY

It is essential that first responders combine efforts in an attempt to deal more effectively with victims of violence. Services at best have been fragmented, and the service delivery system within any particular community has suffered the consequences of overly specialized, direct contact. Recognizing the similarities which exist among victims of rape and domestic violence and attempting to deliver a more cost effective, quality-based service, it is critical that communities begin to demonstrate the need, design the plan, and deliver the service.

Society's recognition of violence has justified the need for first responders and community planners to create specialty violence units not only in an attempt to afford intervention for victims, but as a force in support of social reform.

REFERENCES

1. Zweig FM, Morris R: The social planning design guide: Process and proposal. Journal of Social Work (National Association of Social Workers) Vol. 11 No. 2, April 1966, pp. 11-20
2. Stern H, Sannoll I: A Framework for Analyzing Social Workers' Contribution to the Identification and Resolution of Social Problems. New York, Columbia University Press, The Social Welfare Forum, 1961
3. Warner CG: Chairperson of Subcommittee on Sexual Assault and Intrafamily Violence, City of San Diego. Proposal submitted to San Diego Police Department for consideration, May 1977

INDEX